D1440777

WITHDRAWN

CRAIG EVAN BARTON   EDITOR

sites of memory

PERSPECTIVES ON ARCHITECTURE AND RACE

PRINCETON ARCHITECTURAL PRESS

Published by
Princeton Architectural Press
37 East Seventh Street
New York, NY 10003

For a catalog of books published by Princeton
Architectural Press, call toll free 800.722.6657
or visit www.papress.com.

Editor/project coordinator: Gina Bell & Jennifer Thompson
Book design: Carol Hayes
Cover design: Deb Wood

Special Thanks: Nettie Aljian, Ann Alter,
Amanda Atkins, Nicola Bednarek, Jan Cigliano,
Jane Garvie, Mia Ihara, Clare Jacobson,
Mark Lamster, Anne Nitschke, Lottchen Shivers,
Tess Taylor, and Deb Wood
of Princeton Architectural Press—
Kevin C. Lippert, publisher

Cover photo: "Water, Memories, Civil Rights" by M Lin,
Montgomery, Alabama, 1998. Photo: L. Lokko

Printed and bound in the U.S.A.

Library of Congress Cataloging-in-Publication Data

Sites of Memory.
Perspectives on Architecture and Race /
edited by Craig Evan Barton.— 1st ed. p. cm.
Includes bibliographical references.
ISBN 1-56898-233-X (alk. paper)

1. Afro-Americans—Social life and customs.
2. Afro-Americans—Social conditions.
3. Afro-American architecture.
4. City and town life—United States
5. United States—History, Local

I. Barton, Craig Evan.
II. Title. E185.86 .S595 2000
305.869073—dc21
00-008110
Rev.

contents

preface

When I was a small child, in the 1950s, my family lived in South Carolina. Among my most vivid memories was that of a chain gang working alongside the road near Greenville. We moved north about the time I started school and I spent my teenage years mesmerized by the televised drama of the civil rights movement. I returned to the South to live in 1974, expecting to see the battle-scarred ruins of the strange society and alien landscape I remembered from childhood.

There was a tumble-down sign south of Charlottesville that advertised the "Albemarle Hotel for Colored" and there was a restaurant at the prosaically named crossroads of Central Garage where whites and blacks still used separate, visibly unequal, dining rooms, but these were the only ghosts of the old order, so near in time but apparently completely vanquished, that I found. The residue of what the South Africans called "petit apartheid"—the separate drinking fountains, separate entrances, separate bathrooms and the signs that identified them—was erased remarkably quickly.

As an architectural historian for the Commonwealth of Virginia, I visited places that only a few years before had been the sites of bitter racial conflicts, and I met people who had participated in them—as students in the Prince Edward County schools when they were closed to prevent integration, as major and minor members of the notorious Byrd Machine that controlled the state's politics for decades, devising and implementing the strategy of massive resistance to the federal courts. Yet both places and people seemed curiously ordinary.

From the perspective of the beginning of the twenty-first century, it is hard not to think that a heroic epoch of African-American history has ended. The confident independence of returning black veterans of World War I, the artistic ambitions of the Harlem Renaissance, the cultural authority jazz achieved at mid-century, the renewed activism of World War II-era veterans all seemed to climax in the heady years of the 1950s and 1960s, when it appeared that African-American political and cultural ambitions could not be denied. Forty years later, Martin Luther King, Jr., Ralph David Abernathy, James Forman, Fannie Lou Hamer, Malcolm X, Stokely Carmichael, Huey P. Newton, and other key players in the movement are dead, while Strom Thurmond remains in office and Joe Smitherman, mayor of Selma in the 1960s, was only recently turned out of it. Petit apartheid is gone, but grand apartheid, the routine social and residential separation, the disparities of wealth and political power that were so deeply naturalized in me as a young white man in the 1970s that I didn't associate it with the evil Southern racial order whose traces I sought, remains with us.

As the great events of those years recede into memory, as its principal figures pass through middle age and old age into death, it is not surprising that we should pause to evaluate them before we move on. If the legacy of the epic struggles of the mid-twentieth century seems ambiguous, their moral force remains so compelling that even right-wingers embrace it. The wave of construction of civil rights museums and memorials that marked the 1990s and that has not yet broken marks one such effort. Like the wave of construction of Civil War memorials in the 1890s, these new memorials to a second civil war are meant both to commemorate and to lay to rest the racial conflicts and contradictions that marked twentieth-century society, and to herald a new racial order—or in the modern case, a non-racial order—in the twenty-first.

The memorials are also part of a larger movement to redefine the nature of American society by re-viewing and re-imagining the historic landscape—by reconstructing memory. Seen through our new eyes, the landscape and its builders no longer seem monoracial, monoethnic, monocultural, and monogendered as they did half a century ago. Historic sites no longer focus exclusively on the lives of élite white men. At their houses we also learn of the women and children and workers and servants who lived there. Our national parks and historic sites now commemorate African-American life in Boston, the life of Martin Luther King, Jr., the first Women's Rights Convention, the integration crisis in Little Rock, the concentration camps where Japanese Americans were interned during World War II, the Selma-to-Montgomery March, and, most recently, the racially and sexually mixed labor force of the World War II homefront.

These efforts would have been inconceivable a few years earlier, and they owe their origins to the civil rights and other democratic movements of the 1960s. Without the popular acceptance of cultural pluralism—or what is now called multiculturalism—no legislator would have voted to establish these parks. But the sites we choose to commemorate and the ways we interpret them also owe much to the evolution of academic studies of the American landscape in the second half of the twentieth century. Scholarship usually takes its cues from popular culture, and the opening up of American society in the popular and political realms led to a corresponding broadening of scholarly vision. Scholars began to be interested in the way the built environment reflected human culture. Prompted by the populism of the 1960s, this new generation of scholars no longer understood culture as a unitary thing: they understood their task to be the study of American cultures, not American *culture*, of American minds, not the American *mind*.

To say that the landscape embodies cultures is one thing, to say how is another one altogether, and our answers have changed over the past thirty years. Broadly speaking, one might say that an older, reified view of culture as something groups of people "have" and that they inevitably bestow on their architecture and landscape until they are assimilated to another set of cultural ideas and their culture is diluted or even eradicated, has been challenged by a more fluid sense of culture as contingent, contradictory, willed, and performative. In the newer view, culture is individually based, largely conscious, and created and changed in the acting out rather than existing as an essential, largely unconscious quality of racial, ethnic, or national populations.

These models of the relationship between culture and landscape have been worked out with particular eloquence in the study of African-American architecture and material culture, which is supported by a historical, anthropological, and theoretical literature that is much deeper and more sophisticated than any yet developed for other racial or ethnic groups in North America. Beginning in the 1970s, for example, scholars who were inspired by romantic cultural nationalism in African-American arts and popular culture and by the populist politics of the 1960s resuscitated the pre-war anthropology of Melville Herskovits, exemplified in *The Myth of the Negro Past* (1941). They began to search for "Africanisms" or "African retentions" in landscapes inhabited by African-Americans, particularly in the South and particularly on slave plantations. John Michael Vlach's landmark work *The Afro-American Tradition in Decorative Arts* (1978), for example, identified nine classes of artifacts ranging from houses to ceramics to textiles that represented either a continuation of African artifact types or the application of an African-derived aesthetic philosophy to Euro-American artifact types. Other scholars, taking a cue from the concept of working-class cultural resistance advanced by the English social historian E.P. Thompson in his landmark work *The Making of the English Working Class* (1963), looked to those same settings to understand ways that enslaved Africans and their progeny evaded, undermined, and sometimes openly rejected the planters' authority. Rhys Isaac's *The Transformation of Virginia*, 1740–1790 (1982) dramatically demonstrated the importance of landscape to the dynamics of black-white interaction and conflict in the Old Dominion. In both cases, the emphasis was on group identity and group action.

In the 1990s, the study of race and cultural landscape has moved toward a more complex analysis that emphasizes the everyday performance of identity. Influenced by the interest in cultural diversity and personal identity in popular culture and by critical race theory, "whiteness" studies, and semiotic-oriented postmodern theory in the academy, scholars of the landscape, as the essays here show, acknowledge the elusiveness and allusiveness of racial identity, and think in terms of culturally based attitudes and approaches rather than fixed cultural premises or practices.

My simplified account points to some continuing patterns of cultural identity that seem to cut across racial and ethnic lines in the American landscape. The first we might call the tension between memory and experience. Earlier students of the landscape stressed cultural memory, searching for evidence of material practices that were remembered from home cultures in Africa, Europe, and Asia. Geologists called these "relict" landscapes. Eventually, though, the cultural effects of experience came to seem more important as landscape historians realized that once a cultural practice is transplanted, it is changed by the very fact of its introduction into a new context. Historians of African-American landscape, for example, have debated whether African memories or the experience of enslavement and racism defined the antebellum scene most sharply. Or is some more synthetic and nuanced account necessary?

The interweaving of memory and experience becomes even more complex when we add a second dichotomy, between imposed and adopted conditions and identities. In a pluralistic society, cultural identities arise from a discourse—sometimes an argument—that pits identities assigned by outsiders against those defined by insiders. Where simple models of memory and experience can both seem relatively passive, the tension between imposition and adoption emphasizes the active agency of outsiders and insiders, acknowledging the insiders' powerful, but not if all-powerful, self-defining voice.

The practice that the historians Eric Hobsbawn and Terrence Ranger called *The Invention of Tradition*, in their 1983 book of that title, is a common strategy for working out the tensions between memory and experience, imposition and adoption in the cultural landscape. Every tradition was invented sometime, of course, but Hobsbawm and Ranger were interested in the self-conscious cultural innovations that were recent enough to date and to identify a creator. Some invented traditions are created out of whole cloth, but in ethnic and racial landscapes they tend to be older forms and practices that may be rescued from obscurity or raised from minor to emblematic status by being assigned new or greater meaning. They might be practices that historically were restricted to one historic era, one region, one class, or one ethnic group within the home society, but now are held forth as a distinguishing sign of the entire group. In African-American material practices they might be as disparate as the wearing of kente cloth, the painting of Ndebele-style murals (derived from a region of southern Africa far from the homelands of most African-Americans' ancestors) in a Washington, D.C., alley, or the elevation of shotgun houses to a cultural emblem in the paintings of John Biggers.

These processes of agency and self-definition, of the self-conscious interweaving of memory and experience, and of the invention of traditions characterize the historic landscapes that we study, but they also encompass our own study: the codification of memory in history is a form of racializing the landscape and inventing tradition. My simplistic search for signs of an older Southern racial order in Virginia in the 1970s was one example. So is the search for signs of African retentions and cultural resistance in the landscape. So is the tendency, in the face of disappointed expectations, to romanticize the insular world of the pre-World War II African-American urban middle-class and even (as in Maya Angelou's recent film *Down in the Delta*) the pre-civil rights rural South as an African-American Eden.

What is different, though, what popular cultural politics and scholarly practices in cultural landscape studies over the past thirty years have done to sites of memory is to expand and diffuse them. As the essays here demonstrate, if the relation of race and culture to the landscape is no longer as clear as it once was, if its meaning is no longer as simple as it once seemed, neither are the sites of memory confined any longer to a segregated corner of the landscape; they are everywhere that Americans have built.

CRAIG EVAN BARTON   VOLUME EDITOR

acknowledgments

This volume has been many years in the making. The initial idea for this project surfaced in a brief conversation I had during a year spent at Harvard University as a Loeb Fellow. I left Cambridge with an idea for an anthology about race, architecture, and memory and found in Charlottesville at the University of Virginia a unique intellectual environment in which to develop it.

As with any collaborative project there are many people to thank. First, I wish to thank my colleagues at the School of Architecture. Without their support and assistance neither the original symposium nor the development of this volume would have been possible. I am especially grateful to former Dean William McDonough and the current Dean Karen van Lengen for their assistance and encouragement.

The Graham Foundation for Advanced Studies in the Fine Arts, the George Gund Foundation of Cleveland, Ohio, and the Institute for Sustainable Design generously funded this project. I am particularly thankful for the confidence and support which Richard Solomon of the Graham Foundation and David Berkholtz of the Gund Foundation provided to the project. Bob Lasher was especially helpful securing early support for the symposium. I am indebted to Susan Ketron for her guidance, friendship, and assistance funding this project.

Colleagues within the University of Virginia and beyond aided both the symposium and the publication. I am grateful for the support and encouragement offered by Professors Reginald Butler and Scot French of the Carter G. Woodson Institute for Afro-American and African Studies, Henry Louis Gates of Harvard University's W.E.B. Du Bois Institute for Afro-American Research, Professor William Harris of Jackson State University, Dolores Hayden of Yale University's School of Art and Architecture, Ghislaine Hermanuz of the School of Architecture at City College in New York, and Donna Robertson, Dean of the Illinois Institute of Technology.

This project has benefited from editorial guidance, and this project has gained tremendously from the insights and criticism offered by colleagues and collaborators. I am grateful to Nathaniel Belcher for inviting me to participate in the Jazz Architectural Workshop at Tulane University and subsequently offering me the benefit of his experience. Mabel Wilson has consistently been one of the project's strongest advocates and her insights have helped shape it.

I owe a particular debt of thanks to Professors Deborah McDowell, Elizabeth Meyer, Ruben Rainey, Camille Wells of the University of Virginia and Professor Daniel Friedman of the University of Cincinnati for their thoughtful and rigorous criticism of the project in its various stages of development. Jayne Riew and Boyed Zenner have been great friends offering advice and editorial assistance at many crucial junctures throughout the process. Marthe Rowen was among the earliest and most enthusiastic advocates and her support as an editor and confidante were invaluable to the development of this volume and to the entire project. Angela Blocker, Emily Gee, and Jacqueline Taylor fulfilled many tasks required to transform the project from idea to reality. Professors Daniel Bluestone, Clifton Ellis, Christopher Fannin, Earl Mark, Elissa Rosenberg, and Kenneth Schwartz of the University of Virginia's School of Architecture and Wallis Miller of the University of Kentucky offered valuable insights gleaned from their participation in the symposium.

Finally, I wish to thank the editorial staff at Princeton Architectural Press, particularly Eugenia Bell and Jennifer Thompson for their confidence in the project and their patience in helping it come to fruition.

CRAIG EVAN BARTON   VOLUME EDITOR

foreword

In "New Cultural Politics of Difference," Cornell West proposes that in attempting to gain control of the means and practices of representation, the late 20th-century cultural worker faces
three critical challenges which he defines as intellectual, existential, and political.

> *The intellectual challenge ... is how to think about representational practices*
> *in terms of history, culture and society. How does one understand, analyze*
> *and enact such practices today? An adequate answer to this question can be*
> *attempted only after one comes to terms with the insights and blindnesses of*
> *earlier attempts to grapple with the question in light of the evolving crisis in*
> *different histories, cultures and societies. The existential challenge requires*
> *that the cultural worker acquire the requisite cultural capital necessary to*
> *produce and survive. The political challenge necessitates a view toward the*
> *coalescing of black and white peoples based upon a commonality of moral*
> *and political intent.* [1]

It is in light of West's existential challenge that the project culminating in this volume was conceived and executed. *Sites of Memory* is the result of a symposium bearing the same name,
held March 25–28, 1999, at the School of Architecture, University of Virginia. The symposium
was organized around the broad themes of landscape, race, and memory, and sought to facilitate public discourse around these issues, specifically examining their impact upon the
design and interpretation of African-American cultural landscapes.

     This anthology explores the historic and contemporary effects of race upon the develop-
ment of the built environment, and to examine the realities and myths of America's dual racial

[1] Cornel I. West, *Keeping Faith*
Philosophy and Race in
America, (New York: Routledge
Press, 1993), "Cultural Politics
of Difference," 5.

landscapes. As a social construct and concept, race has had a profound influence on the spatial development of the American landscape, creating separate, though sometimes parallel, overlapping or even superimposed cultural landscapes for black and white Americans. The spaces forming these landscapes were initially "constructed" by the politics of American slavery, and subsequently "designed" by the customs, traditions and ideology emanating from the Supreme Court's "separate but equal" finding in Plessy v. Ferguson, as well as 20th-century "Jim Crow" statutes. The result was a complex social and cultural geography in which black Americans occupied, and often continue to occupy, distinct and frequently marginalized cultural landscapes. Consciously diverse in the scope of its inquiry, this text is distinguished by its multi-disciplinary analysis of the spatial manifestations of black cultural practices, and their legibility and interpretation in the built environment. While other anthologies have successfully linked gender to the built environment (notably Colamina & Wigley, eds., *Sexuality and Space*), and have examined the relationship of African-American cultural practices to identity (MIchelle Wallace, ed., *Black Popular Culture*), *Sites of Memory* offers a complex multidisciplinary view of the intersection of race and cultural identity and their representation on the American landscape.

Within the disciplines of architecture, landscape architecture, urban design, and cultural geography, there is an emerging body of theoretical, historical, and design research which recognizes the capacity of the built environment to serve as a repository of our collective and individual cultural history and memory. Yet contemporary methodologies of design often ignore the power of the landscape to evoke the history and memory of place, homogenizing the diverse cultural forces resident in the landscape, and thus reinforcing a peculiar sense of collective amnesia.

In recent years an increasing interest in documenting and preserving black landmarks has drawn greater attention to individual buildings. Preservation efforts have tended to focus on sites such as churches, houses, and institutional buildings, often interpreting them as fragments isolated from larger social, historical and spatial contexts. Much of the black cultural landscape, however, was shaped by spaces "designed" by appropriation, custom, or use. As a result, such critical components of the physical past and present have remained outside of the analytic view of historians and designers. Often obscured over the course of time, these larger cultural landscapes, defined by customs and events as much as by specific buildings, and represented in text, images, and music, offer invaluable insights into the memory of a place.

For centuries black Americans have supplemented narratives of history with memories—protected, nurtured, and shaped into expressive artifacts as chronicles of their powerful influence upon the American landscape. Contemporary scholarship has begun to make greater use of these artifacts, including literature, music, dance, art, film, vernacular architecture and cultural geography, to explore the construction of a modern cultural landscape defined as much by memory as by physical artifact.

This is a pivotal moment to explore the issues of spatial identity and representation of black culture in the contemporary urban landscape. Thirty years ago the Civil Rights movement reshaped the customs and the traditions which defined both the black and white cultural landscapes. Today, we as planners, designers, writers, artists, and historians continue to explore the problems of America's urban landscape, confronting its multiple histories as well as the physical and cultural elements that separate us by race, class and gender.

The essays in *Sites of Memory* present the recent fruits of such research and collectively and individually address these crucial questions: How are the ideology and political history of race represented visually and spatially in the built environment? What are the visual and spatial elements that distinguish the black cultural landscape, and by what means can these often ephemeral, cultural manifestations be documented, preserved and interpreted? *Sites of Memory* offers critical and provocative responses by those who view the built environment as an artifact capable of rendering a more complex interpretation of the influence of black cultures on the history and memory of place.

CRAIG EVAN BARTON

one   duality and invisibility

RACE AND MEMORY IN THE URBANISM OF THE AMERICAN SOUTH

In his 1947 novel *Invisible Man*, Ralph Ellison chronicled the tension and ambiguity that pervades black life and culture in America. Two passages from that text articulate his interpretations of the physical and ephemeral landscapes occupied by blacks in the twentieth century. In the prologue Ellison characterizes the cultural landscape of black America.

"I am an invisible. No, I am not a spook like those who haunted Edgar Allan Poe; nor am I one of your Hollywood-movie ectoplasms. I am a man of substance, of flesh and bone, fiber and liquids—and I might even be said to possess a mind. I am invisible ... "[1]

Describing a nation bound by both institutional and traditional racism, Ellison defined the black landscape in terms of the visibility (or lack thereof) of black culture. This interpretation still resonates with the contemporary architect or urbanist seeking to explore the historic and contemporary effects of race upon the development of the built environment and to examine the realities and myths of America's dual racial landscapes. Ellison later articulates the importance of spatialized memory to the comprehension and interpretation of twentieth-century black culture. In this later passage the narrator suggests that black history is invisible because of where it resides and may be interpreted through selected vernacular landscapes.

In order to explore some of the effects of race upon the development of the black cultural landscapes in the late nineteenth- and twentieth-century South, it is critical to examine how Ellison 's concept of invisibility was built and spatialized. For Ellison, the ability to render the world visible and invisible is a concrete form of power, and is a part of the social construction of race.

The author would like to thank Mrs. Louretta Wimberly and Mr. J. L. Chestnut for their contributions to and assistance with this essay.

1 Ralph Ellison, *Invisible Man*, (New York: Vintage Books 1995), 3.

Franklin Street, Selma, Alabama

Ask your wife to take you around the gin mills and the barber shops and the juke joints and the churches, Brother. Yes, and the beauty parlors on Saturdays when they're frying hair. A whole unrecorded history is spoken then, Brother.[2]

RACE AS A SOCIAL CONSTRUCTION We understand race to be a means of establishing cultural hierarchies, determined by social rather than biological criteria. In America, race defines us in terms of skin color (and all its associations) and we have historically conceived of "blackness" in terms of negation and opposition. Black culture has been defined not so much by what it is but by what it is not. To be black is to be not white, and as such to be inferior, politically powerless and culturally impoverished. Defining blackness exclusively in terms of opposition is a useful strategy, for it reduces black life and culture to a series of generalities far more susceptible to subjugation by established authority. The irony, of course, is that black culture serves as an avant-garde testing ground for popular culture in America. Fashion, music, art, and even language draw heavily and directly from historic and contemporary aspects of black cultural practices.

Though largely considered a regional phenomenon, race as a social construction has had a broad and pervasive influence upon the spatial development of the American landscape. The connotations conveyed through the perception of race in

2 Ibid.

America have created separate, though sometimes parallel, overlapping, or even super-imposed cultural landscapes for black and white Americans. The spaces forming these landscapes were initially "constructed" by the politics of American slavery, and subsequently "designed" by the customs, traditions and ideology emanating from the Supreme Court's "separate but equal" finding in Plessy v. Ferguson,[3] as well as twentieth-century "Jim Crow" statutes. The result was a complex social and cultural geography in which black Americans occupied, and often continue to occupy, distinct and frequently marginalized cultural landscapes.

In the introduction to his 1978 text, *In the Matter of Color, Race and the Legal Process*, A. Leon Higginbotham aptly summarizes the legal and political structures which have defined the state of black men and women in America. Throughout the text he describes the various judicial and statutory "mechanisms of control. . . . the special limitations imposed upon free blacks . . . generally restricting any activities or aspirations of blacks that might threaten groups in control."[4]

The legal mechanisms of control to which Higginbotham refers are implicitly spatial, reinforcing the visible and invisible boundaries distinguishing white and black space. These boundaries have effectively established the political, social and productive space available for occupation and control by the black population.

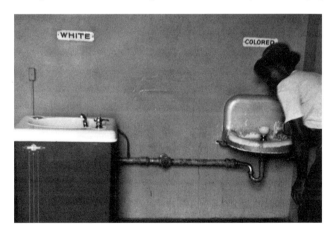

Wilmington, North Carolina, 1950. © Elliott Erwitt / Magnum Photos, Inc.

3 Plessy v. Ferguson was argued before the United States Supreme court in April of 1896 and decided in favor of the plaintiff later that year. In this case the court affirmed a lower court ruling supporting the constitutionality of a statute enacted by the State of Louisiana which provided for separate railway cars for white and black travelers. The ruling by U.S. Supreme Court provided for a revised reading of the obligations of the Thirteenth Amendment (which made illegal the practice of slavery) and modified the scope of the language of the Fourteenth Amendment to the U.S. Constitution (which provided for equal protection under the law for all citizens). In the case of the Fourteenth Amendment the interpretive revisions of the scope of the amendment's language allowed the doctrine of "separate but equal" to be articulated .

4 A. Leon Higginbotham, *In the Matter of Color Race and the Legal Process: The Colonial Period*, (New York: Oxford University Press 1978), 14.

Ironically, one of the subtle implications of these boundaries in the South was that, while the social distinctions and hierarchies of race remained intact, whites and blacks often were required to inhabit the same physical space. The necessity to co-exist in the same room, building, or city required strategies for the construction of space, which by delineating social and spatial hierarchies could differentiate visibility. These spaces reiterated the relationships of power to space and obscured the presence of the black population.

Descriptions of Thomas Jefferson's plantation home, Monticello, often refer to eclectic and idiosyncratic qualities contained within the building and of the Jefferson's skillful manipulation of building and landscape. Much has been said about the views and vistas Jefferson created through the thoughtful placement of windows and doors. Typically, Jefferson is credited for a design sensibility often elevating the mere pragmatic to the level of the sublime. A close examination of the view created from Monticello's east portico provides insight into the pragmatic issues of power and control negotiated through the design of the landscape. The view from the portico looks out over the various sections of Monticello's diverse landscape. Like other working plantations, Monticello was dependent upon an enormous labor force of black slaves. Yet the views created from the east portico actively deny the presence of the black body. Through the manipulation of the landscape section and placement of the volume of the winged dependencies, Jefferson skillfully rendered invisible the slaves and their places of work from the important symbolic view of the property. Ironically,

left: **Monticello view to the south from West Portico;** *above:* **Monticello view of south wing of dependencies.**

there are few locations within the composition where black and white bodies were in closer proximity.

Whether it was Jefferson's manipulation of the landscape and his program to conceal from view the black slaves working at Monticello, the separate "colored" entrance to the cinema, or simply the denial of access to certain facilities, the effect was to render the black person invisible. Negotiating both the concept and the realms of invisibility became central to a construction of black cultural identity.

SPATIALIZING RACE IN THE URBAN LANDSCAPE There are many sites in America where it is possible to discern landscapes charged with the social and political constructions of race. In the American South's Black Belt region, questions of identification, analysis, and the interpretation of racial landscapes preternaturally exist because of the historic presence of a large black population. Identified primarily by its agricultural productivity, the region was also closely identified with the Civil Rights Movement, because of its large politically under-enfranchised black population. Cities like Selma, Alabama, which were critical to the staging and the development of the movement, provide an opportunity to examine the evolution and transformation of racial landscapes.

Set on the banks of the Alabama River, the city of Selma was founded in 1820 by William Rufus King (a former U.S. Senator and Vice-President under Franklin Pierce). Its riverfront location and development of railway links to the ports of New Orleans and Mobile established Selma as a major transfer point for agricultural exports and manufactured imports. This riverfront town, sometimes known as the "Queen City of the Black Belt," was destined to become the site of one of the Civil Rights Movement's most significant struggles.

In Selma, the spatial legacy of *Plessy v. Ferguson* and the various ensuing Jim Crow statutes led to an urbanism of duality, and a city composed of two distinct urban landscapes, which as they evolved became codified by race.

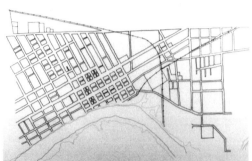

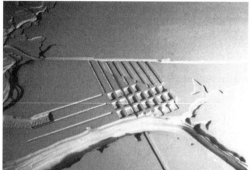

clockwise from left: **Aerial photo, Selma, Alabama; Diagram of town plan and river, Selma, Alabama; Model of Selma circa 1820 showing original plotting and development of civic core.**

Early maps of the city illustrate a number of key elements that fostered the city's growth and the evolution of its dual landscapes. In its original 1820 plan for the city, the Selma Town and Land Company laid out a grid of streets forming a square that became the civic core of the city. Surrounding this area are two street grids. West of the core there is direct access to the river, while the street pattern to the east of the core runs perpendicular to the river. An 1866 map of the city clearly shows this 12-block plan, the two grid patterns, and the nascent beginnings of the city's racial division.

The original town plan established the city's primary residential enclave of west Selma, positioning it between the civic core to the east and Live Oak Cemetery to the west. Race played a significant role in the spatial organization of this precinct. Nineteenth-century census records indicate that this neighborhood had a significant resident black population. Because their residences were typically located at the back of property lots with limited street access, West Selma's black population remained largely invisible.

Race also configures the hierarchy of Live Oak Cemetery, a key component of the precinct's cultural landscape. The cemetery contains the city's Confederate Memorial, the interred remains of many of the city's founding white residents and is a critical link to portions of Selma's antebellum history and memory. Live Oak Cemetery also provides poignant insight to the dual landscape occupied by blacks and whites. The graves of the cemetery's black occupants are not clearly recognizable, for unlike those of their white counterparts, they carry no surnames. Deprived of the recognition offered by a surname, these headstones illustrate the peculiar limited space blacks occupied in antebellum Selma. It was a space in which they were present yet not wholly visible. With its physical connection to both the historic and civic cores as well as the presence of sites celebrating the history of its founders and defenders in the Civil War, West Selma was positioned as a cultural landscape of power and authority for Selma's white population.

left: **Live Oak Cemetery.**
above: **A headstone of a black man.**

The eastern portion of the city lies east of the twelve-block core and continues to the city's eastern boundary, differing in many significant respects from West Selma. The grain of its major streets run north to south, effectively connecting the Alabama River with the city's major commercial and industrial precincts and the rural sites to the north. Initially platted as another residential precinct for the white community, East Selma evolved into a mixed-use area containing commercial, industrial, and residential components. The presence of industrial and commercial facilities undermined the value and the quality of the adjacent residential areas, making them less desirable for whites and therefore available for occupation by the city's black population.

While it is possible to point to similar aspects of racialized geography in American urbanism, what distinguished Selma's dual racial landscapes was the manner in which the city's black population was isolated from both Selma's formal political center and its cultural zone. West Selma contained the city's significant public political spaces, such as the county and federal courthouses which were both located west of Broad Street in the 12-block core area. East Selma evolved into the landscape of the black community because it was disconnected from these sites. The result was to render the black population socially and politically invisible by both consigning them to a series of separate and inferior spaces and limiting their access to the city's symbolic political/public spaces.

Model of civic core and differential graining of urban fabric in West and East Selma.

INVISIBILITY AND THE CONSTRUCTED LANDSCAPE By the early 20th century, the cultural and spatial boundaries inscribed by the city's design had evolved into two racially distinct landscapes, complete with separate housing, street typologies, and schools. The private, and more importantly, public spaces created in the twentieth century reinforced the nineteenth-century traditions of Jim Crow, determining that separate facilities for each race was the preferred method of exercising control and authority over the city's black population.

Housing as defined by its location, typology, and quality, characterized one of the substantial boundaries between black and white Selma. Other features distinguished the black residential area east of Broad Street and north of Jefferson Davis Avenue, such as housing types, which were generally limited to shotgun houses and to public housing projects built in the late 1950s, though remnants of nineteenth-century middle-class housing survived. Among the most distinctive features of this landscape were the streets, the majority of which remained unpaved as recently as 1960.

Perhaps the most important issue of these landscapes with respect to the issue of the invisible black population concerns the idea of dual political and civic spaces. Legalized segregation in the twentieth century sought to remove the black population from the public gaze by creating separate and distinct social and political spaces. While many black men and women regularly moved through the residential and commercial spaces of Selma's white community, negotiating these spaces was a complex affair. The public and civic spaces of West Selma describe a "space of appearance,"[5] a space which Hannah Arendt defined as a symbolic political realm where an individual may be seen through speech and through action. Political visibility and identity in this space were defined by Jim Crow laws, so that while blacks might literally occupy these spaces, their collective inability to vote and therefore access the political process rendered them invisible in these "spaces of appearance."

The Dallas County courthouse and the federal courthouse face one another from opposite sides of Alabama Avenue and, in conjunction with the former City Hall and public safety building, respectively mark the western and eastern boundaries of the city's historic twelve block core. Defined by short, square blocks, this area could be considered the white population's cultural, religious, and commercial center, distin-

5 Hannah Arendt, *The Human Condition*, (Chicago: University of Chicago Press, 1958), 199.

guishing it as the symbolic public space, or "space of appearance" in twentieth-century Selma. Its location, scale, and collection of important buildings allow this space to be interpreted as the "real" civic center of Selma.

The fact that Selma is comprised of two racial landscapes extended the opportunity for the development of an equivalent symbolic civic and political space in its black neighborhood. In East Selma this space is found on the street which connects two of the city's oldest black congregations, First Baptist Church and Brown's A.M.E. Chapel. These churches served as markers in a landscape that emerged during Reconstruction when the black population was again politically disenfranchised. Like many other black churches, First Baptist and Brown's A.M.E. fulfilled a dual role, providing spiritual sanctuary as well as a symbolic political representation for the black community. Just as the courthouses charged the meaning of the street in white Selma, so too did these churches in East Selma. During the voting rights demonstrations their verve spilled out from the sanctuary and onto Sylvan Street, the street these two communities shared, claiming this space as the symbolic political space of the community.

Anchors of Selma's black civic core.
above: **First Baptist Church;** *right:* **Brown's Chapel.**

While its counterpart in West Selma derived its significance, visibility, and power directly from urban structure, this space was much less visible largely because it is superimposed onto a morphological structure that was never intended to support it. This space does not read as a "space of appearance," yet within the dual landscapes of the city where access and visibility to the more formal public realm were denied to blacks, this is precisely the role that it served.

The voting rights movement ultimately dissolved the boundaries of Selma's civic and political space. The Dallas County Courthouse and the Edmund Pettus Bridge became focal points of the movement's strategy to achieve political inclusion for the city and county's large black population. Both the Dallas County Courthouse and the Pettus Bridge represent components of Selma's political and cultural landscape not easily adapted to the strategies of duality and invisibility. Anchoring the city's civic and political precincts the county and federal courthouses represented the inability of black residents to be both figuratively and literally visible within the formal political space of the city and the county.

above: **Martin Luther King Street (originally Sylvan Street)—the civic space of Selma's black community;**
right: **View of Dallas Avenue, Selma, Alabama.**

View of Edmund Pettus Bridge, Selma, Alabama

The Pettus Bridge crosses the Alabama River and is the literal and symbolic entry into the city of Selma. Ironically, given its prominent position in the city's urban structure, it is one of the few components of the urban landscape that did not easily lend itself to the racialized geographies established throughout the city. Neither by design nor by traditions of use does the bridge avail itself of the distinctions of the dual, differential scale of the typological distinctions that define primary entry with white users and secondary entry with black users. In a city replete with redundant cultural systems and whose urban landscape was designed to create spatial, political hierarchies designated by race, the bridge is eloquent in its simplicity. It is in fact the bridge's lack of "flexibility" in negotiating the dual geographies of Selma's racial landscape that caused it to be the focus of the events of 'Bloody Sunday.'[6] The Bloody Sunday confrontation and its aftermath were a challenge to the long standing political hierarchies established by the strategies which had previously rendered blacks "invisible."

6 On Sunday, March 7, 1965, a group of black residents of Selma and Dallas County attempted to march to Montgomery to dramatize their lack of political enfranchisement. This first march from Selma to Montgomery was led by John Lewis and was violently concluded at the foot of the Edmund Pettus Bridge by Alabama State troopers. The date became known as "Bloody Sunday." A second unsuccessful march followed and ended peacefully. Two weeks after Bloody Sunday, a third march left Selma and was successful. The marchers, led by Martin Luther King Jr., followed Highway 80 to Montgomery, camping along the way. They arrived five days later at the State Capitol. In 1996 Congress designated Highway 80 (including sections of Selma and Montgomery) a National Historic Trail.

MABEL O. WILSON

two   between rooms 307

SPACES OF MEMORY AT THE NATIONAL CIVIL RIGHTS MUSEUM

Train tracks crisscross Memphis, so that no matter where you turn you see tracks—tracks whose cars brim with coal, tracks with clicking and clacking cars lumbering across the horizon. Memphis is and has always been a city of comings and goings, of goods and peoples who travel through its rail yards, its depots, and its hotels. Clicking and clacking, crissing and crossing, echoing the blues and the sounds of rememory.

Under the sway of slavery and racism, generations of African-Americans were forced to sever family and communal bonds under the brutal yoke of enslavement or expected to bury a past steeped in violence and anguish. As part of the healing process and in hope of securing a better future, many African-Americans re-imagine the painful past. This imaginative effort permeates black oral, musical, and artistic traditions. For African-Americans, collective history and lore have traditionally been passed on through non-monumental, ephemeral means—for instance, the haunting refrains of the Memphis blues. As novelist Maya Angelou has written:

> *If we were a people much given to revealing secrets, we might raise monuments and sacrifice memories of our poets, but slavery cured us of that weakness. It may be enough, however, to have it said that we survive in exact relationship to the dedication of our poets (including preachers, musicians and blues singers).* [1]

Given the legacy of African-American's 400-year presence in the United States, it is astonishing that most of these monuments, memorials, and museums are so young. The phenomenon of erecting monuments has become popular for African-Americans only recently, because while the 1863 Emancipation Proclamation granted enslaved blacks the imaginary juridical space of constitutional rights, it was not until the Civil Rights Movement a century later that the physical spaces of the nation—schools, hotels, and public institutions—were made accessible. Today "Black Heritage," as it is termed, has ballooned into a multi-million dollar tourist industry. [2] Cities, historical societies, and citizen groups have identified locales where key events in the struggle for equality occurred and have undertaken preservation measures for the homes of eminent figures and the buildings of important institutions. Although

I would like to thank Craig Barton and Ulrick Désert for their helpful comments on this essay.

1 Maya Angelou, "I Know Why the Caged Bird Sings," *The Anatomy of Memory.* ed. James McConkey, (Oxford: University of Oxford Press, 1996), 264.

2 Nancy C. Curtis, *Black Heritage Sites, the North and the South,* (New York: New Press. 1996); Beth L. Savage. *African-American Historic Places.* (New York: Preservation Press, 1994); Wayne C. Robinson, *The African-American Travel Guide* (New Jersey: Hunter Publishing, 1998).

many structures and even some entire communities and towns have been irrevocably lost—leaving only vacant lots and weedy fields—several important historical sites have been established successfully. These include the Black Heritage Trail in Boston, the African-American Museum in Detroit, and the African Burial Ground in New York City. But it is the National Civil Rights Museum in Memphis, Tennessee, that best responds to the concerns in Kobena Mercer's query: What happens on the threshold of [enunciation]?

> *If after many years of struggle, you arrive at the threshold of enunciation and are "given" the right to speak, is it not the case that there will be an over-whelming pressure to try and tell the whole story all at once? . . . What results is an overcrowded chaotic narrative which inevitably tends to simplify what it seeks to describe and explain precisely because it is impossible to condense and contain such a rich and complex history in one brief outburst.*[3]

Built on the site where Martin Luther King Jr. was slain in 1968, the National Civil Rights Museum exposes the complexities that arise when one addresses a culture whose values and practices evolved often in contradiction to those of European America; one popular European-American value is the ritual of erecting commemorative markers.

Tucked behind South Main Street, a formerly bustling thoroughfare fronting warehouses of the crop that was once King Cotton, that now features the galleries and eateries of gentrification, stands the National Civil Rights Museum, neé the Lorraine Motel, neé the Windsor Hotel. Never a prized part of town despite its proximity to the commercial center, the neighborhood has always been industrial, poor, and primarily black. While Memphis' Sanborn insurance maps record the value of real estate, they also map the city's social complexion by conspicuously noting the locations of its "Negro tenements," "colored tenements," and "colored female boarding houses"—all in the vicinity of the NCRM.

In 1947 Walter Bailey purchased the 64-room yellow brick hotel at 406 Mulberry Street from its white proprietor. At the height of its notoriety in the 1950s, the motel

3 Kobena Mercer, *Welcome to the Jungle,* (New York: Routledge, 1994).

View of Lorraine Motel and Museum addition. Author's collection

was a favorite haunt of African-American luminaries and performers, many of whom were top acts at the night spots and theaters around Beale Street, the city's blues haven. The motel was also a favorite layover for Martin Luther King, Jr. as he and his compatriots traversed the South championing civil rights for blacks and the poor. Room 307 was King's usual request.[4]

Memphis' legacy in the struggle for race relations—a 70-year period of productive, but contentious, dealings between white political fathers and the black middle class establishment—allowed the city to avoid many of the fierce civil rights conflicts that had erupted elsewhere in the South. Successful sit-ins and boycotts in the early 1960s brought an end to the legal segregation of the city's public facilities. This is not to imply the absence of a corrosive racial ethos in Memphis—one has only to travel through its still existing "black belts," swathes of shotgun houses bordering cotton warehouses, to comprehend its invasive wrath. Nor is it to suggest that Memphis' African-Americans did not remember the painful and unjust history of living in a segregated, impoverished Jim Crow city—the mournful refrains of the Memphis blues compellingly remind us of that.[5]

At the invitation of local religious and political activists, King journeyed to Memphis twice in the spring of 1968 to rally support during a sanitation workers' strike. The workers demanded fair and equal treatment untainted by racism and

4 David M. Tucker, *Memphis Since Crump: Bossism, Blacks, and Civil Reformers 1948–1968* (Knoxville: University of Tennessee Press, 1980), and Gloria B. Melton, *Blacks in Memphis Tennessee 1920–1955* (UMI, 1982).

5 For an assessment of the reliance of the White-run political machine on highly influential African-American businessmen see David M. Tucker, *Memphis Since Crump* and Gloria B. Melton, *Blacks in Memphis Tennessee 1920–1955.*

For a general history of Memphis see John E. Harkins, *Metropolis on the Nile: Memphis and Shelby County* (Oxford, Tennessee: Guild Bindery Press, 1982).

union representation in order to negotiate with an abusive and implacable municipal authority. King's subsequent civil rights battles integrated labor activism, perhaps an ideological shift that threatened America's racially stratified labor force. For King human dignity had become commensurate with a fair wage. His tactic—the non-violent march—exploded in a deadly melee between a faction of militant marchers and some overzealous police officers. His second trip, in April of 1968, promised to yield a more decisive, unified protest, but on the evening of April 4th King was gunned down by James Earl Ray while standing on the balcony of the Lorraine Motel.

After falling into disrepair in the decades after King's assassination, the Lorraine Motel was transformed into the National Civil Rights Museum in 1991. Since opening, it has attracted local visitors, school children, and tourists from around the world. But to create this memorial to the slain civil rights leader, a coalition of Memphis citizens had to overcome several impasses: they successfully battled foreclosure on the hotel in the early 1980s, lobbied to raise private and state funding, and quelled a political row over the selection of an architect; all before demolition of two-thirds of the motel was scheduled to begin in 1989.[6] An underlying intention, alluded to in the statements of local politicians, was to link the museum to a citywide redevelopment strategy to boost tourism. The transformation of Beale Street into a blues theme park began in the 1980s, and is one outcome of this strategy to promote tourism in Memphis.

To create an edifice that would revitalize both the motel and the image of the neighborhood, the architects, McKissick and McKissick, created a compound—including the museum, memorial, auditorium, and offices—encompassing the entire block. An honorific courtyard to the museum preserves the motel wing where King was assassinated. Behind this, a large nondescript brick addition housing museum facilities takes up the rest of the parcel. Visitors enter the museum between the original hotel building and the 1960s motor court addition. Once inside, they progress through a labyrinth of rooms that culminates in the commemorative vestibule adjacent to King's quarters in the original motel.

6 Interest in renovating the 50-unit motel as a memorial to King began in earnest in the late 1970s after the hotel had begun deteriorating. Owner Walter Bailey had been negligent in maintaining mortgage payments and the hotel was put up for auction in 1982 with the possibility it would be demolished. Over several months a foundation headed by local businessmen raised the $144,000 necessary to purchase the motel. By 1987, $8.8 million dollars had been allocated from various city, county, and state governments.

ORCHESTRATING MEMORY Like many institutions created by and about formerly marginalized groups, the National Civil Rights Museum has established an expansive agenda: it seeks to memorialize not only King, but also the achievements of all Americans who have battled racial injustice. However, by trying to "tell the whole story"—to use Mercer's phrase—the museum unwittingly denies its public the possibility of articulating their own meanings and associations of this complex history. Thus the endeavor to memorialize encourages, albeit unintentionally, a static interpretation of African-American history. The design and exhibitions of the National Civil Rights Museum reinforce an unfortunate fixity of cultural meaning and memory.

As the abandoned warehouses and dilapidated shotguns in the gritty, industrial neighborhood surrounding the Lorraine Motel yield to the forces of gentrification, the National Civil Rights Museum freezes the remnants of the motel in the past. Venturing into the courtyard, visitors encounter an uncanny reconstitution of the Lorraine Motel as it was on April 4, 1968. The signage, balconies, and façade have been meticulously restored according to the memorable photograph that captured the

The National Civil Rights Museum's memorial forecourt. Author's collection

panic of King's final moments. Two vintage automobiles in front of the rooms corre-
spond exactly to those in the photograph. The only contemporary elements are a
wreath of white flowers draped over a railing, a stone plaque installed in front of the
room, and some wrought iron tables. This simulation, while intending to provide a
glimpse into a significant historical moment, preempts the possibility of imagining
the event from a contemporary perspective. Entering the museum, visitors become
passive consumers of an image the media have made iconic. The only intrusion into
this well orchestrated scene comes from the recurring one-woman protest regularly
staged outside the compound by an evicted resident of the Lorraine Motel, who
aggressively reminds visitors that the "bourgeois" aspirations of the museum fail to
carry out King's commitment to bettering the lives of the poor.[7]

Inside the expansive addition, the architects, curators, and museum staff have
designed a series of rooms whose exhibits and full-scale recreations authenticate a san-
itized, institutional account of the Civil Rights Movement. Its linear narrative begins
with the importation of Africans to the American colonies and continues through
Abolition, Reconstruction, and the Jim Crow era. But the museum focuses mainly
upon the intensifying civil rights activity of the 1950s after the Supreme Court's 1954
Brown v. Board of Education decision that outlawed school segregation. Winding
through the exhibition, visitors can view precious few authentic artifacts, since most
of the displays contain reproductions of letters, newspaper articles, and photographs.
Brown tones and sepia hues have been applied to the props and reproductions in order
to cast a "vintage" glow that underscores the "historicity" of the entire exhibition. The
curators and exhibition designers have fashioned full-scale dioramas of pivotal Civil
Rights events—visitors can "participate" in the sit-in at the Greensboro lunch counter
and "march" with the phalanxes of the Freedom March on Washington, D.C.

In one room a panorama of mirrors barrages viewers with news footage of the
brutal assaults against protesters by the Birmingham police. At the Rosa Parks exhibition, museum-goers may board a vintage bus, sit down, and be verbally chastised by
an irate white bus driver who barks, "You can't sit there!" and "I told you to move to
the back of the bus!" These simulations impose a seamless authenticity, and a sense of
inevitability upon the museum's unfolding narrative.

7 Jacqueline Smith's protest
(according to an unofficial
Guinness certificate, the longest
boycott in progress), has garnered
international attention from an
array of sympathizers, scholars,
and activists.

Along with all this imagery, an overwhelming strain of Americanism underscores the exhibition and indeed the institution's mission. Throughout the museum, African-American history marches in cadence with the nation's official grand pageant; the virtues of liberty, freedom, and equality are ritually sounded in a timeless refrain. Emblazoned across the front of the brochure the passage, "We hold these truths to be self evident, that all men are created equal," further confirms the patriotic gloss of the exhibition. Although the trumpeting of this nationalism cannot quite muffle the dissonance that racism has fomented in America, it nonetheless works to repress the widespread conviction that Africans and their descendants have never really been considered equal in America, even after Emancipation. The patriotism of the exhibition also obscures the extent to which blacks were envisioned as the antithesis of whites— as irreparably inferior in character. Indeed, some would even argue that America's concept of freedom was understood, not despite, but through the enslavement of Africans; that although enslaved Africans were in some sense "invisible," they were nonetheless indispensable to the building of a young democracy.[8]

It is regrettable that these difficult and important contradictions are not more forcefully acknowledged and discussed through the museum's exhibits. Instead, the use of certain American myths undermines the memorial's meaning, robbing it of the complexity and immediacy that might encourage engagement.

In the end, the discordant and rigid historical interpretations of the National Civil Rights Museum hinder remembrance. Exploring different strategies for memorializing the Holocaust, James Young cautions us:

> ...that public memory is constructed, that understanding of events depends on memory's construction, and that there are worldly consequences in the kinds of historical understanding generated by monuments. Instead of allowing the past to rigidify in its monumental forms, we would vivify our memory through the memory-work itself—whereby events, their recollection, and the role the monuments play in our lives remain animate never completed.[9]

8 Novelist Toni Morrison offers a useful critique of how racial formations, in this instance articulated through literature, come to serve the formation of America's socio-cultural beliefs, practices, and national identity.

See Toni Morrison, *Playing in the Dark: Whiteness and the Literary Imagination*, (New York: Vintage Books, 1993).

9 James E. Young, *The Texture of Memory: Holocaust Memorials and Meaning*, (New Haven: Yale University Press, 1993), 15.

Whether commemorating the Holocaust or the Civil Rights Movement, we must confront the risk of enshrining any particular interpretation of history; for as Young asserts, by doing so we fail to allow for the mutability of collective meaning and memory. Monuments that resist transformation risk losing their significance to future generations.

THINGS WE FORGET Settled on a strategic bend along the Mississippi River, Memphis blossomed as a center of commerce. The city's tapestry of train tracks not only transported goods to points across the country, but also served as a crossroads for waves of migrating African-Americans for well over 100 years. The lyrical laments of the Memphis blues recall the sounds and emotions experienced by those who traveled along these tracks. Its melodic refrains echo the railroad's modalities of transience and return. For blues virtuosos the music provided several avenues of escape—in one sense it was a means of psychological escape from racism, and in other ways it offered an opportunity for financial flight from the economic shackles of impoverishment imposed by segregation.

In his 1989 film *Mystery Train*, filmmaker Jim Jarmusch eloquently and comedically muses upon the rich blues culture of Memphis. The film tracks the escapades of tourists, transplants, and locals who drift through the train stations, airports, and hotels of the city. This eclectic cadre of travelers criss-cross the dilapidated landscape of warehouses, theaters, and pool halls in the vicinity of Mulberry Street. Though not of African-American descent, Jarmusch imbues *Mystery Train's* story with the poignantly vibrant voice of black Memphis. And unlike the static historical narrative related at the National Civil Rights Museum, *Mystery Train's* playful fusion of local myth, collective memory, and popular culture captures the polyvalent leitmotifs of the blues.

The film is composed of three vignettes, each transpiring over the same 24-hour period. The three stories converge at the shady Arcade Hotel managed by an eccentric black desk manager and bellhop sidekick. The first story, "Far from Yokohama," introduces Memphis from the perspective of two Japanese hipsters on a pilgrimage to the world renowned birthplace of rock and roll. Stylishly hip and aloof, Jun and Mitzko trek through the black neighborhoods adjacent to downtown in search of the haunts of their rock idols Elvis Presley and Carl Perkins. A backdrop of abandoned houses, boarded storefronts, and derelict theater marquees rhythmically flows along as the camera pans parallel to their expedition. Outside of their tourist gaze (and ours) the sounds of daily life—children playing, people talking—can be heard, but are never seen. Exhausted from a day of incomprehensible tours and unseen sights, the weary travelers seek lodgings for the evening at the Arcade Hotel. Negotiating in phrasebook English, Jun and Mitzko secure a room from the Arcade's amused, but unperturbed night staff. Once settled into room 36, Jun and Mitzko debate Japanese-American cultural affinities, and fatigued, after sex, they are eventually lulled to sleep by a late-night disc jockey, only to be startled in the morning by the sound of a lone gunshot. They depart by train the next day.

The second vignette, "A Ghost," tells of a melancholy Italian tourist who finds herself marooned in Memphis for 24 hours. As she meanders through the city, the camera, as in the previous story, pans parallel to her stroll. She arrives at the Arcade Hotel at the same moment as a flustered New Jersey hairdresser who is fleeing a soured relationship with an English millworker nicknamed "Elvis." Intuiting their mutual desperation, the desk manager suggests these two wayward travelers share accommodations. While settling into their accomodations, they overhear Jun and Mitzko making love. Like their fellow hotel denizens, they are serenaded by the sultry disc jockey and rattled in the morning by the sound of a gun discharged elsewhere in the hotel. These two also depart Memphis the following morning.

The darkly satiric final tale, "Lost in Space," introduces two more transplants to Memphis—the hairdresser's brother from New Jersey and the aforementioned Elvis. They are reluctantly accompanied in their adventure by an African-American friend named Will Robinson. The three seek refuge at the Arcade after a spontaneous and unsuccessful liquor store robbery. The post- apocalyptic decor of room 22 befits the mood of their reckless flight from the law. The following morning in a drunken scuffle they misfire a gun. But beyond the misdeeds and mishaps that pepper this story, in this vignette the camera traverses into the everyday spaces of the city: into Robinson's apartment, a pool hall, a liquor store. Pool hall regulars utter despairingly about the hardships of everyday life: ". . seem [sic] like everybody in this town is out of work," laments one distraught brother. Finally, this tale of black Memphis speaks about the harsh economic inequalities and racial discord that resides behind the city's glittering tourist façades.

Watching the comings and goings of these non-natives, and logging the action in an enormous ledger are the hotel's otherworldly night sentries portrayed by blues provocateur Screamin' Jay Hawkins—decked out in a flaming red suit—and Cinque Lee, in full bellhop regalia. A veritable Greek chorus, they reenact the same scene throughout the film. We discover very little about them, (only that Will Robinson is the brother-in-law of the desk manager). While these two remain unnamed, they nevertheless guard the threshold between Memphis' past, present, and future.

Since film readily accommodates non-linear storytelling, a "temporal tourism" of sorts, the brilliance of *Mystery Train* lies in its intertwining narratives and its play of sights and sounds.[10] The hotel room—replete with kitschy Elvis décor—functions as a common denominator linking each tale. If it is the visual landscape, the vibrant night hues clashing against the drab scenes of the city by day, that cuts apart the film's temporal narrative, then it is the aural cues: the Stax sound, blues guitar riffs, and train whistles that stitch the stories back together. Throughout the film's briskly paced dialogue characters misinterpret phrases, meanings transform in translation, and ideas remain opaque to explanation. Along with this linguistic melange, noises and musical refrains also recur. *Mystery Train*, whose title refers to a 1953 blues song written and recorded by Junior Parker and best remembered as an early recording by a brash young Elvis Presley, borrows the polyvalent cadence and kinetic verse of the blues to propel its filmic narrative. As a genre, blues songs shift in sound and meaning through melodic repetition and lyrical double entendres. Recognizing the mutability of the blues, Jarmusch features the tune twice in the film—the popular Presley version begins the film's "lighter" touristic first narrative and the lesser known blues version orchestrates the films "darker" denouement.

With *Mystery Train* Jarmusch scripts a film in which the blues-inspired dissonance and repetition become analogous to the ephemeral spaces of individual and collective memory. In a key scene the retro-rocker Jun contemplates the flow of culture throughout the world which forms sites of remembrance and spaces of forgetting—

10 Anne Friedberg, *Window Shopping—Cinema and the Postmodern*, (Berkeley: University of California, 1993), 94.

the latter constituting gaps in memory that we continually struggle to fill by erecting of monuments and acquiring souvenirs. Responding to Mitzko's query as to why he photographs "the rooms we stay in and never what we see outside when we travel?" he solemnly responds, "Those other things are in my memory. The hotel rooms and the airports are the things we forget." As global culture erodes the individuality of the places we inhabit, Jun photographs them to capture what his mind can no longer retain. Although Jun and Mitzko's journey reminds us that Memphis is a brief layover along the global tourist's itinerary, Jarmusch includes the other tales to allow us to revisit the city once more via other personas and perspectives. The parade of sounds and images interlaced through the three vignettes compels the viewer to connect previous scenes psychologically. By recalling the successive events, viewers assume an active role in animating the temporal and spatial flow of the film. *Mystery Train's* densely woven narrative of events, people, and places activates the collective memory of its audience.

BETWEEN ROOMS 307 In *Mystery Train's* cinematic narratives, the hotel establishes a threshold between the cultural, the historical, the personal, and the urban. Anthropologist James Clifford's evokes "the hotel as station, airport terminal, hospital: a place you pass through, where the encounters are fleeting, arbitrary."[11] Perhaps when experienced as a hotel, the National Civil Rights Museum's Lorraine Motel shares these qualities and transforms into a site of collective memory.

It is the diminutive space of King's Memorial—between the two rooms labeled 307 of the Lorraine Motel—that the visuality, authenticity and ideology of the museum begins to fracture. Before crossing from the museum into the memorial space of the old motel, visitors pass a reenactment in miniature of the Memphis Sanitation Strike; this signals a narrative shift from the grand to the local. Once inside a modest vestibule in the motel, visitors gaze into two of the rooms allegedly occupied by Martin Luther King Jr. The first replicates the decor seen in a 1966 image of King in room 307; in the other room, also identified as 307, we see empty dishes, a turned down bed, and newspapers found in the room on the day of the assassination. Most people mistakenly assume that the first room—labeled in the photograph as 307 (see page 26)—is where King stayed on that fateful night; but then visitors turn and realize

11 James Clifford, *Routes—Travel and Translation in the Late Twentieth Century*, (Cambridge: Harvard University Press, 1997), 17.

that the second room, also identified on the placard as 307, was King's. But neither is accurate. The actual "room 307" was in fact the area demolished to form the vestibule.

At this point it must be acknowledged that the museum's full-scale representations either de-emphasize or, conversely, exaggerate certain characteristics in an effort to portray convincingly the where, when, and how of certain events. The restored courtyard, for example, takes advantage of the authenticity of the motel's locale in order to emphasize its evocation of the 1960s. The linear historical narrative draws the exhibition's geographically diverse cities—Greensboro, Montgomery, Selma, and elsewhere—into the purview of the museum's orderly landscape. With these discrepancies in time and location diminished, the museum's story of the Civil Rights Movement can thus be conveyed to its patrons.

Between the simulations of room 307, however, the spatial and temporal underpinnings of the museum's narrative becomes shaky. On first glance, Room 307 appears to be in the correct place; yet the realization of its duplication and relocation destroys the site's aura of authenticity. Moreover, in this part of the museum time ceases to be a stabilizing factor since, paradoxically, the same room depicts different visits by King. As a result, the strategies of representation that ordered the museum's objectives in the other areas fail to prevail in this important and evocative section.

This criticism is not intended to condemn the memorial entirely; indeed, for perceptive visitors this confusion elicits a strong response. Those provoked by the uncertainty of seeing two facsimiles of room 307 begin to question what they are seeing. And, when comparing the different rooms, museum-goers must struggle to piece together their own interpretation of the events that occurred there, rather than accepting the institution's account. This process allows individual perceptions, along with collective aspirations, to color the formation of memory. Consequently, the ideologies and representational strategies that elsewhere structure the museum's interpretation of history give way to more fluid, mutable remembrances of the Civil Rights Movement.

Although a laudable attempt to celebrate African-American history, the National Civil Rights Museum nevertheless fails to deploy an already well-established local cultural sensibility of the blues. These practices encourage a spirit of placelessness, what Houston Baker, writing on blues culture, asserts as crossing signs:

Fixity is a function of power. Those who maintain place, who decide what takes place and dictate what has taken place, are power brokers of the traditional. The "placeless," by contrast, are translators of the nontraditional. Rather than fixed in the order of cunning Grecian urns, their lineage is fluid, nomadic, transitional. Their appropriate mark is a crossing sign at the junction.[12]

clockwise from left: **National Civil Rights Museum's exhibit of the 1963 March on Washington. Image taken from postcard; Recreation of the Greensboro lunch counter sit-in at the National Civil Rights Museum. Image taken from postcard; Memorial on the site of Martin Luther King Jr.'s assassination at the National Civil Rights Museum.** Author's collection

12 Houston A. Baker, *Blues, Ideology, and Afro-American Literature—A Vernacular Theory,* (Chicago: University of Chicago Press, 1984), 202.

A genre of shifting sounds and lyrics, the blues can be imagined as akin to motels that function as crossroads for migrating peoples and cultures. Unlike the tradition of erecting of monuments and museums that catalog and preserve the past, the cultural practices of African-Americans have flourished in these modes of transience—the modes where words, sounds, and forms shift in the play of remembrance.

> *Memphis is and has always been a city of comings and goings, of goods and peoples who travel through its rail yards, its depots, and its hotels. Clicking and clacking, crissing and crossing, echoing the blues and the sounds of rememory.*

A previous version of this essay was published by Harvard Design Magazine, Fall 1999.

Dr. Martin Luther King Jr., Lorraine Motel, Memphis, 1966. © Ernest C. Withers Panopticon Gallery, Waltham, MA.

three   uncovering places of memory

WALKING TOURS OF MANHATTAN

A stroll along Manhattan Streets reveals almost nothing except dark faces to connect the Negroes with the History of New York City. —M. A. Harris, *A Negro History Tour of Manhattan*

In the tumultuous year of 1968, M.A. "Spike" Harris published *A Negro History Tour of Manhattan* documenting African presence on the island through the span of time. His historical narrative, meant to accompany armchair or real walking tours through discrete neighborhoods, describes an invisible city within New York: the mostly lost and uncommemorated grounds upon which the history of African-Americans has unfolded. His book describes sites that are primarily events and "biographies" listed by address rather than concrete architectural or artistic manifestations of that which is considered historic. As a site of memory, his guide opens a liminal space between history and the urban landscape, provoking a reformulation of the ideologies of the city. As a book about invisible, ephemeral places, the guide offers new definitions of the monumental in the present day American City, a city of perpetual change.

In contrast, *Walking Tours of Manhattan* takes the problem of the radical transformation and reconstruction of spaces within Manhattan as a necessary characteristic of a living city, looking at the absence of historic artifacts as a way to remember and to connect with the past. To walk is the indefinite process of being absent and in search of a place. To make and create a tour or structured narrative from the sites listed is to haunt and remember the city by moving through it, allowing story to cut across map or physically allowing map and location to structure narrative.

In walking, a permanent home position is created as an ever-shifting series of discrete locations from which to understand the city. The use of the terms Negro, African, African-American, and Black in the titling of these sites acknowledges the changing political and social status of African-Americans through the act of naming and re-naming. Three maps are shown, perpetually in progress, illustrating the location of many sites listed by Harris, by I. N. Phelps Stokes in his six volume *Iconography of Manhattan*

Island 1489–1909, and those listed and located by Christopher Moore, an historian of African-American history. Each map consists of a current plan of Manhattan and an overlay illustrating, respectively, the configuration of New Amsterdam from 1623–1664, British New York from 1664–1783, and New York City 1783–1899. Also included are listings of site typologies such as churches and burial sites, African-American owned businesses, farms, schools/orphanages, homes, districts, Underground Railroad stops, and entertainment related sites. Since 1968, because of the work of Spike Harris and historians like Christopher Moore, Dr. Sherrill Wilson at the African Burial Ground Center, and others, many sites have been physically marked and are commemorated. These maps are a step towards understanding a series of stories connecting people and the Manhattan landscape.

"Our Best Society" A scene on Fifth Avenue from the New York
Illustrated News, January 31, 1863. From the collection of the
New York Historical Society.

New Amsterdam 1623–1664

SITE TYPOLOGIES

1) FORT AMSTERDAM AT U.S. CUSTOM HOUSE
1 Bowling Green
Built by first slaves on Manhattan.
First Dutch Reformed Church Inside Fort.
1626

2) HOSPITAL FOR SICK SOLDIERS AND BLACKS
Bridge Street
Castello Plan Section E, Lot 23 & 24

3) "BLACK JACOB'S HOUSE"
Home built by Jacob Hellekers
The Black Carpenter of Gravesend.
Castello Plan Section A, Lot 18

4) JACOB STOFFELSEN OF ZIERICKZEE
Home of the Overseer of the Dutch
West India Company's Slaves.
Castello Plan Section J, Lot 15, 1639

**5) HOUSE OF THE DUTCH WEST INDIA
COMPANY'S SLAVES**
32–34 South William Street
Castello Plan Section J, Lot 15, 1640

6) SUSANNA ANTHONY ROBERT'S HOUSE
Free Black Woman's Home
52–54 Beaver Street
Planted with 8 Small Trees
Castello Plan Secton M, Lot 16 & 17
In 1660 the house was gone.

7) THE HARLEM ROAD
Later the Boston Post Road
Built by the Slaves of the Dutch West India Co.
Currently Includes portions of 5th Ave.,
Park Ave., Madison Ave., and the Bowery, 1658

8) FREE AFRICANS LOTS
Chinatown, Little Italy, Soho, Greenwich
Village, Washington Square Park. Land Granted
to Africans freed from slavery after years of
dedicated service. Prince St. to Astor Place and
from the Bowery to Broadway. Includes the land
of Lucas Santomee, a black physician,
1645–1716

9) BIG MANUEL'S FARM
Greenwich Village, Washington Square Park

10) DOMINGO ANTHONY'S FARM
Greenwich Village, 1643

11) THE AFRICAN'S CAUSEWAY
Minetta Lane and Minetta Brook
The "Negroes" Causeway on historic maps

12) PAUL D'ANGOLA'S FARM
MacDougal & West 4th Street, 1644

13) SIMON CONGO'S FARM
Fifth Avenue, 14th street to Washington Square
1644

14) **GRAMERCY PARK**
(Peter Stuyvesant's widow sells land
to a former slave)

15) **SOLOMON PETER'S PROPERTY**
Now fifth Avenue and 23rd Street

16) **MANUAL SPANGIE AND THE SANTOMEE
FAMILY PROPERTIES**

17) **PETER STUYVESANT'S BOWERY CHURCH**
St. Mark's Church and Graveyard
Second Avenue, N.W. Corner E. 10th, 1650

18) **BLACK PETER ATTEMPTS TO HANG
BIG MANUEL**
1662

above: Site 19) Trinity Church graveyard; *below:* Site 20) African Burial Ground
Memorial. Excavated in 1991 for New Federal Office Tower.

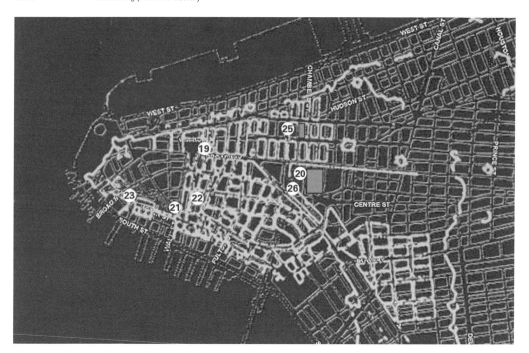

British Colony 1664–1783

SITE TYPOLOGIES

19) TRINITY CHURCH
1697
Later Chartered as St. Philips Church.
Slaves were not permitted burial here,
but were laid to rest in the African's
Burial Ground

20) THE AFRICAN BURIAL GROUND
270 Broadway, 167–1816
Burial place of slaves, free Africans,
and other impoverished people

22) THE SLAVE MARKET
The Buttonwood Tree at
60 Wall Street, 1709

23) SLAVE INSURRECTION
Near pond on Maiden Lane
and Williams Street, 1712

24) FRAUNCES TAVERN
Black-owned tavern, Sam Fraunces, proprietor;
54 Pearl Street, 1719

25) WILLIAMS TOBACCO SHOP
Black-owned shop, 239 Orange Street

26) VAUXHALL GARDENS
Pleasure and Beer Gardens, Chambers Street
to Warren Street to the Hudson.
Owned by Sam Faunces

27) CITY HALL PARK EXECUTIONS
1741

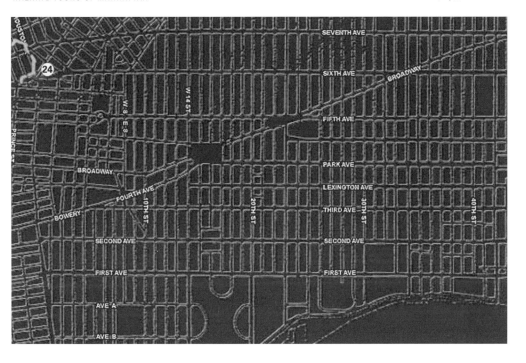

above: **Site 27) Execution on the Commons, lithograph by G. Hayward from the collection of the New York Historical Society;** *right:* **Site 29) John Street Methodist Church Pocket Park with mural copied from painting found in church basement that includes first black sextant, Peter Williams.**

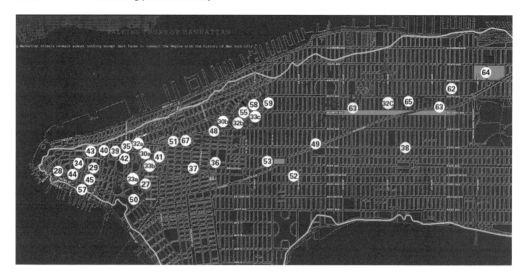

New York City 1783–1899

SITE TYPOLOGIES

28) THE AFRICAN RELIEF SOCIETY
42 Baxter Street. Also Underground
Railroad Station 1786

29) JOHN STREET METHODIST CHURCH
44 John Street
Peter Williams, black sextant.
Later African Methodist
Episcopal Zion Church, 1796

30) MOTHER AFRICAN METHODIST
EPISCOPAL ZION CHURCH
A) 1796, 44 John Street at Cross Street between
Baxter and Mulberry Street. Formed by Sextant
Peter Williams with members of John Street
Church. Founded in 1766 on William Street.
Church Street between Leonard and
Worth Street.
B) 1864, 215 Bleeker Street Corner of 7th Ave
C)1904, 127 West 89th Street between
Amsterdam and Columbus.
D) 1915, 151 West 136th Street between
Powell and Malcom X Blvd.
E) 1925, 140–148 West 137th Street
between Powell and Malcom X.

31) HAMILTON GRANGE,
ALEXANDER HAMILTON HOUSE
1801, abolitionist President of the Society
for the Manumission of Slaves.
287 Convent Avenue.

32) ABYSSIANIAN BAPTIST CHURCH
A) 1808, 40 Worth Street between Church
and West Broadway.
B) 1864– , 164–166 Waverly Place between

6th and Christopher Street.
C) 1903, 240–248 West 40th Street between
7th and 8th Ave.
D) 1923, 132–142 West 138th Street
between Powell and Malcom X Blvd.
Built by Charles Bolton and Son.

33) ST. PHILIP'S PROTESTANT EPISCOPAL
AFRICAN INSTITUTION
(Formed by members of Trinity Church)
A) 1819, 24 Center Street between Worth and
Leonard Street.
B) 1849; summer, 360 Broadway.
C) 1859, Mulberry Street near Bleeker.
D) 1886, West 25th Street.
E) 1911, 208 West 134th Street Built by
Vertner Tandy and George Foster Jr..

34) DOWNING OYSTER HOUSE
3–7 Broad Street
Underground Railroad Station, 1820–1866

35) "FREEDOM'S JOURNAL"
First newspaper in the U.S. owned
and published by African-Americans, John
Russworm and Rev. Samuel Cornish, 150–152
Church Street 1826–1829

36) THE AFRICAN GROVE THEATER
Corner of Mercer and Bleeker Streets
First black theater in New York City
1827–1830

37) BUCKLEY'S ETHIOPIAN OPERA HOUSE
539 Broadway.

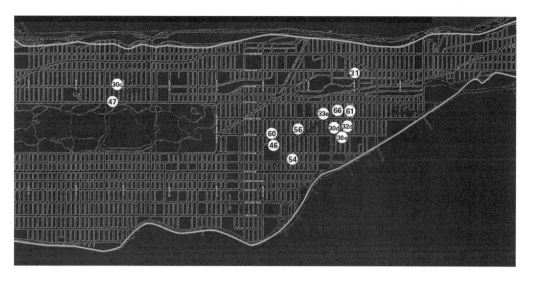

38) COLORED ORPHAN ASYLUM
5th Avenue between 44th and 45th Streets.
Originally at 12th Street.

39) THIRD ASSOCIATE PRESBYTERIAN
CHURCH
41–47 Murray Street.

40) PIERRE TOUSSAINT (ST. PETERS ROMAN
CATHOLIC CHURCH
22 Barclay Street, S.E. Corner of
Church Street.

41) DAVID RUGGLES
36 Lispenard Street.
Underground Railroad Station.

42) SOJOURNER TRUTH
140 Church Street
(Mother A.M.E.Zion Church).

43) DUN AND BRADSTREET
99 Church Street, owned by abolitionist
Arthur Tappan.

44) NAUTILUS COMPANY NEW YORK LIFE
INSURANCE CO.
58 Wall Street.

45) MARY WASHINGTON'S SHOP
79 John Street.

46) ETHIOPIAN HEBREW
CONGREGATIONS SYNAGOGUE
1 West 123rd Street.

47) SENECA VILLAGE
Central Park West between
86th and 89th Street, 1850.

48) CATHOLIC CHURCH OF ST. BENEDICT
THE MOOR
First black Catholic church, corner of
Bleeker and Downing Street.

49) SPORTS AND ENTERTAINMENT ARENA
Madison Square Park.

50) ELIZABETH JENNINGS CHATHAM SQUARE
Underground Railroad Stop, 1854.

51) CIVIL WAR DRAFT RIOTS
Greenwich Village.
Thompson Street and Sullivan Street
north to Canal Street.

52) QUAKER MEETING HOUSE
28 Gramercy Park South.

53) UNION SQUARE
AFRICAN-AMERICAN SOLDIERS
PRESENTED THEIR UNIFORMS, 1864

54) LANGSTON HUGHES HOME
20 East 127th Street,
built by Alexander Wilson.

55) NEW YORK COLORED MISSION
135 West 10th Street.

56) METROPOLITAN BAPTIST CHURCH
151 West 128th Street
(Formerly New York Presbyterian Church),
1880

57) SCOTT AND COMPANY PICKLE
MANUFACTURERS
217 Water Street.

58) THOMAS JENNINGS CLOTHING RENOVATION

59) THOMAS BAGGOT, GROCER

60) ST. MARTIN'S EPISCOPAL CHURCH
230 Lenox Avenue
(Formerly Holy Trinity Episcopal Church).

61) STRIVER'S ROW
138th and 139th Streets between
7th and 8th Avenues.

62) LEWIS LATIMER
African-American electrical engineer
pioneer in Edison's Laboratory.
324 West 55th Street, 1890.

63) TENDERLOIN DISTRICT
Seventh Avenue between
20th and 40th Streets,
1890–1910

64) SAN JUAN HILL
Columbus Avenue to 10th Avenue
between 59th and 66th Streets.

65) GRANVILLE T. WOODS HOME
Near Radio City.

66) THE WHITE ROSE MISSION
Home for African-American women, 1897.

67) KATY FERGUSON'S HOME
51 Warren Street
74 Thompson street off Canal Street,
1853. African-American woman who ran a
Sunday School first out of her home
and then at Third Associate Presbyterian
Church. Adopted and cared for over
40 African-American and other orphaned
children.

Site 53) Presentation of colors to the 20th U.S. Colored
Infantry, Union Square, engraving, 1863. From the collection of the New York Historical Society.

NATHANIEL Q. BELCHER

four

miami's colored-over
segregation

SEGREGATION, INTERSTATE 95 AND MIAMI'S AFRICAN-AMERICAN LEGENDS

COME WITH ME: *Cab Calloway stands center stage smiling as his orchestra plays in the background. He lowers his hand, palm down, and the band rhythmically descends to a whisper. He steps up to the microphone and he looks over the black audience, focusing on familiar faces. The large doors to the rear of Colored Town's Lyric Theater are open and he can just make out the swaying coconut palms in the distance as the soft South Florida winter breeze washes through the room. He snaps his head to toss his conked hair from his eyes and says, "It's Great to be in Miami!" The audience roars!!!*

Within this narrative, both real and imagined, is the essence of Miami's legendary African-American community. The winter home for a sophisticated seasonal society, South Florida is always quick to glamorize itself. From the beginning, Miami's African-American community participated as a willing partner in the bustling tourist village that would emerge as the center of one of the largest metropolitan areas in the southeastern United States.

"Colored Town" was the name taken by a number of segregated black communities; in this article the name will refer to the legends and spaces of segregation that existed in this southern city and to the historic center of the African-American population; a bustling community of commerce, cultural exchange, and housing, that continues to evoke strong memories today.

Colored Town was also a product of vicious labor practices, rank opportunism, and inconspicuous manipulation. It emerged as an essentially quarantined community, whose physical area failed to expand proportionally with the dense population growth of a booming city. Strangely, Colored Town was a vital product of the segregation that existed during the first fifty years of Miami's existence, and it is ironic that it was destroyed by the effects of desegregation and the tremendous physical and cultural changes that occurred in its wake.

Today, Colored Town is officially known as Overtown and will be referred to as such in this article. It embodies the same physical space within contemporary Miami as it once did. Overtown exists despite neglect, migration, and the construction of the federal interstate highway system's

I-95 directly through its center. Overtown is in the center of Miami—Dade County—
(a twenty-minute drive to the Miami city limits) and its population of two million
people. There are ongoing efforts by politicians, community elders, governing officials, and developers to reconstruct historic Overtown. Some adhere reverently to the
legends and myths of Colored Town, others approach the reconstruction with complete ignorance of the community's history, and most approach it with a cautious
combination of community respect and commercial opportunism. Against this backdrop, the words Colored Town continue to survive as a mnemonic device through
which selected narratives evoke the pride of a once vibrant community. The healthy
evolution of Overtown and the African-American community depends on an honest
examination of historic and current conditions. For example, by accepting the historic
conditions of segregation and facing the current condition imposed by the interstate,
a more balanced proposal for the future can be achieved. Just as segregation was the
bane that existed in the first fifty years of Colored Town, I-95 exists today as a similar
interloper, deeply affecting all conditions in Overtown. These external impositions
can be seen to have both sustained and restrained Miami's African-American community. By examining the legendary imagery of the African-American community in
Colored Town, we can trace the events and circumstances leading up to the current
conditions in the African-American community there, with special attention accorded
to the construction and effects of I-95. This examination can be accomplished by illustrating how two seemingly unrelated conditions unwittingly conspired to constrain,
project, and define the future of the African-American community in Miami.

THE IRONY OF SEGREGATION AND VITALITY   In the first half of the twentieth
century, Jim Crow legislation further ghettoized Miami's black community by segregating Colored Town, combining with one stroke all trades and classes. The result of
this was the development of a vibrant, thriving community; in the rosy light of retro-
spection those years seem golden. Indeed, Colored Town experienced a sweet era of
prosperity under the oppression of segregation and perhaps ironically was prized as an
escape destination heralded for its tropical weather and tranquillity.

However, in its second fifty years Miami changed dramatically. Between 1947 and 1967 several significant events caused turbulence in the black community, and combined these events recreated the landscape and texture of the city by changing the nature, means of interaction, and characteristics of the built environment and the population of South Florida. Within the short span of a generation the legal infrastructure that had maintained Jim Crow was dismantled (1947) and black consciousness was raised. The cultural/ethnic make-up of the population changed completely with the increase of immigrants from Cuba in the 1960s and the construction of the interstate highway system significantly altered the urban infrastructure. The reverberating effect of these events had a direct impact on the quality of buildings, the texture of streetscapes, and the cloistering of neighborhoods. An examination of changes that occured in the physical fabric of Colored Town and Overtown, its destruction in mid-century, and its recent reconstruction as legend, illustrate both the endurance of the black Community and the ironies of its identity in the face of legislated abuse.

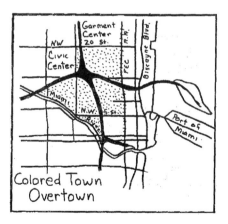

Sketch of Overtown and I-95 as illustrated by Dr. Dorothy Fields, Founder of The Black Archives of South Florida.

The Miami City Downtown Bayshore in the 1930s.

BEGINNINGS Following a destructive freeze during the winter of 1894-95, entrepreneur and railroad magnate Henry M. Flagler decided to extend his railroad interests south to the mouth of the Miami River. Sensing an opportunity, Flagler, Julia Tuttle (a Florida land baroness), and other local business leaders conspired to incorporate the area as the city of Miami and in subsequent years to move the Dade County seat to the young city. A large population of black laborers was employed to extend the railroad, clear land, and build a hotel for Flagler. By 1896 a semi-permanent encampment that housed the black laborers and their families formed upriver from the hotel and west of the railroad line. Flagler and his colleagues relied heavily on the loyal support of the black population, many of whom were registered voters, as their own success continued to grow.

In 1896, the same year the City of Miami was founded, the Supreme Court ruled in Plessy v. Ferguson, the landmark case that legalized segregation and the so-called Jim Crow laws. As the growing population of black laborers and black businesses formed, a defacto segregated community evolved out of the original encampment and came to be known as Colored Town.

Stories from that era tell of individuals like Nat "King" Cole and Ella Fitzgerald leaving a segregated Miami Beach after evening performances in the Whites Only beach clubs, and returning for after-hours shows in the clubs and hotels around Colored Town. Known as Little Broadway, the clubs along Ninth Street hosted performers who entertained late into the night to lively reception. Early mornings saw a young Cassius Clay (Mohammed Ali) jog from the Mary Elizabeth Hotel, located in the heart of Miami City's Colored Town, to Miami Beach before fights. The Lyric Theater, developed by a black entrepreneur for vaudeville performances, entertained the black community. Colored Town also offered the best education black youth could attain in southern Florida at the Booker T. Washington High school, the only school offering a full highschool education. Many of the professionals in the community enjoyed fine homes, clustered around schools, churches, and businesses that were owned by and catered to the black community. The powerful and mythic tales of black Miami that emerge from this legendary and idyllic place hold hostage the reality of its past, present, and future. In an effort to praise its history these legends project a place that never was or that exists only by isolating less desirable images of Colored Town.

Activity along Colored Town's "Broadway," circa 1925, courtesy of the Black Archives, History and Research Foundation of South Florida.

From the 1920s until the 1950s Colored Town was the center of black culture in Miami. Slowly the community crept south to Perine, west to Brownsville, and north to Liberty City through controlled strategies such as red lining narrow bands of development to prevent blacks from buying in non-black neighborhoods. Yet even within such parameters, expansions were always marked by instances of violence against black homes, the timid migration of blacks locally, and the interests of cynical developers seeking to inflate rents falsely and maximize density in the few neighborhoods that accommodated local black migration. Colored Town remained the central and most prosperous black community in the area. The name was officially changed to Overtown—a name derived from the common phrase "going over to town," which when uttered by blacks, meant going to Colored Town. Thus, it is through such narratives that both the real and imagined history of Miami's black community is defined into a benign mythology.

It is clear that Colored Town was a paradox. It contained the best that Miami could offer black culture, yet sustained the worst of conditions and contradictions imposed on the black community in the city. While Colored Town offered fine homes

above: Celebration at Overtown's Sir John Hotel, courtesy of The Black Archives, History and Research Foundation of South Florida; *opposite*: Colored Town's "Little Broadway" in the 1920s.

for the wealthy, it was also a warehouse for the least desirable urban housing stock in South Florida. Within the boundaries of the segregated city the population was always held at or above capacity and expansion was constrained to maintain density. When the population of the community grew, the old wooden shotgun houses were replaced with narrow concrete tenement buildings. These concrete bunkers vented poorly and were designed to minimize apartment size while maximizing the number of units. The rents and taxes for these buildings were inflated by demand, yet public services from the city were minimal, or non-existent. Density often meant sacrificing existing tree canopies to make way for construction. A system of canals that ran through Colored Town was placed there to service other areas of the city, often to the detriment of Colored Town's infrastructure. Stifling heat, poor services, and unsanitary conditions in the summer created health problems for the residents, and they endured continual indignities by local authorities. The city police department was known for its brutality, often sending in large groups of untrained officers to "control" the community. There were also curfews and ordinances that controlled the daily activities of the black population, including one that prevented blacks from driving through certain neighborhoods, forcing them to leave their cars at the city edge. All this runs counter to the positive image of lively night clubs and a sophisticated cafe society that existed alongside the general populace. In reality, the indignities of the Jim Crow South are numerous yet are often forgotten in sympathetic yet sincere rhetoric, which seeks to model history solely on the most positive memories of a community.

The education of Overtown's children was hardly a priority of Miami either; nearly twenty-five years after the founding of the city and long after the opening of the all-white Miami High School, the Booker T. Washington High School was finally built to accommodate the black population. The school was criticized as an unnecessary expenditure and vandalized during its construction, further delaying its occupation. A more balanced examination of the history of this era is needed to produce a more realistic understanding of the conditions that exist today. Long after the removal of legal land estate segregation in Florida (1947) and the Civil Rights Legislation of the 1960s, Miami remains a city that consistently ranks high amongst the most segregated cities in the nation. An increasingly diverse area, Miami has erupted in race riots—four significant times between 1968 and the present alone—during which much of the destruction occurred in Overtown and the largely African-American communities Liberty City and Brownsville.

At present, the communities of Overtown, Liberty City, and Brownsville operate as de facto segregated communities that fluctuate between the state of their present condition and the mythology of their past. Overtown, Liberty City, and Brownsville are physical places, neighborhoods in the traditional sense; the communities that occupy these places are economically mobile, and culturally, if not racially, diverse. The population at one point was actually legislated to be exclusively African-American and for a time these neighborhoods, along with their cultural institutions, were defined as such. In the past fifty years the legislative and cultural mechanism that held the place and population together has been dismantled. However, because the history and the myth of ownership of these places are still associated with its black past, the future of the neighborhood is defined by this community's perception of its past. The people of this community are linked to the fate of this place, and their identity is tied to it even as they flee Overtown for the suburbs.

In the winter of 1997, President Clinton formed a special commission to examine a series of suspicious fires at African-American churches. As the media interviewed individuals in the African-American community affected by these incidents, church officials were often heard pointing out that the materiality of the church does not exist in the place or building, but rather in its people. Despite the physical destruction of a

A funeral processional through Colored Town, 1930s.

church, the spirit survives, the people survive, and often the congregation emerges stronger and more resolved to rebuild in that physical location. It is helpful to con-sider this phenomenon in relation to Miami's present-day African-American urban community. Legislated segregation created a significant dynamic that artificially maintained the community known as Colored Town. In a segregated Colored Town the diversity of professionals, intellectuals, and laborers created a pressurized energy that informs our legendary ideas of the city. In a desegregated Overtown the diversity within the community has changed dramatically, yet the attempts to develop and transform these areas are held in the memories of these legends and the strength of the nostalgia they engender. The community, with all it nuances, which created Colored Town, no longer exists in what is now Overtown. However, it is this exile community that holds sway and politically controls the perception of development and change there. As sympathetic overseers of the community, this new population has amassed resources to rebuild the community of Overtown by creating a benign patriarchy.

In the 1950s a political, developmental, and societal bravado led to the devasta-tion of Colored Town in the name of progress. For reasons that were at times sincere, but often patriarchal and cynical, the Dwight D. Eisenhower interstate highway system was constructed literally through the heart of this community. Just as it was naïve for supporters of the interstate system to believe that I-95 would benefit the community, it may also be unwise for the well-meaning exiled community of Overtown to perceive that their visions for rebuilding will re-establish a mythological history. A more specific examination of the decisions and conditions that surround the construction of the interstate system reveals the full impact of Interstate 95 on Overtown.

THE WILD, WILD SOUTH   Florida has always held a unique position in the South. Though planned segregation in the Jim Crow South is hardly exceptional, Colored Town gains distinction as part of an eclectic mix of people, events, and landscape that constitutes southern Florida. Relishing a role as the forgotten corner of the nation, southern Florida has always been a refuge for the inconspicuous, and the wildly exotic edge of the South. While a relatively normative population sustains it it is also distinguished as a temporary haven for energetic immigrants, modern pirates, low-key transients, sun-happy vacationers and the flamboyantly wealthy. The cultural pluralism that results from migration and immigration only adds to the dynamic nature of the region. This pluralism goes far to explain the persistent transformation of the social infrastructure, but also metaphorically outlines the similar conditions that transform the built environment.

From the interstate highway system to the Everglades the general environment of southern Florida exists as a collection of projects. These projects can be as normative as buildings, bridges, highways, lakes, community developments, and dams, or as complex as the network of canals that drains the Everglades. Much like the diversity in the population the elements of infrastructure in southern Florida are haphazardly executed and exist awkwardly alongside one another. Southern Florida is a completely fabricated landscape. The environment has been drained, quarantined, and stratified to support habitation to such a degree that qualities of the natural are indistinguishable from the artificial. In southern Florida the highway is a major physical entity and in a geography that is basically flat, the berms, overpasses, interchanges, and viaducts that emerge as part of the interstate system stand as stoic and fixed as mountains.

I-95 today in the core of Overtown.

The massive draining of the Everglades, preexisting flood plains, and the creation of extensive canal systems have been used to create artificial boundaries of water and to support development on dry land. Man-made objects break the canopy of trees and redefine the profile of the sunrise, sunset, and breezeways. The blurring of natural and artificial confuses the roles of the permanent with the temporal. In turn, periodic hurricanes divide the weak from the strong by forcing this ephemeral and artificial environment to meet the standards imposed by these violent storms. The structures of the roadways easily survive hurricanes and become powerful symbols of the permanent landscape.

The experience of driving in southern Florida is exemplified by the rhythmic lazy certainty of I-95. The interstate straddles a ridge of high land, which runs north-south and parallel to the coast. Traveling south from Ft. Lauderdale the interstate charges carelessly through what was undeveloped land in the 1950s and slides easily around or over the few geographic elements in its way. New developments snuggle quietly next to the roadway as it enters Miami-Dade County. Once inside county lines the road-way skyrockets over, around, and within a massive interchange called "the Golden Glades." The periodic shifts and banks in the road increase in frequency as it encounters and caresses more populated areas. It quietly bounces through the north side of the county and sways occasionally as its course fixes toward the city of Miami and the terminus of the most expensive and longest north-south interstate in the nation. As the highway drops into Liberty City it grudgingly lunges through the urban fabric, alternately resting on the ground and becoming airborne, to allow for arterial access and underpassing streets. It is at this point that you see how the demands of the inter-state and the realities of the city are intensified and pitted against each other in con-tinual conflict. At the I-95 interchange between Liberty City and Overtown the road soars into a web of ramps, one seven stories high, standing on thin supports over an empty field. This field is a serene landscape currently being manicured with palms, grass, and flowering trees. Beyond the interchange the highway once again drops to the ground, cutting a wide swath through the terrain and splitting the city's warehouse district, then straightening, as if to gain momentum, toward Overtown. As the road-way again becomes airborne it veers only yards form Booker T. Washington High School and forms a viaduct that slices through the remainder of Overtown and Miami's downtown business district. It then plummets south to its end, bleeding into a four lane, tree-lined parkway at Coral Gables, one of the wealthiest communities in southern Florida. The built forms of neighborhoods left in the wake of the interstate often appear awkward, nervous, and stripped naked.

HIGHWAY'S ROBBERY The federal interstate transportation system is often blamed for the fracturing of urban neighborhoods. Demographic, governmental and developmental forces conspire indirectly and directly to increase mobility and connect central business districts to suburban expansion. The image of six-lane concrete highways laid haphazardly though traditionally scaled communities is accompanied by images of a dilapidated city fabric destroyed in the wake of urban renewal. Whether intentional or not, this destruction has the effect of severing a lifeline; the areas in the path of these new roads struggle to survive and are often left abandoned.

The most active years of highway construction coincided with a general relocation of population along racial and economic lines. This quasi-desegregation of shopping, residential, educational, and cultural facilities through both legal and spontaneous actions came on the heels of many Interstate constructions through formerly segregated districts—in Florida and elsewhere. In many of these areas the traditional African-American community was unprepared for these simultaneous occurrences and simply could not withstand such an onslaught; neighborhoods quickly fell into disrepair as uprooted residents moved to more accommodating suburbs.

Today many of these neighborhoods have slowly and silently deteriorated into shells of their former selves. These neighborhoods form a landscape of sparsely populated streets, open lots, barricaded businesses, walled-in homes, and collapsing buildings. It is a fabricated landscape that has begun to claim permanence and encourages continued sprawl. The interstate is part and parcel of this predicament and, as both the symbol for escape and the symbol for the cause of its destruction, I-95 becomes an inseparable yet unwelcome part of the Overtown Community. The Interstate is vilified for the destruction of the community that was Overtown over other significant factors, such as civil rights, black suburban flight, and immigration, which could be seen as being more at fault for the dispersion and redefinition of the neighborhood. I-95 becomes an effective object of blame in stirring up interest in projects to resurrect Overtown in an image based on the mythical imagery of a community that no longer lives there. Traveling north along NW Seventh Avenue from downtown Miami in the 1950s and 1960s you would pass through the center of vibrant, thriving communities. An unintended effect of the building of I-95 parallel to NW Seventh Avenue was the

severing of the urban context east and west and the subsequent amplification of segregation patterns which forced local migration east towards the beach. In the process the
community of Overtown was essentially split to move certain populations west and
expand the neighboring central business district east towards the interstate. The impact
and brutality of the federal interstate transportation system is in reality one of a series of
factors that define Overtown today. By examining it as a component of these defining
forces our understanding of the Overtown community may be broadened.

A SYSTEM OF CONSEQUENCES Systems theory proposes that any system changes
and evolves once it is put into practice and that the intentions of the said system fail to
predict the totality of the outcome. The system in all cases is open and in Miami the
interstate highway system interacts with the environmental, social, and cultural systems to create qualitative new properties. It is the nature of the new qualities that
defines the true systematic functions of the interstate and the communities they
affect. All parties involved in the impact of I-95 have implemented systems based on
varying degrees of noble intentions. However, the ability to control and predict outcome through an effective implementation of these systems is challenged by the fact
that no system operates in isolation and the interaction with other systems causes continuous random results.

The system of interstate highways in the Miami area was initially manipulated under urban development incentives for isolating a passive and un-empowered black community in the name of progress and expansion of the city center. The proponents of development unwittingly conspire to create a political, social, and cultural organism that exerts a great deal of control over the areas affected by the interstate highway, becoming, as it were, de facto stewards of Overtown. These community leaders and "concerned" citizens seek to return the neighborhood to what is merely a glorified perception of the past. They become focused on developing the community in a way that is sympathetic to what is perceived as the needs of the local community. The residents however, hold little sway over the decision making and the development of their community is controlled by a dispersed population that maintains a great deal of influence as a sort of socially acceptable patriarchy.

A STITCH IN TIME As these forces converge on Overtown its future is defined by a patchwork of agendas that assert influences and foster opportunities. The projects that do emerge are simultaneously sympathetic to and systematic of the patchwork of conditions involved. In fact, the community becomes strangely dependent upon I-95 both as a major victimizer and as an excuse for community development projects. For example, at many points along the interstate rejuvenation projects have been attempted to, in effect, stitch together the community beneath the expressway and reconnect the east and west axes of the city. Running perpendicular to the interstate the streetscape on 62nd Street illustrates this condition with a center island of palm trees that connect the business center of Liberty City, west of I-95, to the schools and neighborhoods that lie beneath the Interstate and fan east toward the bay. In other areas gardens and outdoor theaters are proposed as infill. In Overtown itself, a folkloric village and pedestrian mall are proposed as a bridge between west side and east side communities. These urban sutures act to undermine the axis of the Interstate and reestablish the fabric of the fragmented neighborhood. Such projects also become symbolic gestures toward rebuilding the community affected by the interstate. However successful these measures are, it is still unclear whether the African-American community can heal and continue to exist in myth or in reality as we understand it.

clockwise from left: The Ninth Street Pedestrian Mall as designed to reconnect Overtown to the Central Business District; the Historic Overtown Folk Village, view of Second Avenue; landscape beautification project adjacent to I-95.

Caught in a web of good intentions, legendary history, and political patronage, the goal of reinvigorating the idealized center of Miami's African American community finds itself dependent on an infrastructure it despises—I-95, as well as on its dubious history. The future of this community lies in the creation of new forms that are based on existing complexities, rather than in the resurrection of an idealized past. These new forms are the only way the richness of Overtown can be preserved. The irony is that just as Colored Town was anesthetized to become Overtown, an attempt to promote a history clean of segregation runs the risk of ignoring the true conditions and needs of a contemporary community. It also is at risk of repeating a pattern of detached patriarchal dictates, despite well-meaning intentions.

above: Period rendering of the Mary Elizabeth hotel, courtesy of The Black Archives, History and Research Foundation of South Florida; *right:* Present day view of Overtown.

five   negotiated space

THE BLACK COLLEGE CAMPUS AS A CULTURAL RECORD OF POSTBELLUM AMERICA

INTRODUCTION   In 1923, when President Harding's administration decided to locate a segregated hospital for colored veterans adjacent to Tuskegee University's campus near the town of Tuskegee, in Macon County, Alabama, local whites were outraged because Tuskegee's black principal, Robert Russa Moton, refused to yield to their demands that whites be placed in exclusive control of the hospital. Up to this point Moton, like his predecessor Booker T. Washington, was regarded as an unwavering accommodationist who appreciated the social dictates of the Jim Crow South. Now, however, probably buoyed by the wave of militancy flowing from returning black veterans of World War I, he dared to stay his ground even in the face of threats against his life. Increased security on the campus and at Moton's home did not deter a band of the town's irate citizens, who, failing to win President Harding's sympathy for their cause, sought to take matters into their own hands. They marched along Old Montgomery Road, past the ravines that separated town and gown, to confront the defiant Moton at his doorstep, demanding that he sign a statement endorsing white management of the hospital. "Booker T. Washington," one member asserted, "gave thirty-five years of his life to build up this school. You, unless you are too stubborn to sign a little paper here, are going to have it all blown up in twenty-four hours. We have the legislature, we make the laws, we have the judges, the sheriffs, the jails. We have the hardware stores and the arms."[1]

In this moment, what came to a head was more than simply the conflict between town and gown in Tuskegee; it was also the conflict between the goals of black college campuses and the status quo expectations of whites who held the reigns of power. The chasm between town and gown in this violent episode indicates a different spatial relation between black campus and white community than what might be expected in the familiar phrase "town and gown." The ravines traversed by the angry mob may help us understand something about the spaces occupied by the races and how each race negotiated such spaces during this time.

Notes are located at the end of the essay

This essay will look at how the campuses of historically black colleges and universities record through space the African-American struggle for higher education and, more generally, the cultural history of race relations in the postbellum South.

Historically black colleges and universities (HBCUs) emerged between the 1860s and the 1930s in response to the desire of African-Americans—and their supporters—to build a system of higher education to facilitate their social, economic, and political uplift. Their concerted effort to achieve this goal, however, frequently sparked threatening responses from some white southerners. Such southerners felt that black education undermined the agricultural economy of the region by endangering the supply of agricultural labor, which blacks still provided in the postbellum South—a claim that resided within the larger requirement that blacks remain under the control of a white power structure.[2] Booker T. Washington's negotiation of this conflict was expressed by his educational philosophy, which emphasized vocational training for blacks. As a landscape architecture scholar, I am interested in how such conflicts and accommodations were also expressed spatially by Tuskegee's and other HBCU campuses. How did Tuskegee's planners anticipate the possibility that the product of their labor could be "blown up" because of some perceived infraction against the delicate social, economic, and political boundaries of the time? Can we unearth from such features as the location and layout of the HBCU campus a spatial record of this conflict and of the more subtle day-to-day forms of racial subordination? Can the built environment, a mute form, serve as a primary source for history to compensate for the paucity of written records about ordinary and marginalized people or the silence that typically shrouds the memory of painful events in the African-American experience?[3]

In his 1934 essay, "The Negro and His Plantation Heritage," Robert E. Park incidentally touches on the importance of geography in understanding the peculiar separation and connectedness of black and white in the Jim Crow South. Park, who by 1934 had become famous as a co-founder of the Chicago school of sociology and as one of the pioneers of American urban sociology, had lived in Tuskegee while he served as the publicity agent for Booker T. Washington from 1905 to 1912, during which time he was the "ghost-writer" for Washington.[4] Describing, in particular, Tuskegee's Macon County, Park provides a revealing "bird's-eye view" of the marginalized "backways" used by African-Americans spatially intermingled with, yet hidden from, the "official," "public" highways of dominant culture: outside of the plantation the only centers of Negro life are the rural churches and rural schools. The social situation is reflected in the human geography of the county. Plantation, hamlet, and town, still rather widely dispersed, are connected by a network of rural roads which, except for a few stretches of recently constructed thoroughfare, wind their way leisurely along rolling ridges in order to escape as far as possible the perils of the sometimes heavy spring rains. Closer observation of this same countryside discloses the existence of another, narrower, and less obvious network of footpaths which— unplanned, unplotted, and without official recognition—intersect, connect, and supplement but never compete with the public highways. These two systems of transportation—the public highways connecting the towns and the plantations and the footpaths connecting the humbler habitations of the Negro tenant farmers—suggest and symbolize the complicated interrelations and divisions between the two races in Macon County and in the South generally, suggest also some of the complexities and difficulties of studying one section of a population without taking some account at the same time of the other.[5] Park, who helped to establish the use of demographic maps to study the interaction of the multicultural neighborhoods in urban spaces, clearly understands how the cultural hierarchies of postbellum Macon County are expressed spatially. What Park very astutely uncovers is the peculiar pattern of back pathways that wind obscurely within, around, and behind the sanctioned spaces of dominant culture. Park is also very perceptively pointing to the inequity of public development in the New South as he contrasts recently constructed thoroughfares with the unplanned, unplotted, and unsanctioned humble footpaths to which African Americans were restricted. Park picks up on the way the "public" highways occupy the comfortable ridges, while the humble footpaths must traverse the other terrain in obscure, seemingly erratic patterns. The disparity between the "backways" and the "highways," indicating also the subordination of the bottom group spatially, served as a constant reminder to blacks and whites of their respective places on the road to a New South under Jim Crow. Thus, Park's 1934 essay draws our attention to some crucial spatial implications of postbellum Southern culture that we have subsequently overlooked, forgotten, or sublimated in the positivist and artifactual focus of much criticism on the built environment. In critiquing the campuses of HBCUs, we must heed Park's insights and not ignore the implications of their economic marginalization and other aspects of their cultural and natural contexts, which factor in their development, as indeed in the development of all built environments. Understanding these contexts as encoded not merely by buildings but more profoundly by "landscape," engaged as a system of interrelated parts, we can begin to gain a fuller understanding of the historical significance of the HBCU campus. This essay examines campus planning and landscapes in relation to three overlapping cultural-historical concepts particular to the African-American experience: first, the "black bottom"; second, the "backway"; third, the "other side of the railroad tracks." Separately and together, these elements suggest a wealth of insights into the cultural history of the HBCU campus. Among these, my essay will highlight primarily how apparent constraints or obstacles to building these campuses became vehicles by which campus leaders created dual meanings, mollifying white "readers" of the colleges while motivating and protecting the progressive educational goals of the HBCU's black constituents.[6] Two main principles of my approach need to be delineated further. First is the focus on "landscape" rather than strictly on buildings. Understood in its broadest sense as connoting the built environment, landscape is conceptualized not so much as "the grounds" or even as "a collection of artifacts" but more in the sense of ecology, as a system of interrelated parts consisting of buildings and other human constructions within their various changing contexts.[7] These include, for instance, circulation elements (roads, paths, vehicular entries), utility corridors, plantings, land-sculpting, and physical barriers, considered along with buildings in their changing contexts of nature (topography, soil, vegetation) and culture (politics, law, economics, race, class, gender). Most important, as an ecosystem landscape is more than the sum of these parts. Its historical significance cannot be appreciated strictly by detailed study of these parts as, say, a curator might study the artifacts in a museum collection. Instead, because the parts of landscape are usually fixed in space, historical meaning resides not so much in autonomous objects or "things" but rather in how spatial relationships change over time. Interrogating the still prevailing formalism of architectural and landscape architectural discourse, I shift the emphasis here from things—be they buildings (vernacular or otherwise), the "grounds surrounding them," garden ornaments, or historical plants—to understanding landscape as a system of altering relationships.

As an extension of this, a second principle of my approach relates specifically to how I engage HBCU campuses as "multicultural" spaces. Like feminist architectural critics who interpret architecture through women's history, I borrow from contemporary cultural criticism, particularly the method of "history from below," to engage college campuses as "landscapes from below."[8] Rather than assuming that history can be understood from a purely objective position—that is, from a position that assumes that things can be perceived with total ideological neutrality—I make clear the point of view that frames my understanding of history. I interpret the HBCU campus as the cultural product of a recently emancipated people, who, with relatively limited resources and institutions under their control, had to negotiate complicated social, political, and economic constraints—and opportunities—to house their institutions of higher learning. It is not my desire to unearth some essential African-American quality in "African-American" sites. Nor do I wish to extend the canon of architecture and landscape architecture to accommodate these newly recognized sites.[9] Rather, I am interested in these landscapes as cultural-historical phenomena with ideological implications for social conflict, interpreting them as a record of the experience of a marginalized group in the postbellum South and of this group's relationship to the broader American society.

To achieve this goal, I have had to push beyond the traditional limitations of my discipline; specifically, I meld theory and methods from landscape architecture, architecture, and cultural geography with cultural studies and social history—particularly history from below—in synthesizing graphic, field, and literary methods. I treat the landscape itself as a primary source, analyzing it directly through field observation and indirectly through the study of primary and secondary written material, as well as through such graphic materials as regional and local maps, site and building plans, photographs, sketches, elevations, and cross-sections. These materials document the current as well as the historical landscape. When it is helpful, I even draw on "tertiary" written sources such as fiction and make use of literary critical methods to clarify what is happening with these campuses, of which so little has been written or formally assembled. I synthesize all of the information I can gather to reconstruct historical site plans—an activity that is often necessary because most of the campuses in my study have kept few campus planning records. [10] I look for spatial relationships, such as relations between town and gown, and pay particular attention to how these relationships change over historical time. I consider physical science, such as physical geography and geology, to understand some of the cultural attributes of landscape history. As most critics cite written sources in conventional historical scholarship, I use graphic images—plans, photographs, and so on—extensively not only as a tool for analysis but especially as a vehicle for argument. My work, therefore, explores an interdisciplinary approach to constructing history in which landscape serves as a primary source, directly and indirectly providing critical evidence for understanding history. Given that the particular forces that shaped HBCU campuses are mostly no longer "visible" to us today, without honing such tools we are very likely to miss many of the signs of history, of careful negotiations of circumstances, that are significant in those landscapes.

Even architectural and landscape architectural historians and critics have not given this idea sufficient consideration in constructing histories. With a focus of "the college campus as art," most scholarship relating to the American college campus has been directed by the prevailing concept of campus as a collection of artifacts giving less attention to cultural-historical meanings of these spaces. [11] For example, focusing on the style, typology, and artistic significance of individual buildings, the best studies of the Tuskegee campus have been interested in, for instance, how its Carnegie Library speaks an architectural language that "break[s] into full and elegant 'Latin and Greek' with the handsome Ionic portico … complementing but not overpowering the usual fine brick detailing" or how the back of the same building is adorned with "brick pilaster strips … echoing the portico and giving the building interest from the public road behind … [and showing the] appealing thoroughness of … [architect Robert R. Taylor's] talent." [12] This "objective" critique of the building is in the tradition of the predominant discourse on architecture, landscape architecture, and historic preservation. With this approach, the building is constructed as an autonomous entity, whereby the only relevant context for appraising its significance is its architect's "cultural" enlightenment, signified by his or her knowledge and application of Roman and Greek architectural motifs. [13] This dominant paradigm of focusing on classical lineage of buildings as things isolated in the landscape fall in line with the assumptions upon which majority campuses were designed and built. Just like a string of great artworks displayed at eye level in a museum, the buildings on these campuses display the greatness of the institutions that have collected them. Each major building serves not only as a testament to the artist who designed it in emulation of classic precedent but also as a testament to the cultural power and centrality of the institution's publicly affirmed mission.

MAJORITY CAMPUSES AND THE DOMINANT PARADIGM OF DESIGN This conventional methodology has proven very useful in the study of majority college campuses in America, which are almost always designed to accentuate their high purpose. Not only are the major academic buildings of these campuses oriented for public view, but also the prominent location typical of these buildings in relation to campus entrances and public thoroughfares immediately announces their importance to the identity of the campuses. For example, Flowers Hall, the striking collegiate gothic show-piece of Huntingdon College, was situated—in accordance with a 1908 campus plan developed by the Olmsted brothers—to dominate the main entrance of the campus of this private women's college in the elegant Cloverdale neighborhood of Montgomery, less than fifty miles southwest of Tuskegee. *(Fig. 1)* Terminating College Avenue, the bilaterally symmetrical building looks directly down the centerline of the avenue—approximately the position from which the photograph is taken. The axis (main line of direction) thus formed is enhanced by entry columns that mark, symbolically, the threshold between town and gown. College Avenue beyond this point becomes a ceremonial drive, a processional toward the center of the building unbroken until a circular garden area just prevents one from crashing into the steepled elegance that commands one's attention. All other buildings on the campus are less imposing than this one both in terms of their architecture, size, and situation in the landscape. On Huntingdon College's *original* campus, which was located in downtown Tuskegee, the main academic building was also oriented toward the public

Figure 1. **Landmark John Jefferson Flowers Memorial Hall on the Montgomery campus of Huntington College (1997). Designed in the Collegiate Gothic style, Flowers Hall was completed in 1909. For several years it was the only building on campus. Reminding us how the building signifies the aspirations of the institution, the college's 1996-1997 catalog points out that the building "compares favorably with the Victorian Gothic at Oxford and Cambridge."**

Figure 2. *(below)* **University of Alabama's landmark axis, 1997.** *(clockwise from upper left)* **View along axis to the president's mansion across College Avenue from Denny Chimes. View along axis to Denny Chimes from the portico of the Gorges Library. View of the portico of the Gorges Library from its feet. View along axis to the War Monument and the portico of the Gorges Library.**

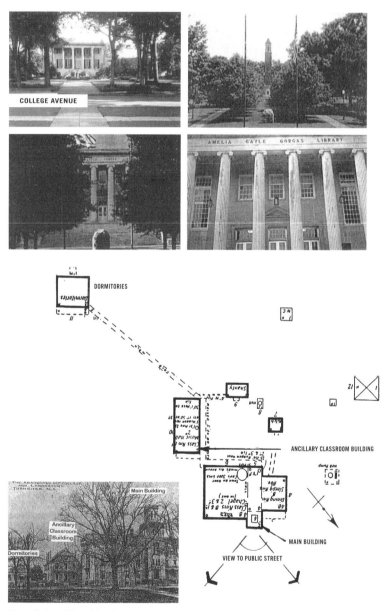

Figure 3. *(above)* **The original Tuskegee campus of Huntington College.** *(left)* **A photograph of campus from Public Street (circa 1920).** *(right)* **A layout of campus based on a 1903 fire insurance map.**

street. This academic building, like Flowers Hall, clearly identified the campus by virtue of its architecture and superior size as compared with adjacent, less grand dormitories and industrial structures. (Fig. 3) The same is also true of public liberal arts institutions built for the white majority. Consider the location of the Amelia Gayle Gorgas Library on the University of Alabama's Tuscaloosa campus, located about 100 miles northwest of Tuskegee and built around the same time. The landmark library building is centered on an immense lawn where it terminates a ceremonial axis that sweeps from College Avenue, past the Denny Chimes—the much photographed carillon tower on the campus—to rest at the feet of the monumental ionic portico of the library building.[14] (Fig. 2) The Gorgas Library was constructed in 1939 on the same site where the school's original library building stood, an equally imposing rotunda. Passersby using College Avenue, on beholding the rotunda, accentuated as it was in the expansive front lawn of the campus, would have suffered no confusion about the University of Alabama's high standing as the flagship of learning in postbellum Alabama.[15] Even the landmark buildings of majority land-grant college campuses, which were being developed during the same period as HBCU campuses, were oriented to command public attention. For example, commanding the focal point of the front lawn of the campus of Pennsylvania State University, the first land-grant college in the United States, Old Main proudly faces what was Main Street—now College Street—in the town of State College.[16] (Fig. 4) Similarly, to use an example of a land-grant institution located in the Deep South, Auburn University's Samford Hall embraces what was Main Street—now College Avenue—in the town of Auburn, just northeast of Tuskegee, asserting the public endorsement of Auburn University. (Fig.5) Samford Hall was built on the same spot where a similarly oriented Old Main once stood before it was destroyed by fire in 1887.

Although conventional art-historical values and methods of design interpretation may have served well to articulate and celebrate the order, purpose, and high aspirations of such majority campuses, the HBCU campus presents a challenge to these values and methods. In fact, such issues as the geographic location, layout, and orientation of these African-American spaces raise questions not only about the applicability of these conventional values and methods to minority and working class

Figure 4. **Orientation of Pennsylvania State's (non-HBCU) landmark Old Main.** *(Left)* **Private, 1997.** *(Right)* **Public, 1997.**

Figure 5. **Orientation of Auburn University's (non-HBCU) landmark Stamford Hall.** *(Left)* **Public, 1997.** *(Right)* **Private, 1997.**

spaces but also about the larger aims of interpreting any built environment from the point of view of the canonical history. By interrogating both majority and minority spaces from the perspective of African-American historical concepts, we may begin to see a larger cultural history of these spaces in relation to each other. Thus, the three concepts used to critique college campuses here—the black bottom, the backway, and the other side of the tracks—reveal not just a cultural history of black spaces, but also an overlooked cultural history of majority spaces as well.

BLACK BOTTOM

In that place, where they tore the nightshade and blackberry patches from their roots for the Medallion City Golf Course, there was once a neighborhood. It stood in the hills above the valley town of Medallion and spread all the way to the river. It is called the suburbs now, but when black people lived there it was called the Bottom …

A shucking, knee-slapping, wet-eyed laughter that could even describe and explain how they came to be where they were.

A joke. A nigger joke. That was the way it got started. Not the town, of course, but that part of town where the Negroes lived, the part they called the Bottom in spite of the fact that it was up in the hills. Just a nigger joke. The kind white folks tell when the mill closes down and they're looking for comfort somewhere. The kind colored folks tell on themselves when the rain doesn't come, or comes for weeks, and they're looking for a little comfort somehow.

A good white farmer promised freedom and a piece of bottom land to his slave if he would perform some difficult chores. When the slave completed the work, he asked the farmer to keep his end of the bargain. Freedom was easy—the farmer had no objection to that. But he didn't want to give up any land. So he told the slave that he was very sorry that he had to give him valley land. He had hoped to give him a piece of the Bottom. The slave blinked and said he thought valley land was bottom land. The master said, "Oh, no! See those hills? That's bottom land, rich and fertile."

"But it's high up in the hills," said the slave. "High up from us," said the master,"but when God looks down, it's the bottom. That's why we call it so. It's the bottom of heaven—best land there is." So the slave pressed his master to try to get him some. He preferred it to the valley. And it was done. The nigger got the hilly land, where planting was backbreaking , where the soil slid down and washed away the seeds, and where the wind lingered all through winter.

Which accounted for the fact that white people lived on the rich valley floor in that little river town in Ohio and the blacks populated the hills above it, taking consolation in the fact that every day they could literally look down on the white folk. [17]

Establishing the setting of her novel *Sula* in what was once the "Bottom" of the town of "Medallion," Ohio, Toni Morrison draws on landscape to represent the cultural circumstances of her characters and more generally to identify African-Americans as a marginalized group in American society. Her "joke" summarizes not only the class and racial relations that characterize the cultural construction of space but also how space serves both to preserve and to affirm the social status and identity of different groups. This "joke," moreover, alludes to the economic basis of oppression and to America's historical willingness to scapegoat those citizens who have benefited least from the bounty of better times in order to ease the pains of the country in harder times.

Even as the blacks of Medallion sat on top of their world physically, they were still at the bottom socially and economically. [18] When the Medallion region was primarily agricultural, low-lying flood-plain areas—though susceptible to periodic flooding—were highly desirable for homesteading because they offered large expanses of level terrain with fertile alluvial deposits. [19] Therefore, this was where whites settled and where the town eventually grew up—meaning, of course, the white section identified as the town itself. Morrison implies that this geography is taken for granted to such an extent that it seems a force of nature: the gods have sanctioned that the most "valuable" land be the birthright of those with significant resources at their disposal and the institutions of society under their control. Consequently, African-

Americans and poor whites are left with the most difficult and infertile hilly areas—
the spaces associated with hillbillies, whose substandard surroundings both ensure and
affirm their social status beneath members of the dominant group.[20]

Morrison, furthermore, reminds us that the value of land is not intrinsic but
governed by economic motives. The imperative that black townspeople be relegated
to the hills—an imperative that seems so natural—is readily reversed when economic
change dictates. Because they offer, among other advantages for industry, ready
access to rail and water transportation networks, which are critical for inexpensively
moving large quantities of raw materials, fuel, and manufactured goods, the low-
lying flood-plain areas become desirable for locating factories as Medallion's economy changes.[21] Industry, however, brings attendant environmental ills: filthy and
sometimes hazardous air and water, noise, and visual pollution. Because the hills
remain free from these ills, the manifest destiny of the well-to-do dictates that they
now occupy the hills, forcing those at the bottom of society to occupy the polluted
flood-plains, where they can remain the butt of jokes. Regardless of their actual location in the landscape, therefore, the poor and the weak are consistently relegated to
their proper space in the literal or symbolic "bottoms" that are no longer desired by
the rich and the powerful, a phenomenon we can detect repeatedly in American history. This is why African-American neighborhoods across the South—and in the
North as well—have historically been called the "black bottoms," regardless of the
actual location topographically. The bottoms are where they are, for they are the bottom of society.[22]

Morrison's insights remind us that examining the sites of HBCU campuses in
relation to the changing system of assigning value to real estate in the postbellum
South can reveal much about the status of these institutions and, more generally,
about the relationship of blacks to the larger society. What do we do with the fact that
most of Alabama's HBCUs are located on hills or "bottoms," a situation apparently
at odds with their declared functions as—at least in part—agricultural schools?
In order to move towards an answer to this question, we can take Tuskegee as a case
study, beginning with an overview of the school's social, political, and especially
economic history.

The historic section of the campus of Tuskegee is preserved as the Tuskegee Institute National Historic Site, documenting the work of Booker T. Washington and those who followed, modified, and dissented from his philosophy. Washington, the powerful African-American leader and educator, between 1881 and 1915 negotiated the rancorous cultural terrain of the postbellum South to head the development of one the most famous schools for blacks in the United States at the time. The campus is located in Macon County, near Montgomery, the center of Alabama's Black Belt, a region that was the economic, political, and social hub of the Deep South before the Civil War. The rich, black calcareous soils of the Black Belt were ideal for cotton cultivation. Thus, during the 1850s and 1860s when cotton made up 60 percent of the United States' exports and Alabama produced 25 percent of this output, the ten Black Belt counties of the state accounted for more than half of Alabama's total production. As a result, the planters of the Black Belt enjoyed great prosperity. This was a dual society, as Frederick Law Olmsted and many others have described it, consisting of very rich at the top and very poor in the bottoms.[23] Enslaved Africans were brought to the region in large numbers to provide the labor that fueled this prosperity, leading to the unusual demography of the region, in which blacks generally outnumbered whites.[24]

Before it was completely disenfranchised by 1900, this black majority enjoyed a brief period of political influence. At the height of Reconstruction, virtually no representative to the Alabama legislature from the Black Belt could be elected without the support of the black vote. It was in this moment that Alabama finally approved legislation to establish the Tuskegee Normal School for Colored Teachers on 12 February 1881. With the spirit of public education in the air, the passage in 1862 of the First Morrill Act by the federal government instituted practical and applied education for the masses. Even before that—and despite the fact that they were generally locked out of the system in the region—higher education was one of the strongest black imperatives. Blacks believed education to be the best means of uplifting themselves. Thus, in Macon County, as in many other parts of the Deep South, they used the power of their vote to secure state assistance for their schools.[25] With the passage of the legislation to establish Tuskegee in Macon County, therefore, they had finally harnessed their political resources to achieve one of their most intense desires.

This triumph, however, came after several failures over the previous years, because Southern plantation owners were equally intense in their discomfort with and resistance toward black education, which they felt threatened the availability of agricultural labor that blacks still provided after the war. Washington wrote:

> *There were not a few white people in the vicinity of Tuskegee who looked with some disfavor upon the project. They questioned its value to the coloured people, and had a fear that it might result in bringing about trouble between the races. Some had the feeling that in proportion as the Negro received education, in the same proportion would his value decrease as an economic factor in the state. These people feared the result of education would be that the Negroes would leave the farms, and it would be difficult to secure them for domestic service.*[26]

Hence only a sum of $2,000 annually was appropriated for the school. This was to be taken from "the general school revenue, set apart to the colored children."[27] Moreover, with these funds set aside for teachers' salaries only, providing funds to develop the physical plant fell on the shoulders of the community designated to benefit from the enterprise. Of course, African-Americans, just sixteen years out of slavery, were generally without financial means. These provisions were typical for black schools in Alabama during the period. For example, the Alabama Agricultural and Mechanical University, which opened in 1875 as the Huntsville State Normal School for Negroes, received an appropriation from the state of $1,000 annually under the same conditions as Tuskegee.[28] At the time, this institution became the state's first black land grant school in 1891—under the provisions of the 1890 Morrill Act—the level of state funding was at $4,000 per annum.[29] The state funding levels for these black schools pale next to an annual yield of more than $20,000 from the endowment that Auburn University received as Alabama's white male-only land-grant school two years before Alabama A&M and eight years before Tuskegee.[30] Similarly, the University of Alabama received an appropriation of $24,000 annually from the state, as well as $30,000 for building in 1878—three years after Alabama A&M opened—and another $60,000 for the same purpose in 1883.[31]

Working within the economic impositions of Tuskegee's limited grant, Washington chose an apparently less-than-ideal property for the beginning of his school. The one hundred-acre property on which Tuskegee's campus was built was an abandoned cotton plantation known locally as the "Burnt Place" since its Great House had burned down during the Civil War. The only structures remaining on the site were three ancillary buildings—a stable, a chicken coop, and a kitchen. These roughly constructed buildings were made of wood as was typical of the out-buildings of less well-to-do Southern plantations.[32] For land that was to provide opportunities for farming, its soils were not only inherently poor for cotton cultivation by Black Belt standards but were also severely eroded.[33] Alluding to the condition of the property at the time it was acquired, as he made a case for preserving the tax-exempt status of a prospering Tuskegee University in the early 1900s, Charles Hare points out in an article to the *Advertiser* that "Tuskegee was located in its first year in a district where no whites had lived for a quarter-century, on a farm known as the Big Hungry."[34] Hare, in attempting to pacify a suspicious public, exploits the fact that when it was acquired by blacks the property was no longer desired by whites. Moreover, he exploits another local name of the property, "the Big Hungry," to evoke the image of land, which was so rough and infertile that George Washington Carver, apparently on seeing the campus for the first time, insinuated that it was fit to support only the school's roaming herd of razorback hogs "that looked as though they were built for speed rather than for the table."[35]

Tuskegee's land is so poor because Alabama's heavy rainfall does not easily penetrate the clay-rich soils that predominate in counties such as Macon, which lies in the hilly fringe of the ten counties considered to constitute Alabama's true Black Belt. When clay-rich soils become saturated with water, they swell and, so, tend to prevent additional later from passing through them. This excess water flows over the surface as it makes its way to rivers, wetlands, and lakes. As it flows, it erodes the surface, taking valuable topsoil from uplands and depositing it in low-lying bottoms discussed earlier. In so doing, it gradually carves gullies and ravines in its path. The sinuous ridges that occur in the region are remnants of uplands that were dissected in this way. The Tuskegee Ridge, an example of such a remnant, is the highest section of Macon County. (Fig. 6) The flat top of the ridge, though impoverished in terms of soils, pro-

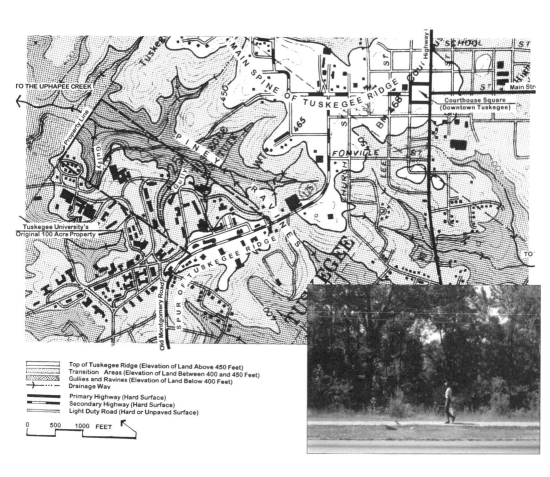

Figure 6. The relationship between town and gown in Tuskegee.
(top) The base of the drawing is a USGS topographic map,
which was photo-revised in 1983. *(bottom)* A walk from campus along Old Montgomery Road past the Piney Ravines, 1993.

vides some of the most suitable area for building because, as Robert Park pointed out, such locations avoid the risk of flooding. Thus, the downtown area of Tuskegee was sited on the main spine of the Tuskegee Ridge and the original one hundred-acre section of the Tuskegee campus was sited on the northern side of a spur that extends from this main spine.[36] Connecting town and gown, Old Montgomery Road—belonging to the older network of secondary rural roads Park described—runs along the crest of the spur and forms the southern boundary of the one-hundred-acre property. We can see how the spur flanks the southern part of that section of the campus. Two gullies dissect the spur creating finger-like promontories. The gullies join to create a ravine that occupies the northern and eastern part of the property and is part of a larger system of ravines that dissect the region. These gullies and the ravine are difficult and expensive to "develop" not only because their steep slopes necessitate expensive earth movement to create flat spaces for building but also because, in addition to being poorly drained, they are susceptible to land-slips. Since they account for about one third of the total extent of the one hundred-acre property, we can understand that this was by no means prime land.[37] Thus, the campus's buildings, by and large, are sited on the tops of the spur and its promontories, turning this way and that with the folds of the land. (Fig. 6 & Fig. 15)Such "spontaneous" layout creates a visual display dramatically different from most majority campuses, which generally are arranged formally.[38] As I will discuss later, an observer could easily mistake this informal layout for merely a lack of planning. A better explanation is that the campus was planned in concert with the most cost effective technological uses of this kind of topography. To reach this understanding, we must use the historical context of physical evidence, which can help us rethink common assumptions about these campuses and those who built them. Rather than merely looking at the buildings and how they do or do not form the expected straight lines and quadrangles, when we examine the buildings in relation to their physical and cultural contexts, we see a different kind of order, one developed in relation to specific geographic and historical pressures. Due to the race and class strictures of the time, Tuskegee was relegated to this terrain, but given the lapse of time we easily forget the cultural, economic, and design implications of attempting to build on such terrain with few resources.

Like Tuskegee, many other HBCU campuses in Alabama are located in hilly districts. Miles College, established by the Colored Methodist Episcopal Church in Booker City, Alabama, in 1902 enables us to examine the significance of the hilly topography in which HBCU campuses are often located. In 1907 the institution had to move to the hilly site it occupies today.[39] The steel giant Tennessee Coal and Iron (TCI) held mineral rights to the land that the school originally occupied. When TCI was ready to begin mining on that site, it forced a "land-swap" with the school, exchanging this first site for the one on which the campus sits today, which had already been mined. It is significant in interpreting this landscape that the huge operations of US Steel even now dominate the lowlands surrounding the black community that developed on the hilly area around the college. By way of another example, Alabama State University, Alabama's first HBCU, was driven out of the town of Marion, where it was founded, because of racial tensions. The institution finally found refuge on Beulah Hill in Montgomery, where it is located today. Similarly, despite the rhetoric about affording "better opportunities to develop the industries of the school," Alabama A&M's decision in 1891 to move out of town had to be dubious at best. The language of one catalogue gives a different impression from this rhetoric, when it says that the school sold "its Huntsville property at great sacrifice, so that in reality it began anew … at its present location."[40] The sacrifice would have been very evident to the school's personnel long after the property was occupied.

With limited funds available for development, the hills presented the institution with another set of problems. *The Huntsville Times*, in an article entitled "New Buildings Shook in High Winds While Students Prayed," recounts the problems experienced in the 1890s concerning high winds that "whipped against the exposed hillside" of Normal's Hill. According to the article, "The flimsy frame buildings of the early campus often gave concern, especially to those who used the third floor for dormitories, by shaking badly in high winds." Walter S. Buchanan, president of the university during this period, on the occasion of the seventy-fifth anniversary of the founding of the institution, recalled his attempt to calm the frightened students on one of these occasions: "'Don't lose your heads now; we're right here. The building's not going to fall.' Which I doubted very much for the wind was terrible."[41] Today, when one considers the

exposed hilly terrain of Normal's Hill within the context of the surrounding flat agricultural bottomland it now owns, one could appreciate why William Councill, the black
principal of the school who oversaw this move, was severely criticized by his peers "for
buying that old rocky land for a school."[42]

It is unlikely that blacks would have purchased these properties without appreciating
the limitations of the land for the agricultural purposes they publicly claimed of their
schools. These were an agrarian people after all. Tuskegee's "Farm," Alabama A&M's
"Hill," Miles's mined land, and Alabama State's Beulah Hill all would have required real
work if the new owners of these properties were to realize the opportunities they suppos-
edly offered. So what could have made these properties so attractive to their new owners?
First, their relatively low cost as abandoned places would have been an advantage for
these poorly funded schools, a fact that in itself is significant in a cultural-historical analysis.[43] Second, the acquisition of marginalized property—or the tolerance of the marginal-
izing of property—would have offered the additional benefit of conveying that these
institutions were not willing to transgress the delicate social boundaries of the postbellum
South, conveying the impression to local white supremacists that, while their missions
were lofty, their proper place at the bottom of society was well understood.[44]

At its most basic and functional level, what these innovators had to achieve was
progress under camouflage. The difficulty of the task is demonstrated by the occasions
when white leaders reacted to black actors that they regarded as not subservient enough.
The exceptionally tactful Washington, for instance, sometimes ran afoul of the
Southern establishment for appearing to be uppity or for inciting that feeling among
his followers. An editorial published by the *Times-Democrat* in June 1902 gives a
perfect instance of Southern hypersensitivity to his actions. The editorial was occasioned
by Washington's meeting with President Theodore Roosevelt to discuss the appointment
of black officials in the South:

> *From whatever point of view these Roosevelt-Washington conferences are
> considered, they are mischievous and wrong. The best advice that Booker
> Washington has ever given his negro brethren has been to leave politics alone
> and go to work; and it is advice that he can very well afford to follow him-*

self instead of devoting so much of his time to the consideration of Federal patronage and to recommending negroes for office in the South. If he is so very earnest in his desire to improve the Tuskegee Institute and to make it an educational centre for the negroes, it will require all his time and he will have none left for trips to Washington to consult with the President, and if he wishes to give his students a good example he will steer clear of politics instead of seeking to convince them that he is the political head of the negro race, with full power to distribute all the Federal offices. …

On the other hand President Roosevelt can learn a lesson in regard to the appointment of negroes from his predecessor. Mr. McKinley appointed a number of them to postmasterships and other positions in the South in the early days of his Presidency. It naturally caused a great deal of resentment and indignation, for it subjected the white people to unpleasant intercourse with these negro officials; and the popular feeling on this point was made so plain that that it soon reached the President. The men and women who mail or receive letters, who pay customs dues, who enter public land are white, and they should not be subjected to unnecessary annoyance or insult by having to arrange these matters with negroes.[45]

The editorial indicates how closely policed were the racial boundaries of Jim Crow. Earlier, Washington's dinner with President Roosevelt had caused such a rash of criticism against him that the *Tuskegee News*—though skeptical of the school in the beginning—had to come to his defense, evincing the degree to which he had succeeded in negotiating the cultural terrain of the postbellum South to that point. "Surely," the newspaper reported, "if Principal Washington were engaged in preaching a propaganda of 'social equality' we believe we should see evidences of such teaching in this little community where his school of 1200 students and teachers is located."[46] Here the campus Washington created becomes central to our understanding of how these two meanings—progress and compliance—coexisted: when one considers that the school was located on an abandoned plantation in a marginal district and that classes had to be held at first in a refurbished stable and hen-house, it is not surprising that the *Tuskegee News* could find no evidence of "social equality." As in the rhetoric, this evidence was also masked spatially at least to those who did not—or could not—consider the possibility of black agency. Perhaps the spaces these institutions occupied were the most flagrant reminder of their place. Just as the ante-bellum plantation houses would continue to represent and assert the rightful status of the former planter class, so these marginally sited campuses acknowledged black sec-ond-class citizenship in the postbellum South. For the black educators and builders of the campuses, however, this land was better than the "huts" behind the Big House. They were symbols of black progress worth nurturing even, quite literally, on the most degraded ground.

This negotiation would have been necessary at the other HBCUs as well. Miles College, in the face of a show-down with the powerful TCI, was wise in accepting the "land-swap." Similarly, one might wonder if Councill's decision to move to the "Hill" would have also been expedient. After being locked out of the great American system of public education for nearly thirty years, the state finally in the same year of the move made the school the first black land-grant institution in Alabama, a federal requirement imposed under the provisions of the Second Morrill Act. This distinction might have been both auspicious and inauspicious since Councill would have had to manage rather gingerly some local resentment for the federal imposition that led to the windfall (relatively) for his school. Leaving town and moving to the "Bottoms" might have been part of the management strategy. On the one hand, Auburn, as Alabama's official white land-grant school, was encouraged to become a model for New South agriculture, finding ways to make the Alabama soil more productive with-out the apparatus of a slave economy. On the other hand, Tuskegee, Miles, and Alabama A&M—the latter despite its status as Alabama's official (state supported) black land-grant institution—were expected to provide overtures evincing their will-ingness to remain implanted in the old ways. The properties they eventually occupied offered not only acres of cheap land but also the surprising advantage of being places that were undesirable or were abandoned by plantation owners and mining compa-nies. Unlike their white land-grant counterparts, the confluence of school and "Bottom" made these threatening black institutions more agreeable to powerful whites. Understanding HBCU campuses in relation to the nature of the property they occupy, we can begin to trace a history from below that is recorded in part in the physical landscape itself.

BACKWAY Not only are they situated in the bottoms; HBCU campuses are frequently also laid out "backwards" according to the dominant design paradigm. Many black campuses put their "best" façades inward not outward. Most, though not as obviously introverted as the Tuskegee campus, reflect the observations of architect A.H. Albertson. His conclusions are documented in a 1916 study of the buildings and grounds of black schools prepared under the supervision of architect Isaac Newton Phelps Stokes for the Department of the Interior, Bureau of Education.[47] Recalling Albertson's assessment of the campus of Hampton University (Booker T. Washington's alma mater in Virginia), the report observes that "the main entrance to the ... institution ... when discovered gives the impression of being a back way in; it certainly does not suggest the main approach to a large institution of high standing."[48] This might also be said of several HBCU campuses in Alabama, such as Stillman College in Tuscaloosa, Alabama State University in Montgomery, and Alabama Agricultural and Mechanical University in Huntsville. While some of their major buildings actually face outward, their "landscape," especially the location and articulation of entrances, does not visually proclaim the high public status of the institutions that they house in the manner of majority schools. The main gates to these campuses, as a rule, are hard to find. When one does find them—these campuses are usually fenced—like Albertson, one is likely to feel that one is arriving on campus by a back or side way.

It is easy to dismiss this observation, as do the authors of the Department of the Interior study, by explaining that "Hampton ... and the other black college campuses were] not built upon a plan ... [being] the ... result of undirected growth under a laissez-faire policy of development ... [giving] no intimation, implied or expressed, of a central controlling purpose."[49] Even if this indictment were true—the historical record does not necessarily support this explanation—the interpretation of these landscapes, I argue, must be extended to explore why these campuses were apparently not "built upon a plan," an inquiry that, to the degree possible, must be mindful of the problems of canonical assumptions that shape the typical critique of built environments. In failing to do so, the interpreters imply that these campuses "sprung up" without social, economic, political, racial, or other cultural contexts. To describe these campuses as "spontaneous" is to imply an inability of the people who planned these spaces to formulate a development policy, an act that requires forethought, vision, and the discipline to stick with a plan, traits that poor people, women, racial minorities, and, at least until only recently, Southerners were seen as stereotypically lacking. According to this assumption, the absence of such elevated abilities is evidenced by the "uncontrolled" manner in which the HBCU campus is laid out and betrays the limited achievements in civilization and culture of the people who planned these spaces. Thus, interpretation of the built environment might be understood as a decidedly political act. Just as Tuskegee's "spontaneous" layout on the ribbon-like spur of the Tuskegee Ridge cannot be divorced from the social and economic circumstances that dictated its placement in the landscape, so the introverted orientations and backway entrances of these HBCU campuses must be reconnected to their political implications.

Examining the actual physical spaces of the campuses themselves, we can test to what extent canonical assumptions like Albertson's are legitimate, or to what extent they are based on cultural biases. Engaging the differing spatial relationships of HBCU and non-HBCU campuses relative to their public contexts enables us to gain a fuller appreciation of these spaces as documents of the American experience. Although most of the campuses in my study never receive the attention or achieve the canonical status represented by mainstream historic sites, their present conditions and their past landscapes reveal the complicated history whose spatial reality is recorded in the buried largess of their physical orientation to their public. As one characteristic aspect of these campuses, the notion of the backway—like the bottom and the other side of the tracks—can easily be overlooked. Once we spotlight it with information from African-American history, however, we discover it to be very suggestive in uncovering the cultural meaning of landscape.

We can gain a deeper understanding of buildings like the Carnegie Library, which I discussed briefly in my introduction, by engaging them in relation to their physical and cultural contexts. Beyond identifying the Greco-Roman forms embodied in the buildings, we need to expand this analysis to examine how these forms operate in the landscape, requiring an examination of such issues as the meanings conferred upon them by their African-American builders and users as well as by those in the dominant culture who engaged with the campus, and how these meanings are mobilized in the building to particular cultural ends. Thus, in the case of Tuskegee's Carnegie Library, we need to ask why the back of this building is turned so decisively to face Old Montgomery Road—the only public road that passes through the campus. (Fig. 7) Buildings like the Carnegie Library clearly adapt architectural details from the buildings of majority campuses, which in turn adapt Greek, Roman, and Gothic models as a sign of their high Old World European aspirations. However, the fact that the Tuskegee buildings turn these details away from the public may be more revealing. Why is so universal a symbol of the academic landscape as the "handsome Ionic portico" oriented so decisively away from public view? Indeed, why is this pattern repeated by all of the major academic buildings on Tuskegee's campus that were erected adjacent to this public road from the 1880s through the 1930s? Other HBCU campuses embody a similar orientation. The layout of Stillman College, for example, has some similarities to its grander and more generously funded neighbor, the University of Alabama. Although on a much smaller scale, it too aspires to an axis, which extends between the Shepard Library built in 1956—analogous to the Gorgas Library—and the sixty-foot-high Strange Bell Tower built in 1983—analogous to the towering Denney Chimes. Unlike such campuses as the University of Alabama or Huntington College, however, rather than acknowledging and celebrating the relatively impressive portico that graces the library, the entry road at Stillman leads quietly from 15th Street, on the outskirts of Tuscaloosa, weaving its way along a nondescript edge of the campus. While at Huntingdon—the white women's college campus introduced earlier—we enter the campus by driving along a ceremonial axis that is terminated by Flowers Hall and at the University of Alabama we can enter by walking along a similar axis that is terminated by the Gorgas Library, at Stillman College one can only enter campus via what seems like a backway, approaching the landmark building from a side angle rather than head-on and so miss its full monumentality. This sequence of entry and arrival fixes the dominant impression with which visitors to the

Figure 7. **Orientation of Tuskegee University's (HBCU) Carnegie Library.** *(left)* **Public, 1997.** *(right)* **Private, 1993.**

campus are left.

Occupying or entering by way of the "back" has always been a pervasive metaphor for the marginal status of blacks in American society. Black captives and their families, in antebellum times and long after, could enter the white households they served only by way of the back door. When churches in the South were segregated, black attendants were required to sit at the back pews or sometimes in the back balconies. While traveling on buses or trains during Jim Crow, blacks were not allowed to use public white restrooms. When there were no "colored only" ones available, as was often the case in small towns, black patrons would have to relieve themselves at the back of the station or out in the woods, out of view, they hoped, of white passersby. Similarly, the practice of blacks living behind the big houses of leading white families continued long after the Civil War—and on occasion can still be found in remote sections of the rural South. During Jim Crow, blacks were required not only to sit in the seats at the back of public buses but also to leave them by way of the back door. By the time of the Civil Rights Movement, "back of the bus" emerged as a rhetorical rallying cry that enjoys currency even today. The concept is more than a metaphor, though it is also that. It is also a concrete, everyday experience of space that becomes embedded in the consciousness of those who experienced these things, and passes down to those born after Jim Crow was outlawed. Given the poignancy of this concept in the black experience, therefore, it is reasonable to ask whether and how it was manifested physically in so potent a symbol of black aspirations and focus of racial hostility as the black college campus in the Jim Crow moment.

Necessarily, HBCU campuses have a sense of "belonging" in relation to the towns that they occupy that is markedly different from the relation of white colleges. The backway not only reflects an earlier history adapted into these campuses, but also facilitates the protection that HBCUs sometimes required from hostile townspeople. Talladega College's Savery Library, for instance, like the buildings along Old Montgomery Road on the Tuskegee campus, also turns its back decisively to West North Street, once a major street leading from downtown Talladega to the campus. (Fig. 8) Built in 1939, the building blocked off the front of Swayne Hall, which, as a structure erected to serve as a school for white boys, was sited, like Huntingdon

Figure 8. **Orientation of Talladega College's (HBCU) landmark Savery Library.** *(left)* **Public, 1993.** *(right)* **Private, 1997.**

College's Flower's Hall, to command the attention of travelers approaching the campus on West North Street. (Fig 9) Like the other black colleges, Talladega College existed in a hostile relation to the town. On several occasions in the 1870s the black community and supportive whites successfully defended the campus from mobs who sought to burn it down. The American Missionary Association, the Northern white organization responsible for the school, armed the residents of the campus with Henry rifles; blacks in the community promised to burn the town if the campus were harmed.[50] By turning its back to the town, the Savery Library building seems to respond to this history of racial hostility.

We should not confuse the peculiar backway orientation of HBCU campuses with more traditional campuses displaying an internal or cloistered orientation. Although the backway and internal orientation both offer a feeling of security and belonging for those within the private space of the campuses, the similarities end here. Once we examine the historical developments, the actual design of the building's façades, and the potential social, economic, and political purposes of the designs, the differences become very apparent. In contrast, Tuskegee's introverted or backway orientation, internally oriented private campuses, such as Yale University's and the University of Chicago's, are patterned on their Old World precedents. Outwardly, they display public façades that assert their high authority to those using adjacent thoroughfares. Cambridge University's St. John's College, for example, presents a continuous stone façade to the public that is broken by the Great Gate, which is so richly decorated that no mistake could be made with regard to the exclusivity of the activities within. (Fig. 10) Above the heavy iron gates that tantalizingly close off the orifice, reliefs of mythical beasts—called yales—hold up the coat of arms of the college's founder, Lady Margaret Beaufort. The display inspires the awe and foreboding of passersby in no less a degree than the gargoyles that watch over the University of Chicago's main entrance off the Midway Plaissance. These gothic campuses cloister those within—guard them from the outer world—as they also serve up an intimidating exterior to outsiders. The façades of these campuses have a double message: one, the institution belongs here and has a right to dominate this space; two, those who belong to the institution must show due respect and those who do not belong must be

Figure 10. (above) St. John's College (Cambridge University) front gate, 1995. *(top)* Public, facing St. John's Street. *(bottom)* Private, facing the first court. *Figure 9. (below)* Talladega's West North Street axis. *(left)* Talladega College's Swayne Hall, which originally housed a school for white boys, once looked down the center line of the town's West North Street. The Savery Library, constructed in 1939, was oriented in such a way as to break this axis, turning its back to downtown Talladega and to the industrial operations that began to populate the once ceremonial space between town and gown, 1997. *(middle)* Along the West North Street axis to Talladega College from downtown Talladega, 1997. *(right)* Along West North Street axis to downtown Talladega from the college area, 1997.

reminded of it. The town-gown relations between Yale and New Haven, the University of Chicago and Hyde Park, Princeton University and Princeton, St. John's College and Cambridge constitute a different order and nature from the explosive racial hostility that HBCUs experienced in the years from their founding through the Jim Crow era.

The location of Talladega College offers an especially concrete example of how an unconventional situation maps out and controls the difficult relationship between an HBCU campus and the Southern town in which it exists. In addition to town-gown orientation, the example of Talladega College elaborates on the issue of the hill as bottom and anticipates my final analytical category relating to the other side of the railroad tracks. It is also an excellent example of how time factors into our ability to understand the cultural meaning of landscapes. The college occupied a building and thirty-four acres of land, which before the Civil War served as the Coosa River Baptist Association's high school for white boys. At the time the building was acquired by Talladega College in 1867, the site had been abandoned for several years, and it served briefly as a prison for Union soldiers during the war—another significant and consistent piece of history.[51] The building was located on a hill. This hill, however, was not like the other hills we have encountered so far—it was no isolated, useless bottom. Instead it was a prominent location that gently sloped down to the city and provided an impressive focal point from the courthouse square area that marked the center of downtown Talladega. The building was sited on the hill in such a way that it looked directly down the centerline of West North Street—the central east-west thoroughfare connecting Talladega to nearby towns such as Anniston and one of the two major streets that runs adjacent to the courthouse square. (Fig. 9) So important was the boys' high school building that it terminated West North Street. When landscape architects employ such axial landscape motifs, they usually punctuate the axis with significant markers. We saw this in the cases of campuses of Huntingdon College and the University of Alabama. Similarly, to use one of the most famous axial landscapes in the United States as an example, the axis along East Capitol between Capitol Hill and the Robert F. Kennedy Memorial Stadium in Washington D. C., is interrupted only by Lincoln Park, an ornamented oasis in the city.[52] (Fig. 11) In a similar way the line

Figure 11. **Washington, DC, the East Capitol axis.**

between the Amelia Gayle Gorgas Library and the President's House on the campus of the University of Alabama is interrupted only by the notable Denny Chimes—the carillon tower erected in honor of a former president of the university—and a split-faced granite monument erected by the Daughters of the Confederacy to honor university confederate cadets who served in the Civil War. (Fig. 3) So sacred are such axial landscapes that recently, at the University of Michigan's campus in Ann Arbor, trees had to be removed in order to preserve the direct line of sight between the Horace Rackham Graduate Building and the Harlan Hatcher Graduate Library. The Ingalls Mall, an axis so certain of its right to belong in its setting that it imposes its brick-banded elegance on the two city streets it crosses, slicing past them as if they did not exist and stooping to recognize only emblems of the institution and the state: a fountain in its court of raised gardens, a monumental pole bearing the American flag, and finally a landmark "M" set in granite that marks the center of the Diagonal, a space that kisses the feet of the Harlan Hatcher Graduate Library.[53] (Fig. 12) Such axial arrangements dramatize the centrality, high purpose, and public endorsement of these spaces and the institutions that occupy them. These axes are very costly, especially when at the heart of cities, because they represent spaces that could have been used for more utilitarian—profitable—ventures. Preserving these axes for lawns, trees, fountains, and monuments with no commercial, industrial, residential, institutional, or even active recreational use indicates that they are sacred spaces intended to symbolize the culture's highest values.

In contrast with these sacred axial spaces, Talladega's former West North Street axis between the old boy's school and the town has become a broken or abandoned axis that sharply reconfigures the line between the Talladega campus and the town. What now lies between campus and the courthouse? The CSXT Railroad, which crosses West North Street between the campus and the downtown, has literally placed the campus "on the other side of the tracks." (Fig. 9) The Wehadkee Yarn Mills Cotton Receiving Plant, located so as to span West North Street, breaks further the once direct axial connection between town and gown. A Cotton Receiving Plant—ironically, one of the historical icons from which blacks had sought deliverance through education—now serves as an object of contemplation for the occupants of

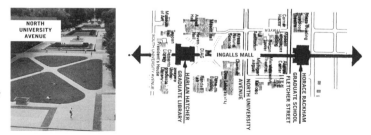

Figure 12.(left) View along mall to the Hatcher Library from the balcony of the Rackham building, 1997. *(right)* University of Michigan's Ingalls Mall axis.

the campus, who must go around its fenced compound industrial buildings and stock-piles if they wish to use West North Street to go downtown from what was the front door of their campus. While motorists and pedestrians using Washington, D.C.'s, East Capitol axis must go around a lovely Lincoln Park on the processional to the U.S. Capitol, users of Talladega's West North Street must go around a cotton receiving plant on the processional to Talladega College. Would this axis have been preserved if the school had remained in the hands of the Southern élite? Like railroad tracks, the cotton plant suggests the lack of value, or the depreciated value, that the white power structure of the town placed on the campus—the desire to "break" the direct connection with the town's identity. Although we cannot say for sure, we can speculate that the present relation between town and gown indicates the actual hostility the campus endured at the hands of white citizens during the height of Jim Crow. The primary and secondary sources attest to the incidents when the residents of the campus had to defend it from the encroachments of a hostile mob. The question must be asked—do the industry and railroad blocking the axis embody this history of hostility? Perhaps the blocked landscape indicates not only the power of the dominant group to block off the campus but also the agency of the marginalized group to exploit that blockage for its own purposes of protecting itself from this hostility. In other words, might there have been reasons why blacks and their colleagues would have wanted their campuses blocked off from easy public access?

OTHER SIDE OF THE TRACKS Pierce Lewis described the historical roots of the expression "on the other side of the railroad tracks." Many small towns that sprung up along railroads as they penetrated the American continent were laid out in simple, bilaterally symmetrical plans. The railroad itself formed a central axis that divided these towns into two sections. The trouble is that service facilities, such as the fire station, could be located only on one side of the railroad. In the unfortunate event of an emergency occurring while the train was in town, therefore, the side without the service facilities was at the mercy of the gods. This was the other side of town to which African-Americans, Latinos, and poor European Americans—America's others—were relegated, a good illustration of how the location of landscape tells much about the cultural circumstances of the people associated with it. In historic preservation, however, we have been so focused on describing or explaining objects in landscape as museum artifacts that we have rarely interpreted the historical significance of the neighborhoods or campuses in relation to their contexts of regional geography.

Much as we have not examined comprehensively the meaning underlying the orientation of college campus buildings in relation to their local contexts, so we have not interrogated the actual location of college campuses in their regional contexts. Consider the location of the Tuskegee campus.[54] Given that the town of Tuskegee was the seat of Macon County and the home of two other institutions of higher learning—including the Tuskegee Female College discussed earlier—one would have thought that Tuskegee University, as a state-funded school, would have been located in downtown Tuskegee. While the school was first opened in a building adjacent to the African Methodist Episcopal Zion (AMEZ) church on Zion Hill just off Highway 80—one of the two county roads leading to downtown Tuskegee—within months of its opening, the institution moved out of town to its present site. Described as being "conveniently located" by Washington, not only was the property about one mile from downtown but also it was separated from it by an area of piney ravines carved by running water that eventually feeds the Uphapee and Callebee Creeks.[55] (Fig. 6) A section of the walk from the Tuskegee campus to downtown Tuskegee along Old Montgomery Road, shows that this area at least to that point had remained undeveloped probably because of the difficulties discussed above relating to building in the gullies. Vehicular access between town and gown during the postbellum period, moreover, was limited to Old Montgomery Road. As the drawing shows, access to the campus is still quite restricted due to the difficulties posed by the ravines.[56] (Fig. 13) In terms of the natural and cultural geography, therefore, the campus is dramatically separated from town. Town and gown, unlike the case of many other campuses of this era, are separated by distance, limited vehicular access, and land so dissected that it has been largely left alone to this day. Historian Louis Harlan has observed this in passing, pointing out that there were no connections between downtown Tuskegee and the black campus. This he attributes to "an ingenious town planner [who] arranged the through and dead-end streets in such a way that the Institute students could travel into town only along a single street [Old Montgomery Road]."[57]

Looking at Harlan's conclusion from a somewhat different perspective, could it be that the new black owners of the property understood the advantages of locating their campus on property that was potentially difficult to connect with the town? Separation offered the advantage of autonomy against the proscriptions of the potentially hostile town. Looking at the campus in relation to its context of physical geography, then, caused me to take the total controlling agency Harlan assigns to the white town-planners and reconsider it in relation to the black campus planners who were busy going about the business of building their civilization even as others were busy trying to thwart their ambition. Harlan assumes the imperative of protecting white townspeople from the black community associated with the school. Looking at the town and gown relationship from below, I suggest an alternative imperative of the black planners of Tuskegee to protect their campus from potentially hostile white townspeople. We know from Washington's papers that the leader of the young institution was deeply concerned about students leaving the campus to go to town. The leader had pressing reasons to restrict movement both ways (black students to town and white townspeople to campus). Isolation from town offered some degree of protection to the campus while appearing to appease the anxieties of the status quo.

While the need for protection was a concrete and powerful motivation for campus planners, the deliberate distance between town and gown also managed a subtler strategy and meaning that were integral to the survival of HBCU campuses: the ability to maintain high educational goals within the framework of an acceptable "agricultural" school. Similar to Tuskegee, Alabama A&M University, as I pointed out above, was also originally located in town. It occupied a four-acre property on West Clinton Street in the city of Huntsville, which it purchased in stages beginning in 1881.[58] After this institution became Alabama's black land-grant school in 1891, however, it sold this valuable property and acquired instead the 182-acre Henry P. Turner place on Normal's Hill, which is located four miles north of the city, where the campus sits today.

> The commissioners of the school thought it better to sell the valuable property in Huntsville and invest the proceeds in land further removed from town, where there would be more and better opportunities to develop the industries of the school.[59]

All-white male Auburn University, on the other hand, was located on Main Street in downtown Auburn, which it eventually claimed and renamed College Avenue.[60] When it gained land-grant status, it retained its location in town, addressing the space requirements for such industries of the school as farming by buying additional property well away from the campus, the path taken by many other historically white land-grant colleges to solve the "farm problem." At first glance, this distinct separation of farm and school might be considered at odds with the institution's official mission to advance practical and applied education of the white male population. The more pressing imperative for this and other white land-grant colleges, however, was to assert their authority as respectable institutions of higher learning, requiring careful management of the image projected by their campuses. Given that farming, at least until the passage of the Morrill Acts, was in many ways the antithesis of academic pursuit, conflating farm and school could not have been a good thing for the status of these institutions. Auburn University solved its problem of perceived conflicting mission by retaining the original location of its campus in downtown Auburn, with the impressive academic façade of the campus facing the town—even if less aggressively than, say, Huntingdon College's private campus. With this front face, the institution asserts its rightful place among institutions of higher learning and in the city that houses it. The farms, which it placed well beyond like an expansive backyard, indicate the other state mission of the university. This audacity to claim and hold on to its prized location in the town is not surprising, for what was then the school was founded for the sons of the "courageous and ambitious settlers … who had risked the hazards and hardships of frontier life … [and were] now reaping the reward of a bountiful nature."[61]

Much to the chagrin of the parents of the students of many "industrial" black schools, merging farm and school in space as in rhetoric and program appears to have been advantageous to these schools, which capitalized on the message of accommodation to racial inferiority that such juxtaposition evinced. Thus, in the rhetoric popularized by Washington and adopted by many black schools, "head" and "hands" were

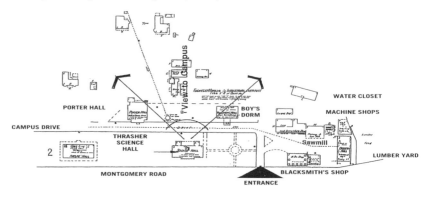

similarly juxtaposed as the targets of black education. Chapter VII of Washington's tribute to manual labor *Working With the Hands* is entitled "Head and Hands Together;" a merging of school and industry representing the HBCU's negotiation of Southern attitudes toward its quest for higher education.[62] It is not surprising that the new campus of Tuskegee in 1881 was referred to by its owners, donors, and the public not as "the College," as was the East Alabama Male College (Auburn University) but strategically as "the Farm," so that southerners and northerners, pleasantly surprised by Washington's vision of the new "educated Negro," began to throw their support behind the fledgling institution.[63] In *Making of a Black Leader*, Louis Harlan documents that a friend from the North gave $100, stipulating that it be used to purchase a horse to work the farm (128). Similarly, the conflation of school and industry is evident in the layout of the entrances to Tuskegee's campus at the turn of the century, which were consistently industrialized. Thrasher Science Hall, the only academic building located near the entrance, was oriented away from public view, much like the Carnegie Library. (Fig. 13) Furthermore, it shows how the school's industrial buildings, including its sawmill, were located in such a way as to command a direct line of sight as one entered the campus via Tuskegee's main entrance from the public road. Its blacksmith shop and foundry were also located near the entrance, an instance of the masking of the academic mission of the institution with industry. In support of this claim, the historic record provides numerous instances of the delicate relationship between black ambition for higher education and white southerners' discomfort with this matter. Tuskegee, like other black schools at the time, established strict rules of conduct for students and faculty to observe while visiting town. Wolters, for instance, documents that one of Tuskegee's faculty members from the North, unused to southern traditions, was admonished by the dean for carrying too many books—the dean feared that whites "would get the impression that Tuskegee was training the intellect rather than the heart and hands."[64]

Figure 13. Tuskegee's main entrance at the turn of the century. *(above, bottom)* Public, façade of Thrasher Hall facing Montgomery Road, 1997. *(above, top)* Private, façade of Thrasher Building facing interior of campus. *(opposite)* The Main entry area at the turn of the century. The base is a 1897 Sanborn Fire Insurance map. *(left)* Main entry area on the occasion of President McKinley's visit to campus in 1898. Even on this auspicious occasion, the pile of logs is prominently displayed.

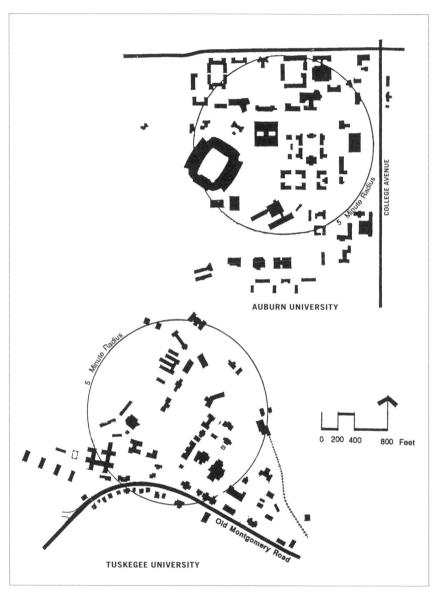

Figure 14. Comparison of the layout
of Tuskegee and Auburn Universities.

The manifest destiny belonging to the sons of white settlers, the only individuals who enjoyed full citizenship in the United States at this moment in American history, undergirds Auburn's right to assert its claim to the town of Auburn. The idea of manifest destiny, however, was an aspiration of African-Americans as well. However, it was played out under different cultural constraints. Unlike Auburn, Tuskegee and Alabama A&M, like many other HBCUs in the Deep South, located their campuses where they would have been less likely to affront those who were uncomfortable with their missions. Unlike the new land-grant schools serving white people in Alabama, the campuses of black schools represented a conflation of the culturally conflicting missions of educating the "heads" and "hands" of their students. Faced with mounting southern intolerance for their mission, black schools found it advantageous to showcase their role in training the "hands" of their students for use in the postbellum southern economy, thus providing cover for their more radical role in developing the heads of their students in the interest of black uplift.

Even if black educators saw these marginal spaces as symbols of race uplift and progress, they were still left with the problem of how to develop a campus on them with limited funding. How could they communicate to their students this symbolism against the grain of white hostility and a history of racial inferiority? The unusual ribbon-like layout of the Tuskegee campus, which accommodated the dissected topography of the site, might provide a hint. With the buildings sited on the high ground, they are related to one another not in the geometrical ways we associate with college campuses but in seemingly "unpredictable" ways that reflect the lay of the land.[65] The rambling layout gives the campus a special ambiance that is rooted, not in the conventional notion of the college "campus as a work of art," but in the physical geography and cultural circumstances of place.[66] The layout represents the necessary pragmatism of a people who had to make the best of their financial and social constraints and in this sense takes on additional historical significance. Moreover, even after they could financially afford to do differently, they still kept at bay any inclination toward establishing a more formal design motif, such as was adopted by the more generously funded Auburn University. (Fig. 14) The obviously studied formality of Auburn's campus communicates immediately and forcefully the institution's function as an academic institution. The design has become associated with rationality, progress, and high civilization. It could be argued, however, that the cost it takes to manipulate and manage ground to achieve this effect also embodies the privilege and worth of the place. While Tuskegee, too, aspires according to these values, its plan, mitigated as it was by particular constraints facing African-Americans of the period, means that any hint of formality is restricted to the flattest sections of campus upon the ridges where they could be accommodated with limited earth movement and thus limited cost.

But it is the large unmannered gully at the heart of the Tuskegee campus that most gives the campus its identity. This was where the school's farms were located at the turn of the century and where the famous Tuskegee Negro Conferences were held.[67] (Fig. 15) Immersed in the rolling spaces of the gully, one is reminded of "campus" by the porticos, domes, and cupola of campus buildings that sit on its edges. In the early days one would have had difficulty seeing these façades from the public road because of the line of buildings that sat along Old Montgomery Road. The façades, however, are clearly visible from the interior of the campus. Tantum Hall, a women's dormitory on the edge promontory, is the best example of this. The façade of the building facing the gully, is considerably more monumental than the façade facing the campus road. (Fig. 4) In describing its details, architectural critics have often overlooked the significance of the building's orientation relative to the gully. Some of the other buildings around the gully, such as James Hall, another women's dormitory, also show this curious relationship to it. From their balconies one can imagine seeing the grazing cattle and other farm animals in the rambling space. One could have a box-seat view of the Farmer's Conference, all of this providing an unusual focus for contemplation. Viewers, be they student or farmer, would have seen here an unprecedented juxtaposition of high architectural forms (such as the classical ionic portico of Tantum Hall), which signify high cultural and academic aspirations, with the "simple" rambling pasture of the gully, which signifies the familiar rural Alabama landscape. This prospect, this seeming conflict of meaning, could have provided a coherent dual meaning. On one hand, these buildings facing the gully could have served to inspire the multiple constituents who beheld them—the black students living in them or working on the farm below them and the black public who saw them as

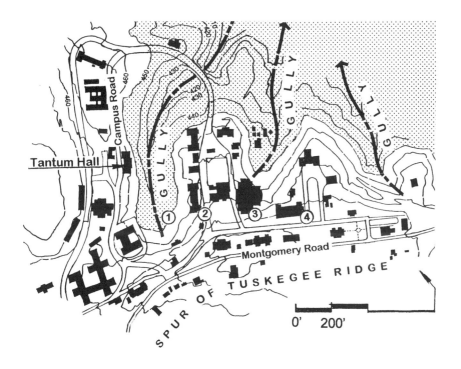

Figure 15. "Spontaneous" layout of Tusakegee's campus,
circa 1940. The overall structure of this section of the campus can still be observed today. (bottom left) Façade of
Tantum Hall facing the gully, 1907.

they participated in the annual Farmer's Conferences—to respect the authenticity of their locale. On the other hand, the conventional emblems of the campus encouraged these constituents to retain their highest aspirations, and to do so by factoring in the place with which they were most familiar.

"Cast down your bucket where you are" was Washington's metaphorical lesson to his audience at the Atlanta Exposition in 1895, at once apparently giving in to élite demands for blacks to stay in the fields but at the same time giving veiled direction for higher achievement, education, acquisition of land, business, and the like—all of the qualities that he believed undergirded the progress of any race. As the landscape of this campus surely spoke lessons to the newly emancipated people of Washington's time for whom it was built, so the HBCU campus—and the histories it records—should continue to speak to us today.

Grandison, Kenrick Ian. *Negotiated Space: The Black College Campus as a Cultural Record of Postbellum America. American Quarterly* 51:3 (1999). 529-579." The American Studies Association, Reprinted by permission of the Johns Hopkins University Press.

NOTES

Funding for my project has been provided by the University of Michigan's Office of the Vice Provost for Academic and Multicultural Affairs and Horace Rackham Graduate School and the Graham Foundation for Advanced Studies in the Fine Arts of Chicago who provided funding for this project. I am indebted to Marlon Ross, Ondine Le Blanc, Lucy Maddox, Michael Vlach and the many other to colleagues and friends who made invaluable contributions to this manuscript.

1 For further details on this episode, see Raymond Wolter, *The New Negro on Campus: Black College Rebellions in the 1920s* (Princeton: Princeton University Press, 1975), 11.

2 This history is documented definitively by such works as W.E.B. Du Bois's *Black Reconstruction in America*: An Essay Toward a History of the Part Which Black Folk Played in the Attempt to Reconstruct Democracy in America, 1860–1880 (1935; reprint, Cleveland: World Publishing Co., 1962); and Horace Mann Bond's *Negro Education in Alabama, A Study in Cotton and Steel* (1939; reprint, New York: Octagon Books, 1969). James Anderson's *The Education of Blacks in the South, 1860–1935* (Chapel Hill: University of North Carolina Press, 1988) is a recent work on the subject of black education in the South during this period.

3 For further discussion of the theoretical and methodological context of this essay, especially in relation to studies of the cultural-historical significance of the material world, see note 3 in my article "Negotiated Space: the Black College Campus as a Cultural Record of the Postbellum South South," *American Quarterly* 51.3 (1999): 529–579.

4 His essay introduces *The Shadow of the Plantation* (Chicago: University of Chicago Press, 1934), a book written by Charles S. Johnson—Park's former student at Chicago. The essay being cited here is reprinted in Robert E. Park, *Race and Culture* (Glencoe, Ill.: Free Press, 1950), 66–78.

5 Park, *Race and Culture*, 72.

6 By "readers" I refer to those contemporary visitors or passersby to these campuses who observed or attempted to understand the campuses. This could be extended to later scholars who have offered interpretations.

7 The importance of landscape understood as "the grounds" has been raised by such scholars as landscape historian Cynthia Zaitzevsky. She argued in "The Historian and the Landscape:

Focusing New Emphasis on Documentation and Synthesis," *Preservation Forum* 7 (1993): 16–25, that "the grounds surrounding the historic house might be of as much historical importance as the structure itself." Renee Friedman in her essay "For the Curator of Trees and Teacups: The Landscape as Artifact," *CRM* 17 (1994): 5–6, 9, took this idea further. Theorizing parity between house and grounds, she argued for a "holistic" pproach to interpretation based on understanding "the entire site," which she conceptualized as a "collection" of artifacts comprising "what's inside the house, what's outside the house, and the house itself." In making an analogy between landscape and museums, she follows the direction given by such scholars as Thomas Schlereth (see note 3). Less restricted by the assumptions of art history, cultural geographers such as Peirce Lewis have come even closer to employing a holistic approach to interpreting the built environment. See for instance his piece, "Common Landscapes as Historic Documents," in *History from Things: Essays on Material Culture*, ed. Steven Lubar and W. David Kingery (Washington, D.C.: Smithsonian Institution Press, 1993), 115–139.

8 The approach of doing scholarship "from below" was initiated in the disciplines of architecture and landscape architecture by scholars of vernacular studies, especially after Bernard Rudofsky's Museum of Modern Art exhibit and book *Architecture without Architects* (New York: Museum of Modern Art, 1964). Extending this tradition, Delores Hayden's first book, *The Grand Domestic Revolution: A History of Feminist Designs for American Homes, Neighborhoods, and Cities* (Cambridge, MIT Press, 1981), is one of the works applying the method to study architecture from the vantage of women's history. Similarly, but more broadly embracing the cultural politics of space, Hayden's most recent book, *The Power of Place: Urban Landscapes as Public History* (Cambridge: MIT Press, 1995), begins to integrate the concerns of cultural studies with historic preservation in the urban setting. See, for instance, Wright's *Building the Dream: A Social History of Housing in America* (New York: Pantheon Books, 1981). Scholars of landscape architecture, such as J. B. Jackson and John Stilgoe, helped to define the field "vernacular" landscape studies, centering their investigations on the landscapes of "ordinary people" previously ignored in the discourse on the built environment. See, for instance, Jackson's *Discovering the Vernacular Landscape* (New Haven: Yale University Press, 1984) and Stilgoe's *Common Landscape of America, 1580 to 1845* (New Haven: Yale University Press, 1982).

9 This was a goal of my earliest article on the HBCU campus, "From Plantation to Campus: Progress, Community, and the Lay of the Land in Shaping the Early Tuskegee," *Landscape Journal* 15 (1996): 6–32. The article sought to make a case for including the Tuskegee University campus in the landscape architecture canon—a goal that is consistent with the formalism that still prevails in much architectural and landscape architectural criticism.

10 The official keeping of such records, which has been routine on élite majority campuses, could not be a pressing priority for HBCUs. This is not because of a lack of concern but rather because of scarcity of financial and human resources. Thus, it is all the more important for scholars to retrieve and help assemble and preserve records of the black campus.

11 Thomas Gaines's *The Campus as a Work of Art* (New York: Praeger, 1991) provides a good example of this. The HBCU campus has been considered by such works as Richard Dozier's "Tuskegee: Booker T. Washington's Contribution to the Education of Black Architects" (Ph.d. diss., University of Michigan, 1990), and Ellen Weiss's "Robert R. Taylor of Tuskegee: An Early Black American Architect," *Journal of the Southeast Chapter of the Society of Architectural Historians 2* (1991): 3–19. These studies are pioneering and important. However, they have emphasized either individual buildings and their designers (Weiss) or the history of architectural education (Dozier).

12 Weiss, "Robert R. Taylor of Tuskegee," 10.

13 I offer more on this critique of the art-historical focus of campus criticism in my articles "Challenging Formalism: The Implications of Contemporary Cultural Theory for Historic Preservation," *Landscape Journal* 18 (1999): 22–36.

14 The cultural implications of the axis will be discussed in more detail later.

15 Because Auburn University and the University of Alabama at Tuscaloosa were both state funded white male institutions in the Black Belt during the postbellum period, these institutions are important for comparison with the historically black institutions considered in this study. Auburn University, located in Lee County adjacent to Tuskegee's Macon County, was established by the Alabama Conference of the Methodist Church. The institution opened as the East Alabama Male College in 1859. Alabama accepted the provisions of the Morrill Land Grant Act in 1868, selecting Auburn as the state's first land-grant college in 1871. The Board of Trustees of the institution accepted the state's offer in 1872. While the University of Alabama—located in Tuscaloosa County in the western section of the Black Belt—was opened in 1831, much of the present-day campus was built during the postbellum period. Huntingdon College, as a private white women's college located in Montgomery County adjacent to Macon County, is also interesting for comparison. The institution was opened in 1856 as the Tuskegee Female College by the Methodist Church in downtown Tuskegee just one block south of Main Street. It was moved to its present location in Montgomery in 1910.

16 Pennsylvania accepted the provisions of the Morrill Act in 1863 and selected Pennsylvania State University (then called the Agricultural College of Pennsylvania) as the state's first land-grant institution in the same year. Thus, Pennsylvania State University claims to be the first land-grant institution in the United States.

NOTES

There is some competitive argument about this matter, however, since Iowa State and Michigan State Universities also appropriate this distinction. Whatever the case, the layout of Pennsylvania State University's campus is a useful example here not only because it was an early land-grant institution but also because its campus is an archetype for the land-grant college campus with its prominently situated Old Main and other academic buildings in relation to public thoroughfares. It is useful to consider both southern and northern land-grant college examples to suggest the consistency of their design across regions—a fact that also marks their aspiration to become national institutions competing with private and public liberal arts colleges.

17 Toni Morrison, *Sula* (New York: New American Library, 1973), 4–5.

18 Toni Morrison's joke also alludes to how interior spaces were utilized according to race and class. Before blacks built their own churches, they worshipped in the balconies of white churches. Later when cinemas, theaters, and opera houses were segregated, blacks were again forced to sit in the balconies—the "nose bleed" sections, which though physically "on top" were considered the least desirable seats. These balconies, in the early 1900s, were referred to as "nigger heavens." In characterizing the hills as the "bottom of heaven," therefore, Morrison is drawing on and referring to an even wider African-American spatial and cultural experience.

19 Ironically, the periodic flooding of such low-lying flood-plain areas is a good thing because such flooding continuously replenishes the fertility of these areas. As flood waters retreat they leave behind thick deposits of rich topsoil that was eroded from the hilly areas.

20 A whole cultural analysis could be done on the typology of the word "hillbilly" in relation to the historical biases of hilly topography in American culture.

21 Rail and water transportation are considerably less expensive than transportation by road. Locomotives cannot operate on very steep terrain, which is why railroads generally follow river flood plains—the broad, flat, alluvial-rich valleys carved by rivers in their lower courses as they meander across the terrain before they pour into lakes and oceans.

22 See Clarence Major's entry for "Bottom," in *Juba to Jive: A Dictionary of African American Slang*, (1970; reprint, New York: Penguin Books, 1994): Bottom: n (1870s–1930s) the black (Negro? colored?) section of town; a rundown, disreputable area in a black community; Poor Pond. Also known (especially by whites) as "Coon Bottom" (59).

23 See Olmsted's *The Cotton Kingdom: A Traveler's Observations on Cotton and Slavery in the American Slave States*, ed. Arthur Schlesinger Sr. (1861; reprint,New York: Modern Library, 1984).

24 While the Black Belt of Alabama has been variously delimited, J. D. Pope's definition has been most influential. Pope subdivided Alabama into ten physical geographical areas in "Types of Farming Areas," included in *Agriculture of Alabama* (Montgomery, 1930), 53-65. He classified ten counties as actually belonging to the Black Belt. Tuskegee's Macon County was classified as belonging to the Upper Coastal Plain subdivision, a slightly more hilly region that fringes these ten counties. Since cotton cultivation gradually expanded into this region in the 1850s and 1860s, the population of blacks in this region as in the ten counties is generally higher than that of whites. Thus, from a cultural-geographical stand-point, it is reasonable to consider this region as part of the Black Belt.

25 W. F. Foster, a veteran of the Confederate Army and the Democratic contender to the Alabama Senate in 1879, approached Louis Adams, a former slave and a highly regarded man in the Tuskegee community, regarding securing the black vote for his candidacy. Adams pledged this support with the understanding that Foster and A. L. Brooks, the Democratic contender to the Alabama House, if elected, would secure the passage of a bill to establish a "Negro Normal School" at Tuskegee. For documentation see Grandison, "From Plantation to Campus," 8.

26 Booker T. Washington, *Up From Slavery: An Autobiography* (1901; reprint, Garden City, N.Y.: Doubleday, Doran & Co., 1929), 119-20.

27 Act of the Legislature establishing the "Normal School for the Education of colored teachers at Tuskegee," reprinted in Anson Phelps Stokes, *Tuskegee Institute, the First Fifty Years* (Tuskegee, Ala.: Tuskegee Institute Press, 1931), 59-60.

28 Historian Richard D. Morrison documents this in *History of Alabama A&M University, 1875 to 1992* (Huntsville, Ala.: Liberal Arts Press, 1994), 12–13. The school's black founder and first principal William Hooper Councill supported the Democrat George S. Huston for the governorship of Alabama in 1875, thereby helping Democrats to regain control of the state for the first time since the Civil War. This action did not endear him to African-Americans. However, in return for his support, like the case of Tuskegee, the state passed legislation to establish the school, appointing him as its Principal and three Democrats to its Board of Trustees. Given the presence of the ruling Democrats on the Board of Trustees and Councill's role in helping to restore Democratic rule in Alabama, one would have thought that a more generous appropriation could have been worked out for the institution. The meager sum that was provided, like the case of Tuskegee, conveys the attitude of the southern establishment toward black education.

29 Richard D. Morrison, *History of Alabama A&M*, 38. The federal government's 1890 Morrill Act required the segregated South to provide funding for black land-grant schools. Almost all of the states in this region excluded blacks from benefiting from the 1862 Morrill Act.

30 The annual yield from the land-grant endowment is recorded in Authur Klien's *Survey of Land Grant Colleges and Universities*, vol. 2 (Washington, D.C., 1930), 101.

31 See Bond, *Negro Education in Alabama*, 106–110; Robert G. Sherer, *Subordination or Liberation? The Development and Conflicting Theories of Black Education in Nineteenth Century Alabama* (Tuscaloosa: University of Alabama Press, 1977), 7–8. Figures for Alabama A&M University are also documented in Richard D. Morrison, *History of Alabama A&M*, 12–13, 15–19.

32 See Washington, *My Larger Education: Being Chapters From My Experience* (1911; reprint, Miami: Mnemosyne Pub. Inc., 1969), 23, for historical photograph of the property around the time it was purchased. Also see Washington, *Up From Slavery*, 130, for his description of property.

33 The United States Department of Agriculture and Alabama Department of Agriculture and Industries, Soil Survey: *Macon County, Alabama*, ser. 1937, no. 11 (Nov. 1944), 31, classified 80 percent of the soils of the property as "eroded phase."

34 This is documented in Louis Harlan's *Booker T. Washington: The Wizard of Tuskegee, 1901–1915* (New York: Crowell-Collier Press, 1983), 169. Harlan states that Hare's article was a rebuttal to local whites who complained that Tuskegee was "trying to buy up the whole county." This criticism, Harlan suggests, was precipitated when whites became anxious about the school's success in the 1900s with "its big buildings, neatly dressed students, air of bustle, and affluence. . .[in contrast to] the shabby downtown and the flaking paint of the old mansion houses"(165–167).

35 Rackham Holt, *George Washington Carver: An American Biography* (Garden City, N.Y.: Doubleday, Doran & Co., 1943), 132.

36 As in Tony Morrison's fictional Medallion, the town refers to the "official" or white identified section of the community, where the facilities of white power are located, such as the courthouse and private homes of the prominent—powerful white—citizens.

37 The limits of the original property were determined from the verbal and graphic description of the property included on the deed for the property photographs, which are included in L. Albert Scipio, *Pre-War Days at Tuskegee: Historical Essay on Tuskegee Institute 1881–1943* (Silver Spring, Md., 1987) 12–13.

38 For more description and explanation of Tuskegee's layout See Grandison, "From Plantation to Campus," 15–20 .

39 The campus is now located a few miles from downtown Birmingham.

40 For information about Normal, Alabama,or theState Normal and Industrial School for Negroes (located at Normal, near Huntsville,

Ala.) (Montgomery, 1896?), 3; see the University Archives, J. F. Drake Memorial Learning Resources Center, Alabama A&M University.

41 "1975 Centennial Edition," The Huntsville Times, Sunday, 27 April 1975, 6; held at University Archives, J. F. Drake Memorial Learning Resources Center, Alabama A&M University.

42 Richard D. Morrison, *History of Alabama A&M*, 49. Ironically, today Alabama A&M's campus, sitting on the hill as it does, appears imposing. We need only remember the negative attitude toward "hillbillies" to understand the cultural historical significance of the site.

43 Tuskegee's farm at $5 an acre, for instance, was inexpensively priced even for 1881. Given the financial constraints of the early school, it would have most likely been the best property the school could have afforded. In this and other instances when blacks were allowed to acquire real estate, their financial privation, the result of their circumstances, was one of the factors that restricted them to the most marginal property available.

44 This understanding of the social dictates of their time would have been particularly true for black leaders like Washington and Councill, who were native Southerners. Washington was born in Franklin County, Virginia. His formative years were spent both in this state and in West Virginia, where his family moved after Emancipation. Councill was born near Fayetteville, North Carolina. Most of his formative years were spent there and in Jackson County, Alabama.

45 Booker T. Washington Papers, Manuscript Division, Library of Congress, Container 980.

46 Harlan, *Wizard of Tuskegee*, 5.

47 Isaac Newton Phelps-Stokes was the Harvard-trained architect who designed most buildings funded by the Phelps-Stokes Fund. He was the nephew of Olivia D. Phelps-Stokes, the donor of the fund.

48 Department of the Interior, Bureau of Education, Negro Education, "A Study of the Private and Higher Schools for Colored People in the United States," *Bulletin* 38, vol. 1 (1917): 205.

49 Department of the Interior, Bureau of Education, *204–205*.

50 See Maxine D. Jones and Joe M. Richardson, *Talladega College: The First Century* (Tuscaloosa: University of Alabama Press, 1990), 11–17.

51 This is documented in Buell G. Gallagher, *Sunrise o'er Alabama: The Report of the President, 1935–36* (Talladega, Ala., 1936), 8; Jones and Richardson, *Talladega College, The First*

NOTES

Century, 248. The fact that the property served as a prison for Union soldiers probably also helps us to understand why it fell into the hands of the American Missionary Association for use as a black school.

52 Washington, D.C., provides some of the finest examples of axial landscapes in the United States. The example is drawn from the nation's capitol city because many readers are likely to have encountered these landscapes and would be able to recall how these spaces convey the power and authority of the State. Thus, this example, perhaps better than any other, should help to place the aspirations implied when this device is used in the landscape.

53 The donor who provided the money for the Rackham Building—one of the most costly academic buildings in the country constructed during the Depression—prescribed that no object should block its view toward the library, which is located several blocks to its south.

54 See Grandison, "Landscapes of Terror," 340–351 for more discussion of Tuskegee University's separation from downtown Tuskegee.

55 Booker T. Washington, *Southern Workman* 10 (Sept. 1881): 91.

56 The drawing is based on USGS map of the Tuskegee area, which was photorevised in 1983.

57 Harlan, *Booker T. Washington: The Wizard of Tuskegee: 1901–1915*, 423.

58 The initial purchase is documented in H. Clay Armstrong, *Report of the Superintendent of Education of the State of Alabama for the Scholastic Year Ending September 30th*, 1882 (Montgomery, Ala., 1883). The particulars about the property at the time it was put up for sale in 1891 are documented by the announcement of sale carried by the 27 May 1891 edition of the Huntsville newspaper *The Weekly Mercury* (Alabama State Archives, Microfilm no. MN672).

59 Catalogue of the State Colored Normal and Industrial School, Normal, Alabama (near Huntsville), 1895–96 (30); held at University Archives, J. F. Drake Memorial Learning Resources Center, Alabama A&M University. Also see John G. Harris, *Thirty Seventh Annual Report of the Superintendent of Education of the State of Alabama for the Scholastic Year Ending September 30, 1891* (Montgomery, Ala., 1891).

60 See Grandison, "Landscapes of Terror," 344–351, for more discussion and a map illustrating Auburn University's integration with downtown Auburn.

61 This is according to Auburn's Centennial Committee on the occasion of the institution's centennial celebration as recorded in *Auburn's First 100 Years, 1856–1956* (Auburn, Ala., 1956), 5.

62 Booker T. Washington, *Working with the Hands: Being a Sequel to "Up From Slavery" Covering the Author's Experience in Training at Tuskegee* (New York: Doubleday, Page and Co., 1904), 82.

63 For further discussion of this issue in relation to the Tuskegee campus, refer to Grandison, "Landscapes of Terror: A Reading of Tuskegee's Historic Landscape," in *The Geography of Identity* ed. Patricia Yaeger (Ann Arbor, Mich.: Univesity of Michigan Press, 1996), 347 and 362–366.

64 Walters, *The New Negro on Campus*, 144. In another example documented in the same source, when a sociologist from the University of Chicago offered his resignation because he could not understand why the administration, in the old-fashioned style of Mr. Washington, was so anxious to keep the good will of the white community, Tuskegee's principal Russa Moton's response hit the mark. He accepted the professor's resignation, adding that "most teachers from the North don't fit in. We have a peculiar situation down here, and I imagine you have to be born in it to really understand it" (144).

65 Overtly "formalist" critics, who insist on the aesthetic standards defined by canonical campuses, would be hard pressed to consider this layout as anything but chaotic. Those who favor "multiculturalism"—as evidenced by their desire to extend the canon to include once ignored places such as Tuskegee's campus—are usually more generous, invariably characterizing the campus as "spontaneous." The term, however, still implies that the campus is in some way "unplanned," an inevitable conclusion given that they too continue to assume as "harmonious" and "proportioned" the form of campus that displays the geometrical—orderly—arrangement of buildings to define quadrangles, malls, axes, and other signifiers of the "planned." Holding on to these assumptions, therefore, we are faced with the dilemma of somehow justifying why Tuskegee's campus deserves a place in the canon.

66 The reference is to Thomas Gaines's art historyl critique of the American college campus cited in note 11. Published as recently as 1991, this book, like so many other contemporary criticisms of the built environment, suggests how, despite multicultural impulses, formalism still perseveres in architecture, landscape architecture, and historic preservation.

67 Though these began as informal meetings of black farmers and workers from the Black Belt area, by 1892 the first organized annual conference was held at Tuskegee, attracting some 500 farmers from all over the region. They discussed problems and explored solutions with the benefit of the practical and applied work done on the campus. The Tuskegee Negro Conference was the forerunner to subsequent farm congresses hosted by agricultural colleges as part of their extension work all across the country. See B. D. Mayberry's *A Century of Agriculture in the 1890 Land-Grant Institutions and Tuskegee University—1890-1990* (New York: Vantage Press 1991), 64–75 for more on this.

AMY WEISSER

six

marking brown v.
board of education

MEMORIALIZING SEPARATE BUT UNEQUAL SPACES

The mark of race and its mark on the American built environment is a catalyst for individual and collective memory. It is also dependent upon these memories. The sites most commonly associated with African-American history, if landmark registers and guidebooks are the arbiters, are houses and churches. In effect, these designations herald African-American private spaces, places that could be called home. With the Civil Rights era, and the conflicts surrounding the public identity of African-Americans at its heart, public sites associated with protests or strife enter the list—lunch counters, bus depots, parks, highways, schools, and the like. This equation disavows the ordinary presence of African-Americans in the public landscape and, in effect, writes large a lack of place that African-Americans have long experienced.

Brown v. Board of Education of Topeka, the Supreme Court case whose decision is often cited as the opening of the Civil Rights era, offers a venue for addressing placelessness. The Supreme Court's 1954 judgment, which proclaimed segregation in schools unconstitutional, pioneered

the attack on a legally mandated system of segregated public accommodations in the American south. At the heart of *Brown* is realizing the Constitutional right of all children, regardless of race, to an unexceptional walk to the neighborhood public school. A consolidation of five cases challenging segregation in public education, *Brown* centers on a number of school buildings in Topeka, Kansas; New Castle County, Delaware; Clarendon County, South Carolina; Prince Edward County, Virginia; and the District of Columbia.[1] That *Brown* , a case of landmark status with respect to social change, centers on public facilities prompts an exploration of the meaning of segregation through the vehicle of architecture. This discussion includes the recipr cal impact of architecture and social values and the possibilities for marking African-American presence for the future.

With *Brown*, the Supreme Court affirmed the Fourteenth Amendment of the Constitution which guarantees all citizens "equal protection under the law." To counter the trend by southern

I am grateful to Craig Barton for the opportunity to participate in the Sites of Memory symposium. I would like to thank Craig, Alyssa Rosenberg, Ann Fabian, Adam Yarinsky, and my colleagues at the American Museum of Natural History for their comments and support.

1 Brown, as heard by the United States Supreme Court, consolidated the case from Topeka with similar appeals from New Castle County, Delaware (Gebhart v. Belton); Clarendon County, South Carolina (Briggs v. Elliott); and Prince Edward County, Virginia (Davis v. County School Board of Prince Edward County). A related case from the District of Columbia (Bolling v. Sharpe) joined the case under a writ of certiorari.

school boards of dodging integration, the National Association for the Advancement of Colored People (NAACP), which masterminded the *Brown* suit, avoided questioning the equality of physical facilities "and other tangible factors." Instead, the NAACP presented expert witnesses who testified that segregation itself caused emotional and psychological damage that negatively impacted the educational experience of African-American children. This position led to the key finding in the *Brown* decision, written by Chief Justice Earl Warren, that "in the field of public education, the doctrine of 'separate but equal' has no place. Separate educational facilities are inherently unequal.² The Court's judgment overthrew the precedent established by *Plessy v. Ferguson* in 1896.³

In order to achieve its legal aim, *Brown* assumed equality of accommodation, but nearly all public schools built in the 21 states that required or permitted segregated facilities illustrated two unequal systems of education and facilities. These physical realities are evident in even the best examples of school architecture, for example the two highly praised elementary school buildings in Vicksburg, Mississippi—the Bowmar Avenue School for white children and the Cherry Street School for African-American children. These schools were constructed concurrently in 1937 by the same architects (Overstreet and Town, arguably the premier school architects in the state), by the same school board, and under the same bond issue and grant from the federal government.⁴ Though built for children separated by race, Bowmar Avenue and Cherry Street provided the same ordinary experiences (despite their aesthetic exceptionality) that were at the basis of *Brown*.

To a critic examining the Bowmar Avenue and Cherry Street schools today, the physical differences between the buildings corroborate their identity as the product of a racially divided social structure. Although the two schools have a similar façade organization and style, they differ markedly in character and complexity. The plainness of the façades at Cherry Street School contrasts with the sophisticated composition at Bowmar Avenue School. Bowmar Avenue, with its low-scale reiteration of its surrounding neighborhood, its delicate emphasis on the entranceway, and its simplified portico, is identifiable as a public accommodation rooted in its community. Cherry Street, on the other hand, replaces this subtlety with a simplistic articulation

---

2 From the Supreme Court decision: *Segregation of white and colored children in public schools has a detrimental effect upon the colored children. The impact is greater when it has the sanction of law, for the policy of separating the races is usually interpreted as denoting the inferiority of the Negro group. A* *sense of inferiority affects the motivation of the child to learn. Segregation with the sanction of law, therefore, has the tendency to [retard] the educational and mental development of Negro children and to deprive them of some of the benefits they would receive in a racial[ly] integrated school system.*

3 In 1951, the NAACP challenged school segregation before the United States District Court for Kansas. The suit was assembled by McKinley Burnett, head of the Topeka NAACP, and Lucinda Todd, a former school teacher then serving as secretary to the local NAACP. Thirteen parents, on behalf of their twenty children, served as plaintiffs in the suit. The plaintiffs had been instructed by the NAACP to attempt to enroll their children in the nearest (white) public school in the fall of 1950. So advised, the Reverend Oliver Brown, a 32-year-old welder in the Santa Fe Railroad shops and an assistant pastor and sexton at St. John

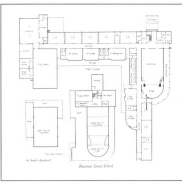

top left: **Overstreet and Town, Bowmar Avenue School, Vicksburg, Mississippi, 1937. Rendering from N.W. Overstreet Architectural Records, Special Collections Department, Mississippi State University Library.;** *top right:* **Bowmar Avenue School. Plans from N.W. Overstreet Architectural Records, Special Collections Department, Mississippi State University Library.**

bottom left: **Overstreet and Town, Cherry Street School, Vicksburg, Mississippi, 1937. Rendering from N.W. Overstreet Architectural Records, Special Collections Department, Mississippi State University Library.;** *bottom right:* **Cherry Street School. Plans from N.W. Overstreet Architectural Records, Special Collections Department, Mississippi State University Library.**

A.M.E. Church, walked Linda, the oldest of his three daughters, to the "whites only" Sumner Elementary School only to have his request to enroll her denied. (At that time, Ms. Brown was a third grader at the all-black Monroe Elementary School.) Of all the plaintiffs, Brown was the only male, and so received the honor of donating his name to history.

The Kansas court acknowledged the "Separate but Equal" precedent established by Plessy v. Ferguson and found that the school facilities in Topeka were substantially equal, although segregated, and denied the plaintiffs case. In 1952, the NAACP appealed the case to the United States Supreme Court, were it was consolidated with the similar cases from Delaware,

South Carolina, Virginia, and the District of Columbia.

The consolidated *Brown* case was argued before the Court in December 1952. With the death of Chief Justice Fred Vinson and the subsequent appointment of Earl Warren as Chief Justice, the cases were reargued in December 1953. On May 17, 1954, the Court issued its verdict—a unanimous decision with only a single opinion of the Court.

The Delaware, Kansas, South Carolina, and Virginia cases challenged Plessy as a violation of the Fourteenth Amendment (1868). The Amendment, which extends federal citizenship to African-Americans, states: "No State shall make or enforce any law which shall abridge the privileges or immunities of citizens of

the United States; nor shall any State deprive any person of life, liberty, or property, without due process of law; nor deny to any person within its jurisdiction the equal protections of the laws." As the Fourteenth Amendment does not apply in the District of Columbia, the NAACP brought suit there under the Fifth Amendment's "due process" clause.

Ms. Brown never attended the Sumner School. By the time Topeka integrated its elementary schools, she was a student at an integrated high school. (School systems in Kansas were segregated based upon an 1879 law granting communities with more than 15,000 residents the authority to segregate schools, except high schools.)

4 Application to the Public Works Administration [Docket Miss. 1337-F], August 2, 1938, in Adjourned Meeting, August 5, 1938, Board of Aldermen, Archives, City Clerk's Office, City Hall, Vicksburg, Mississippi; Amendatory Application to the Public Works Administration, March 7, 1939, Miss. X1337, Roll #6276, Records of the Public Works Administration, Record Group 135, National Archives, Washington, D.C.

of an institution—formidable and rootless in its surroundings. An examination of the process that produced these schools makes clear that the two buildings contained two different—and not simply separate—educational systems.

The Vicksburg school board actually set out to build model school buildings for both whites and African-Americans. Vicksburg voters believed that architecture could advance pedagogy, and they saw the new school buildings as community investments. The local paper stated that modern buildings and equipment made the children of the community into "citizens of the future,"[5] and a member of the Board of Education championed the new schools as signs of progress.[6] When the schools were completed, the local press announced, "The Bowmar Avenue elementary school...has been acclaimed the finest of its kind in the south.... [T]he new Cherry Street School is one of the finest in the United States."[7] The construction press added that the schools expressed "the most progressive ideas in education."[8]

Despite the published rhetoric, standards in Vicksburg differed between whites and African-Americans. In a report for the Works Progress Administration, a Vicksburg writer expressed the white conception of the black role in the community.

> The dark thread of [the Negro's] existence in the city is interwoven with the buildings he has helped construct.... Colored help is still exclusively used in the city. Negroes keep our houses, cook our food...; they are one of the factors that made possible the luxurious and charming atmosphere of the antebellum South before it was destroyed to set them free.[9]

To whites the complex inter-dependency of the races extended to educational opportunities as well. State education agents published a parable in which whites played Robinson Crusoe to the blacks' Friday. Like Friday, African-Americans needed to be trained to abandon their natural instincts. They wrote that Friday had to be taught "to like goat's flesh better than human flesh," and thus before "colored people can be of much value in the progress and the development of the state, they must be given something of the culture of the white people."[10]

5 Editor, "The School Bond Issue," *The Vicksburg Evening Post,* September 25, 1938, 4.

6 "Ben Colmery is Junior Chamber Guest Speaker," *The Vicksburg Evening Post,* September 16, 1938, 4.

7 "Prospects Good At Vicksburg's Public Schools This Year," *The Vicksburg Evening Post,* August 29, 1940, special section, 7.

8 N.W. Overstreet, "Two Schools for Vicksburg," *Architectural Concrete* 10, no. 1 (1940): 18–20.

9 "Negroes," Box 423, [typescript,] Folder: Negro, Source Material for Mississippi History, Works Progress Administration, Record Group 60, Mississippi Department of Archives and History, Jackson, Mississippi.

10 P.H. Easom and J.A. Travis, "The Negro Schools of Mississippi," *The Mississippi Educational Advance* 31 (1940): 100.

The architecture of the schools bears out this paternalistic discourse. Bowmar Avenue's plan expresses a dedication to children's delight in discovery. The school stretches across an 8.5 acre site. On the exterior, the intersection of volumes and the large spans of glass foretell a dynamic assembly of classrooms and specialized rooms. The building's more public facilities—offices and an auditorium with a stepped floor and permanent seats—flank the entrance. The two arms of the plan lead to thirteen classrooms, a playroom, a cafeteria, and restrooms on the first floor, with an art room, library, study room, and teachers' room on the second floor. The classrooms for the kindergarten and first two grades face the morning sun and exit directly to the playgrounds. Cubbyholes, bulletin boards, and chalkboards line the interior of these and other rooms, and workspaces, with individual bathrooms, supplement half of the classrooms. With its attention to the orientation of the rooms, its balance between book learning and physical activity in the youngest grades, and its diverse curricular spaces, Bowmar Avenue demonstrates a connection to the progressive pedagogy of the day.

At Cherry Street, however, the dynamic promise of the ahistorical exterior is only skin deep. A compact building at the edge of a mere 1.4-acre site, Cherry Street was planned without regard to solar orientation; its front and rear façades are nearly identical and its side walls virtually blank. While the entrance to the school duplicates that of Bowmar Avenue with the auditorium and offices adjacent, the first floor includes the sole toilet facilities and a classroom-size room that serves as the cafeteria. A double-loaded corridor leads to six classrooms on each of the three floors. These rooms are repetitive bare rectangles without built-in storage, workrooms, toilets, or exits to the playground. As the auditorium doubles as the playroom, its floor is flat and its seats are temporary.

Even the representational systems employed by the architects separate the two buildings and suggest a hierarchy. For Bowmar Avenue, Overstreet and Town constructed an axonometric as the presentation drawing, highlighting the school's expansive plan and broad site. In contrast, for Cherry Street, Overstreet and Town offered a rendering of the front elevation, emphasizing (consciously or not) the building's two-dimensionality.[11]

11 I am indebted to Marthe
Rowen for her comments
on the renderings.

Although the differences between the two school buildings can be partly attrib-
uted to the money spent on them (Bowmar Avenue received twice the construction
funds as Cherry Street, while the black school served twice the number of students[12]),
in comparison with the overall financing of education in the south in the 1930s,
Vicksburg's treatment of African-American education was magnanimous. While the
average investment in school plants across the United States was $250 per enrolled
child, Mississippi's capital investment totaled only $69, and black school facilities con-
stituted less than $10 of this sum.[13] In the entire state, African-Americans had only 119
auditoriums, 46 lunchrooms, and 5 playrooms.[14] Thus, the cost of $127 per enrolled
child at Cherry Street nearly doubled the state average, while Bowmar Avenue's cost of
$566 per enrolled child more than doubled the national average.

In light of the above facts, the willingness of Vicksburg whites to construct a substantial school building for their non-voting, African-American population might
appear to offset the financial inequality. Still, variations in the design and planning
solutions of the two schools confirm that architecture was complicit with a racist system that extended beyond separation. Although Vicksburg whites valued the education of African-Americans, they defined it differently from the education of their own
children. Within the architectural context of the 1930s, the white school's classroom
layouts and special facilities reinforce an educational program based upon the individuality of the student. Whites were educated to be leaders. The black school layout, on
the other hand, represents a mass education in specified subjects. While the exterior of
Cherry Street School, abstracted from its setting, may have provided whites with a visible display of Vicksburg's civic superiority to the rest of the state, the interior affords
African-Americans only a lockstep method of education. Blacks—as imagined by
whites—were educated for service.[15]

Vicksburg, the third largest city in Mississippi, fancied itself "a modern town,"
"progressing and living in the future." As in the rest of the state, white Vicksburg residents in the late 1930s identified African-Americans as crucial assets in a much-needed
statewide modernization, providing the labor force that would build a strong state.[16]
Cherry Street provides a mirror for this civic modernization.

12 Application, August 2, 1938, and Board of Education to the Mayor and Board of Aldermen, August 2, 1938, in Adjourned Meeting, August 5, 1938, Vicksburg Board of Aldermen.

13 Doxey A. Wilkerson, *Special Problems of Negro Education*, The Advisory Committee on

Education, Staff Study, no. 12 (Washington, D.C.: Government Printing Office, 1939): 30–31; W.G. Eckles, *A Survey of the Plant Facilities of the Public Schools of Mississippi* 13 (Jackson, Mississippi: The State Department of Education in cooperation with the Civil Works Administration, 1934): 23.

14 Eckles, *A Survey of the Plant Facilities*, passim.

15 Despite multiple attempts, I have been unable to locate written documents that include the testimony of African-Americans on Cherry Street School; neither have I been able to locate residents of Vicksburg from that time period who have strong recollections of the con-struction of Cherry Street.

As a case study, the comparison between the Bowmar Avenue and Cherry Street schools reinforces a familiar history wherein a segregated program of accommodation existed within unequal support systems, including disparities in teacher salaries, teacher-student ratios, per capita expenditures, and, not least, building facilities.[17] These architectural and other material histories also advance an understanding of social history in that the obvious differences in form provide a route for disclosing the covert differences in educational ideology that are at the core of the school system in Vicksburg and—by extension—elsewhere in the American South.

The schools which were party to *Brown* include, in Kansas, Sumner Elementary School (the white school to which Oliver Brown sought entry for his daughter, Linda) and Monroe Elementary School (the African-American school Linda attended) in Topeka; in Delaware, Claymont's "whites only" high school, Wilmington's "colored" Howard High School and Carver Vocational Annex, and schools for each group in Hockessin; in South Carolina, Clarendon County's white Summerton School and Scott's Branch School for blacks; in Virginia, Farmville's High School for "whites only," and the Robert Russa Moton High School for black students; in Washington, D.C., the "whites only" John Philip Sousa Junior High School and "colored" Shaw Junior High School; among others in these school districts. As in Vicksburg, these schools, which the plaintiffs or their children attended, sought entry to, or cited as comparisons, were products of a segregated system of public facilities. To varying degrees, these buildings internalize disparities in education between the races.

In some cases, differences were so manifest that the NAACP was hard-pressed to expand the case beyond mere equalization of facilities. Sited in the rural Deep South, the South Carolina case included what were perhaps the worst physical conditions. A 1951 report by the NAACP describing the school facilities in District No. 22 in Clarendon County noted that the value of the physical plants for whites was four times that for African-Americans, despite an African-American enrollment three times greater than the white enrollment. Masonry construction was used for the white schools while all of the African-American schools were wooden. The two white schools had running water, electricity, indoor flush toilets, bus transportation, lunch-

16 Editor, "Train the Negroes," *The Jackson Daily News* (October 19, 1937), reprinted in: *Mississippi Educational Journal* 14 (1937): 31–32; George Johnson, Jr., "Vicksburg," Box 425, Folder: Source Material for Mississippi History, WPA, Mississippi Department of Archives and History.

17 Between 1938 and 1939, Vicksburg spent three times as much on white public instruction as on African-American, despite an African-American enrollment thirty percent greater than the white enrollment. Similarly, African-American salaries were under white salaries by about forty percent. In addition, while the white

schools, with their enrollment of approximately 1,200, had fifty-one teachers in 1938, the black schools, with an enrollment of about 1,600, had only thirty-three teachers and one substitute. ["Expenditures for the 1938–1939 Session as Taken from Budgets for that Session," Biennial Report and Recommendations of the State

Superintendent of Public Education to the Legislature of Mississippi for the Scholastic Years 1937–1938 and 1938–1939 (Mississippi: Department of Education, (1939): 107; Meeting, May 14, 1938, Vicksburg Board of Aldermen].

room attendants, janitorial service, adequate desks, specialized classes and classrooms, and a student-to-teacher ratio below twenty-eight to one. By contrast, one of the three African-American schools had lacked water, another had no electricity, and one even lacked desks. Only outhouses were available at all of these schools, and none offered transportation, lunchroom attendants, janitors, or classrooms for group instruction (an auditorium or gymnasium) and the arts. Specialized classes taught at the high school included only vocational opportunities, and the student-teacher ratio ran as high as forty-seven to one.[18]

left: **Thomas W. Williamson, Summer Elementary School, Topeka, Kansas, 1926. From the Kansas City Historical Society.**

below: **Thomas W. Williamson, Monroe Elementary School, Topeka, Kansas, 1936. From the Kansas City Historical Society.**

18 Matthew Whitehead to Robert L. Carter, May 16, 1951, located in the NAACP Legal Defense Fund files on *Briggs v. Elliott,* as cited in: Richard Kluger, *Simple Justice: The History of Brown v. Board of Education and Black America's Struggle for Equality* (New York: Vintage Books, 1975), 332. Kluger provides additional information on the condition of the schools in Clarendon County on page 8; in New Castle County, Delaware, on pages 433–35 and 447; in Prince Edward County, Virginia, on page 489; and in the District of Columbia, on page 521.

19 Like all public schools built in Topeka from 1912 through the 1950s, Sumner and Monroe were designed by architect Thomas W. Williamson. During the initial trial in Kansas, expert witnesses testified to Sumner's superiority, based upon a comparison of neighborhood, sites, and age. However, in 1958, the Bureau of Educational Research at the University of Denver gave Monroe a slightly higher rating (498/1000) than Sumner (459/1000), upon consideration of structural defects at Sumner. [Kluger, *Simple Justice*: 414–15]

In Topeka, which offered the judiciary advantage of extending the case to the moderate Midwest, the differences between the schools were more nuanced and are partly attributable to the difference in their ages (Sumner was built in 1936, ten years after Monroe), neighborhoods (Sumner's is more residential and its site allows greater space for play); and circumstances of commission (Sumner had the advantage of being built under federal funding during the Depression).[19] In retrospect, the differences in neighborhood, acreage, and decorative detail seem less an accident of chronology than a manifestation of latent racial attitudes.[20] A report sponsored by the National Park Service comparing Monroe to a school for whites built in the same year, Clay Grade School, bolsters this conjecture.[21]

Recently, the federal government and local groups in Kansas, South Carolina, and Virginia have pushed for recognition of *Brown*-era school buildings as symbols of the case. The Summerton School in South Carolina has been listed on the National Register of Historic Places, and Sumner Elementary and Monroe Elementary in Kansas, and Moton High School in Virginia, have been named National Historic Landmarks. The National Park Service is creating the *Brown v. Board of Education* National Historic Site in the Monroe School and has initiated a theme study on segregated schools.[22] The preservation of these landmarks to *Brown* not only acknowledges the case as a critical agent in the struggle for civil rights but also provides important visibility for ordinary African-American experiences, and counters the more typical erasure of the physical marks of discrimination. These school buildings join multiple and sometimes conflicting narratives of race, including the inequality of separation; the nurturing power of African-American educational systems, built by legions of parents, teachers, and women's groups despite segregation; the potency of African-American activism; and a multi-racial faith in the founding ideals of the United States Constitution.

While public history has not devoted much space to ordinary moments in the lives of African-Americans, increasing recognition of diverse experiences, as seen in the actions detailed above, is providing a remedy. In their extension of this narrative into the public realm, the *Brown*-era school buildings stand in for much of the surviving school stock in the South that predates the Supreme Court's decision or its imple-

20 Interested African-Americans in Topeka take issue with a characterization of their education as inferior to that of whites, citing teacher education, salary, and dedication. [Cheryl Brown Henderson of the Brown Foundation for Educational Equity, Excellence, and Research, telephone interview with author, March 17, 1999.]

21 Quinn Evans, Draft of "Historic Structure Report: Monroe Elementary School (HS-01)" (Washington, D.C.: Department of Interior, National Park Service, 1998).

22 Pending funding, a museum will open in Monroe Hill School in 2001. Sumner Elementary was not included as part of the National Historic Site as it was, at the time of designation, still serving Topeka as a public school. (Sumner closed in 1996 and currently acts as a warehouse for the City's library system.) The National Park Service commenced its theme study on school segregation in the summer of 1999.

mentation. Even without formal presentation to the public as preserved sites of public memory, these "vernacular" buildings, like Vicksburg's Cherry Street School, which now holds a community outreach center for the Good Shepherd Community Church,[23] whisper stories to their former students and present-day caretakers.

Still, the markers of Jim Crow have begun to fade under the natural effects of age and the more invidious results of inferior construction, materials, and amenities, and delayed maintenance, general distaste, and ignorance. Many formerly black schools have been closed or stripped from the landscape. When Vicksburg integrated its schools twelve years after the Brown decision, factors including declining enrollment due to "white flight" led to the consolidation of school buildings and the closure of all five of the city's formerly black schools.[24] In Topeka, none of the four formerly black schools still serve as educational facilities.[25]

Yet, only two of the four *Brown* schools for which recognition has been sought are formerly white-only schools: Sumner Elementary School in Kansas, the school to which Linda Brown sought entry, and the Summerton School in South Carolina. Sumner was the first structure recognized (in 1987) and is the only one whose recognition was initiated by a federal agency.[26] In South Carolina, Summerton may be the sole surviving architecture of the state's case. Appreciation for the other schools, the all-black schools attended by *Brown's* plaintiffs, came from African-Americans who, forty years earlier, had been key participants in the litigation. For reasons personal, political, and practical, these parties chose to salute the schools they had attended, rather than the schools to which they sought entry[27] Intriguingly, the National Historic Site dedicated to the story of *Brown* resides in Monroe Elementary, a school in which Topeka's African-American community retains great pride for the education members received despite the system of segregation that forced its existence.

These choices raise questions about agency and identity in the early 1950s and today: What histories do the various "black" and "white" buildings contain and who interprets these stories? How does the preservation of a building whose existence was predicated by exclusion make a place for a diverse community? How do buildings gain positive meaning for those who had no voice in their existence but who had primary experiences therein? Can lack of place, or absence, be marked? These questions are

23 In the 1980s, after being decommissioned by the Vicksburg Board of Education, the Cherry Street School was taken over by the Good Shepherd Community Church, a mostly African-American congregation, as a community outreach center. In 1988, then President George Bush named the community center point

#299 of his "1,000 Points of Light."

24 Judgments on the question of relief regarding *Brown* were handed down on May 31, 1955. However, the opinion set no deadline for implementation, demanding only that separate school systems be dismantled "with all deliberate speed."

Many southern school districts did not integrate until the mid-to-late 1960s.

25 In Topeka, Kansas in the 1950s, there were four elementary schools for African-Americans. One has been torn down (Washington Elementary), and the remaining three are no longer used by the Board of

Education (Monroe Elementary, Buchanan Elementary, and McKinley Elementary). As elsewhere, African-American schools were decommissioned earlier than comparable white examples. Monroe Elementary was closed due to declining enrollment in 1975 while Sumner Elementary continued to welcome the children of its neighborhood for another 20 years.

central to the acknowledgment of multiple cultures and moments of conflict, and are shared with other such efforts (including, in the United States, the experience of Native Americans and immigrants).

In addition to identifying agency, or instrumentality, as a key element in marking the ordinary presence of African-Americans in the public landscape, current efforts to recognize the schools of *Brown* highlight several truisms for architectural history and preservation. First, these buildings remind us that architecture is a mnemonic device. It is the evidence by which many of the stories of history are recounted to a community and its visitors. Still, the buildings' historical importance has less to do with their architectural forms than with the manner in which they were seen, used, and appropriated. In their continued existence and with their potential to welcome visitors, the schools extend a single moment in time to include its antecedents and successors. Without preservation, Sumner Elementary would be reduced to its threshold. It would exist as a picture etched in a cultural consciousness of Linda Brown standing on the outside, along with the press photographs of Arkansas' Little Rock Nine being escorted into Central High School by the National Guard and George Wallace barring the schoolhouse door at the University of Alabama. With preservation, Sumner Elementary provides an opportunity for a public airing of concerns.

Second, in posing these queries, Linda Brown's placelessness may provide a strategy for meaning. American educational history is riddled with absences whose exposure might open doors to opportunity. As they illustrate the racial system into which they were born, the buildings may prompt visitors to ask: Do the *Brown* schools herald union or memorialize the gap between segregation and integration? Historic sites might raise awareness of, but do not, in and of themselves, provide answers to such issues.

Finally, though these schools may contain multiple meanings, uncovering these tales is dependent upon the visitor's vantage point, a perspective partially qualified by race, age, and locality. Do the schools mark the power of individual bravery and collective action or the tyranny of the majority? Do they uphold a strong African-American culture or normalize the white experience? By allowing many to step over the thresholds that both contained and dismissed Linda Brown and other African-Americans, preservation of the *Brown* schools, black and white, acknowledges and

26 A survey initiated by the federal government of historic sites related to the Constitution singled out Sumner for its national importance. [Harry A. Butowsky, *The U.S. Constitution: A National Historic Landmark Theme Study* (Washington, D.C.: Department of Interior, National Park Service, 1986).

27 "New NPS Unit Commemorates Civil Rights: Brown v. Board of Education National Historic Site," CRM 16, no. 5 (1993): 1; "Unfinished Business," *Historic Preservation* 46 (1994): 56–61; Cheryl Brown Henderson, "The Brown Foundation Story: Developing Resources to Interpret Public History,"

CRM 19, no. 2 (1996): 7–9; "Farmville: A Burden of History," Historic Preservation 48 (January/February 1996): 62–67.

gives honor to their journey. Theoretical constructions aside, the schools—along with a growing number of institutional buildings that sheltered important events of the civil rights era[28]—begin to mark the presence of race in the American built landscape and to give voice to memories. And in so doing, they contribute to a more complete history, not only for the public but for architects and historians alike.

In February 1999, the National Park Service developed an itinerary of civil rights-era properties that are listed on the National Register of Historic Places. These include twenty-five houses, home sites, residential districts, and churches, and the following public, institutional, or commercial facilities:

Alabama

Selma-to-Montgomery Historic Trail; City of St. Jude (Hospital), Montgomery; U.S. Post Office and Courthouse, Montgomery; West Park (Kelly Ingram Park), Birmingham.

Arkansas

Little Rock Central High School, Little Rock (designated a National Historic Site in November 1998).

Georgia

Atlanta Center University (including Morehouse College, Spelman College, and Atlanta University), Atlanta; Dorchester Academy Boys Dormitory, Midway.

Kansas

Monroe Elementary School, Topeka.

Kentucky

Lincoln Hall, Berea College, Berea.

Mississippi

Tougaloo College, Tougaloo.

Nevada

Moulin Rouge Hotel, Las Vegas.

North Carolina

F. W. Woolworth Building, Greensboro.

South Carolina

All-Star Bowling Lane, Orangeburg; South Carolina College, Orangeburg.

Tennessee

Lorraine Hotel, Memphis.

Virginia

Robert Russa Moton High School, Farmville.

Washington, D.C.

Lincoln Memorial.

28 At the time that Monroe School came under consideration for designation as a National Historic Landmark, the National Park Service hosted three civil rights-related sites (1991): Frederick Douglass National Historic Site, Washington, D.C.; Martin Luther King, Jr. National Historic Site, Atlanta, Georgia; Mary McLeod Bethune Council House National Historic Site, Washington, D.C.

seven

accommodation, resistance, and appropriation in african-american building

The African-American cultural experience can be linked to the development and dynamics of the African-American physical environment and institutions. In observing such relationships with the built environment it is possible to define an understanding and interpretation of community empowerment, neighborhood pride, and social identity within the African-American Diaspora. In the design dynamics of historically black institutions and neighbors a special sense of belonging, control, and ownership is developed by integrating strategies of accommodation, resistance, and appropriation. The role of these strategies in the design and transformation of African-American institutions informs the connection between design input, form, community empowerment, and identity. While accommodation suggests complicity of the dominant aesthetic, it also becomes a negotiated adaptation or a strategy for acceptance through building or environmental design. Accommodation combined with the strategies of appropriation and resistance provides the basis for an adjusted environment and increased cultural identity.

Environmental appropriation as resistance is the reclaiming or redesigning of an existing building or landscape to present a new identity through cultural expression. Appropriation claims and redefines a built environment, ultimately instilling in it a new sense of place and memory, defying its former past by adopting new cultural and social aspects. This resistance strategy is an assertive act opposing the authority of established design standards through the execution of adjusted or alternative environmental design concepts. Environmental appropriation and resistance are integral to the empowerment of communities to promote a cultural identity.

African-American builders, architects, and designers since the era of southern enslavement have carefully practiced the balancing act of accommodation, resistance, and appropriation in design and building. Slave artisans and builders were instrumental in the creation of the southern build environment. The role of slaves as the architects, artisans and builders of the plantations that they served is now being acknowledged by historians and scholars. These same enslaved builders were also often the agents for the resistance and the destruction of the buildings of the southern plantocracy. Several historians of slavery have studied the complex relationship between domination and subordination, accommodation and resistance, as they relate to the demands of slavery. Historian Eugene Genovese asserts that accommodation itself breathed a critical spirit and disguised subversive actions and often embraced and produced its apparent opposite—resistance.[1]

Enslaved artisans and builders were often organizers of the resistance and arbiters of change. Resistance came in many forms, ranging from subtle African details and dimensions applied to building to planned construction flaws and the outright systematic burning of the very plantation buildings that slaves had designed and built. The most significant rebellions were often led by "invisible," literate, skilled slave artisans who had contributed to the creation of the South under slavery, yet their most visible role was as the architects of major slave insurgencies to tear down buildings and institutions, thereby disrupting the economy. Gabriel Prosser, Denmark Vesey, Nat Turner, and Sheridan Leary used blatant and powerful acts of resistance through destruction in order to make changes in slavery society.[2] There was indeed accommodation—the South was built after all—but when the same buildings were occasionally destroyed at the hands of the "complicit" laborers, there is a different story to tell. Resistance was played out daily on the plantation to varying degrees but this physical destruction powerfully illustrates the simultaneous accommodation and resistance in the building process and, more importantly, within the institution of slavery itself.

These environmental and cultural strategies continued to inform the design process after the end of slavery, most notably in black churches and educational institutions. These institutions offered opportunities for the African-American architect and in turn nurtured the architect's economic, spiritual, and intellectual development, and political thought and action by enlisting them in black owned or administered projects. African-American schools, such as Hampton Normal and Agricultural Institute (founded in 1868 and now known as Hampton University) in Virginia, were the birthplaces of a new professional African-American class. This generation of students was trained for assimilation but was also eager to lead and liberate the developing African-American citizenship. Hampton Institute also opened its doors to African-

1 E. Genovese, Jordan Roll: The World the Slave Made (New York: Pantheon Books, 1974) 587–99.

2 H. Ploske and W. Marr, The Negro Almanac: The African-American (Bellwether Publishing, 1976) 608.

and Native American men and women students. Between 1878 and 1923, thousands of American Indians representing over sixty tribal groups were enrolled at Hampton and participated in programs that inspired the federal government's late nineteenth-century boarding school system.[3] During this period the colleges were sites of highly articulated and prolific debates in the African-American intellectual community about the direction, leadership, and advancement of the African-American community, and, in the unique case of Hampton, Native American advancement as well. These debates were often framed by strategies of accommodation, gradualism, or conciliation versus that of resistance, opposition, or change for African- and Native Americans as a defense against and reaction to a racist society. At the same time, similar discussions abounded among the white founders and leaders of the African-American institutions about the proper educational, political, and societal roles of these institutions for the newly freed African-American population. These discussions were supported by ideas of assimilation, acceptance, paternalism, productivity, exploitation, and ethical and proper behavior of the African-American students.

General Samuel Chapman Armstrong, the son of white missionaries and himself a former army chaplain, founded the Hampton Institute as a pragmatic and accommodationist educational institute for African-Americans and Native Americans. Armstrong envisioned a place for the "education of the hand with the education of the mind," a useful and practical educational philosophy, also known as the great Negro experiment.[4] He strongly believed in and promoted the significance of a "manual labor" education system and wrote, "We believe that when a manual-labor system is attempted, it should be carefully adjusted to the demands of scientific and practical education and that the training of the hand was at the same time a training of the mind and will."[5] The succeeding leaders of Hampton Institute continued Armstrong's manual experiential learning concept as a way of training and acculturation of early Hampton Institution students. As highlighted by Dr. Hollis B. Frissell, vice principal:

3 "Enduring Legacy: Native Peoples, Native Arts at Hampton" (Hampton University Museum, 1999).

4 M.F. Armstrong and Helen W. Ludlow, *Hampton and Its Students* (New York: AMS Press, 1971), 39.

5 Francis Greenwood Peabody, *Education for Life: The Story of Hampton University* (Doubleday, Page & Company, 1918), 244.

The need for Hampton work seems to increase every year, and we are endeavoring to extend the school's influence by developing and carrying out General Armstrong's plan of giving these people a practical, industrial education which shall fit them to go out into the south and the west and help their people.... This school founded by General Armstrong soon after the close of the war, has always upheld industrial education as the surest means of fitting these people for useful citizenship.[6]

The physical developments of Hampton Institute and other HBCUs reflect these institutions' seemingly contradictory commitments to producing leaders and liberators while also educating assimilationist and accepted workers. The original Hampton Institute and today's campus design and its buildings can be interpreted here with attention to the principles of accommodation, resistance, and appropriation. The mere existence of educational institutions for African- and Native Americans in the 1870s was a radical and liberating step, yet they also perpetuated a type of African-American subordination with a focus on appeasement, control, and the development of educated labor. The American Missionary Association and the Freedman's Bureau, formed in the post Civil War years, helped create institutions like Hampton by appropriating farmland and plantations.[7] The prevailing concept of segregating Hampton Institute encouraged the idea of physical appropriation, accommodation, and resistance.

Sited on the former Little Scotland Plantation, Hampton Institute was separated from the town by the Hampton River, which endowed the school with a sense of physical autonomy from the town. Armstrong combined the dual mission of "uplifting the Negro" and "civilizing the savage" by educating the "head, hands, and heart," the educational trinity that was the goal of Hampton Institute and the other HBCUs. Architecturally, Armstrong strove to design the campus buildings in the traditional, dominant institutional style and to maintain the aesthetic standards of the contemporary white campuses. He used architecture as a means of bringing acceptance, conformance, and acculturation to Hampton in the service of the mission of uplifting and civilizing.[8]

6 Keith L.Schall, *Stony the Road: Chapters in the History of Hampton University*, (?) 57, 53.

7 Armstrong, 15–23.

8 "The Legacy Continues: A Photo Essay in Celebration of 125 Years of Hampton University History," (Hampton University Museum, 1992) 2.

Armstrong used leading New York and Boston architects like Richard Morris Hunt and James C. Cady, William Ware, and the firm of Peabody and Ludlow to design the buildings of Hampton Institute within the architectural status quo, and these architects used the Institute commissions as a distant site for their architecturally stylistic experiments. These prominent architects found the opportunity to practice, advance, and experiment with their architectural creative movements out of the critical spotlight of architecturally aware New York City and Boston. Along with these noted New York architects and their tendency to experiment, the students and faculty of the Institute's trade school, the early predecessor of the architecture program, also greatly participated in the design and construction of the Hampton campus and buildings. Students in the trade schools, as at other HBCUs, were required to participate in the design and construction of buildings, furniture, and landscape elements of the campus as part of their curriculum and studies or as the realization of Armstrong's philosophy of education and manual experience.[9] While professional architects were formally commissioned to design and experiment on the impressive Virginia Hall, Memorial Church, Ogden Hall, Huntington Library, and several other early buildings, the trade students and faculty actually detailed and constructed these and many other buildings on campus. This collaboration between the architects, the students, and the faculty as designer/builders produced a special type of design team. The combination of the prominent white New York architects working on the obscure and isolated Hampton site and the participation of the African-American students and faculty worked to create the physical environment of Hampton Institute. The physical campus became the product of the cultural interpretations and creative identity or the resistive expressions of the Hampton students and faculty joined to the experimental advances and design statements of the established white architects.

Throughout the campus carefully placed cultural markers can be found in the structural and ornamental details of the student- and faculty-built halls, alongside the more overt planning and designs of later African-American architects. From the playful repeating rhythms of Kelsey Hall's brickwork to the geometrically patterned brick panels of Armstrong Hall and the modernist buildings Harkness and Davidson Hall

9 Armstrong, 41.

by the early African-American registered architects William Moses and Hilyard Robinson, these buildings collectively communicate a story of accommodation, resistance, and appropriation.

The overall design of the Memorial Church, for example, conforms to the dictated Romanesque Revival style of contemporary church design. The plan and style were intended to symbolize the permanence of Hampton and to promote decency, moral uplift, and respect for authority. Completed in 1866, Memorial Church was the original focal point of the campus and remains a landmark and architectural icon of Hampton University. James Cleveland Cady, of New York City, was selected as the architect by Elbert Monroe, the president of the Hampton board and Cady's friend and admirer. Cady's large practice was devoted to institutional and religious architecture. He had designed the Metropolitan Opera House, the United Presbyterian Church of the Covenant, the New York Avenue Methodist Episcopal Church, and several other large New York churches and institutional buildings around the period of the planning and design of the Hampton church.[10] Cady favored masonry for construction and decorative materials and was greatly influenced by the Romanesque architecture styles. It is important to note that Cady's design allegiance was to Monroe, his patron and board chief, not to Armstrong, the founding principal, and that Monroe was not present during the construction of the church.[11] These factors allowed Cady freedom to address the cultural details of the church without the aesthetic scrutiny of the Hampton Board of Trustees.

While the general plan, design, exterior masonry work, and details of the church were inspired by the Boston architect H.H. Richardson and his Trinity Church, the interior details suggest an adjusted and more culturally specific aesthetic. Identity and pride are expressed in the corbel blocks of the arcade under the cornices at twenty feet and forty feet above the floor, revealing alternating reliefs of African-American and Native American busts—spaces traditionally reserved for classical gods or Anglo faces. The interiors are furnished with student-designed-and-built yellow pine pews and other handmade furnishings. Cady was much more concerned with the general space, volume, and plan of the church than with the elaborate surface details and decorations, enabling others involved with the building to design and construct of many of the details and espressions.[12] Memorial church represented the formal ideal of pat-

10 Norval White, and Elliot Willensky, editors, *American Institute of Architects Guide to New York City*, (Macmillan, 1968).

11 Thelma B. Brown, Memorial Chapel, "The Culmination of the Development of the Campus of Hampton Institute, Hampton, Virginia 1867-1887," (Master's Thesis, University of Virginia, n.d.) 109.

from left: **Exterior detail of Kelsey Hall women's dormitory; Front view of Memorial Church showing the Richardsonian architectural style.; Interior details of Memorial Church showing African and Native American busts.**

terns, space, and styles envisioned by Cady, Monroe, and Armstrong while participating in and allowing a display of resistance details that worked quietly within a conformist shell but spoke loudly to those who looked up once inside.

Seventy years later, Harkness and Davidson Halls, womens' and mens' dormitories, built at Hampton Institute in 1954 and 1956, respectively, present us with similar cultural design revelations as with the Memorial Church. These two buildings are the embodiment of the European international movement or the modernist style developed and imported by European modernist architects at the beginning of the twentieth century. Harkness and Davidson Halls were designed by Hilyard Robinson of Washington D.C., one of the early African-American architects working in the Bauhaus style. Robinson and his modern buildings represent the beginning of Hampton Institute's continuing tradition of commissioning established African-American registered architects and architecture firms for many of its major new buildings. Robinson's two dormitories are noted for their well-designed connection to the exterior spaces and their concern about technology, scale, and modernist aesthetics.

The international modernist style is about the rejection of cultural and site specific references in favor of a universal aesthetic language and function for the architecture. Robinson believed in and utilized the modernist theories because of their universal values and, as an African-American architect, he could assimilate his own architectural language and connect to a shared American identity.[13] While the overall

12 Thelma B. Brown, 117.

13 Bond, Max, Jr., "Still Here", Harvard Design Magazine, summer 1997, 52.

plan and exterior design accommodates the prevailing aesthetics, when we look closely at the interior detail that we find, again, culturally expressive design details. The interior lobby ledges are topped with ceramic African-American cultural figures as a repeating detail in the rhythm of the modernist style. Robinson's design clearly has a commitment to and accommodates the prevailing modernist style while celebrating the special African-American context and aesthetics in the details of the building's design.

The debates over the African-American social and aesthetic direction through appropriation and accommodation continue today, reflected in the education and politics of race, space, and the built environment. Cincinnati's Revelation Baptist Church is a dramatic example of a type of empowerment through environmental appropriation. Revelation Baptist Church is located in the African-American West End neighborhood. The West End, once a largely Jewish neighborhood, experienced the typical American urban tradition of ethnic movement and migration in the 1960s and 1970s when segregation was lifted and "white flight" began to concentrate African-Americans in the inner cities. Revelation Baptist Church was originally the Wise Temple, a synagogue which closed its doors in the early 1970s. Shortly afterwards, the African-American Baptist movement took over the space. Upon this transition the structure underwent a major renovation by the architect Jack Roy Gore, with emphasis on reorienting the main axis, entry, and seating of the original temple. The temple's original axis was oriented towards the east as is common in some Jewish traditions. The African-American Baptist church has no similar tradition with regard to siting or axis, thus the congregation and axis could face any direction. This new design reclaimed the space for a Baptist congregation. The church symbolically and physically became an integral part of the African-American community. It was no longer the "Baptist Church in the temple." Through appropriation the church has built its own identity, closely connecting with the neighborhood, and African-American Baptist theology and style.

Like the plantations built and destroyed by slaves, the early HBCUs, the recycled African-American churches, and other modern examples of African-American cultural institutions and buildings, contemporary design practices have coalesced around the negotiated process of design resistance and appropriation. The Martin Luther King Center for Non-Violent Social Change and the Audubon Ballroom project, along with several other contemporary designs from J. Max Bond Jr., now a partner at Davis Brody

Bond in New York City, continue to build upon these concepts. These important buildings were conceived to appropriate the cultural and historic site and experience. The King Center, located in the heart of one of Atlanta's National Historic Site and Preservation Districts, is a comprehensive environmental memorial, tied to the African-American historic district as an urban institution. It contains the library and archives for the world's largest collection of primary source material on the Civil Rights Movement. It is also the burial site of Dr. Martin Luther King Jr. The King Center opens up to Auburn Avenue, a major avenue through the African-American neighborhood, to allow a view of the white marble crypt of the Reverend King for all to see and experience. There are no architectural barriers to seeing or approaching the crypt from the street. This arrangement becomes a symbolic urban gesture of openness, particularly appropriate and consistent with King's memorial.

Interior view of Revelation Baptist Church with realigned axis.; *right:* Exterior courtyard of the King Center for Nonviolent Social Change by J. Max Bond, Jr.

The architecture of the center reflects the non-violent nature of Dr. King's work and the continuing civil and human rights movements. The formal organization of the spaces, the elegant proportions of the building, the introduction of a reflecting pool into the complex and carefully chosen materials each possess a spiritual, cultural, and in some cases economic relationship to the ... goals of the Center.[14]

Architects William Stanley and Roland Wiley, African-American architects, each with established practices in Atlanta and Los Angeles, respectively, are just two examples of several designers working with the negotiated realms of accommodation and resistance. Their work dislocates the African-American architect from the larger cultural group as a means of resistance. In my own experience, designing the Casa Umoja and Fair Oaks Senior Center, in the San Francisco Bay Area, I worked to appropriate cultural aesthetics and to offer a resistive design direction by incorporating geometry and materials that recall the elements of the African-American and Latino neighborhood of the Center. By striving to make this design process a standard and by incorporating specific, cultural aesthetic expressions, we can begin to operate in the context of the African-American experience and influence American art and architecture in practice. Critical architects of color can align with this design philosophy to extend the forms of resistance even as they accommodate, often unavoidably so, the mainstream design order.

The cultural strength of African-American institutions, sites, and communities lies, in part, with the designers' and builders' ability to negotiate the terrain of accommodation, resistance, and appropriation. The ability to conceive and understand African-American sites of memory would be incomplete without an examination of the appropriated space and their means of mediating a resistance while accepting the dominant order. Appropriation, accommodation, and resistance then become integral parts of the empowering process and enable positive, forward-thinking community design while providing cultural and community identity. It is both the making of these resistive buildings and the recognition of the resistance that empowers individuals and communities.

14 Davis, Brody Associates, "FAIA Application to the AIA," (New York: Davis Brody and Associates Architects, 1994)

Front sketch of Casa Umoja, by the author

eight   body.memory.map

A NARRATIVE IN 12 SEGMENTS

I. JUNE, 1994

(the courtyard, Wates House, University College London, c. mid-afternoon)

Diploma (post-graduate) in architecture projects. Bound and gagged. A very good student.

II. TUESDAY, JUNE 20, 2000

(at home in Chicago, 10:45 am)

A little "something" extra about process, about this piece, and particularly about the process of making it is required here.

A year ago, almost to the date, after organizing and convening a conference in Charlottesville, Virginia, Craig Barton asked us to reconstruct our papers for the purpose of making a book. He meant it quite literally, requiring us to fashion our "stuff" from the spoken to the written, from the context of a darkened, crowded specific site—Campbell Hall, Room 153, School of Architecture, University of Virginia, where the conference was held—to the bound and somewhat blank context of a book, sites unknown.

For those of us whose papers attempted to blur or question distinctions (between the written, spoken, and visual, in this case), the request posed an interesting, if not uncommon, challenge. As architects, we are familiar with the transformative and often surprising processes by which one's thoughts are realized: from idea to sketch to construction drawings and finally (and hopefully) to building. As writers or thinkers, however, the transformations are less clear. This difference has been on my mind lately. In the weeks and months following the conference, as I worked intermittently on the paper's transformation to "chapter," I realized two things: one, that the paper was both the process of making the paper and the paper itself, and two, that this would be really hard to

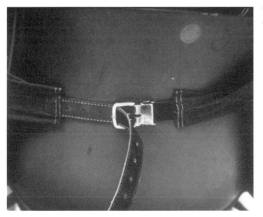

"Chair, Strap" by M Savini, Bartlett School of Architecture, London, 1994. Photo: J. Hill

describe. Being a sort of "lay" writer, as opposed to a writer writer, I'm fishing around for ideas. How best to describe or evoke the multiple sites, contexts, spaces, slippages, and processes that the paper contrived to construct?

Following Catherine Ingraham's eloquent description of "being interested in the equation between words and images, words and things, words and objects,"[1] I myself now understand how the "slippage" in language that occurs when moving among thinking (seeing), drawing (seeing), and building (also seeing) can confound. As the first transformation takes place (from thinking to drawing, let's say), one becomes aware that the gap between thought and thing, what happens in that moment where an idea (ephemeral) becomes an object (tangible) is, in its own right, an event, or at least a minor event alongside the Main Event (the Thought, the Drawing, the Building, etc.). In one's mind is the image, the idea … we take hold of the pen, pencil, camera, mouse, etc., and suddenly something else appears … a drawing—an object, a thing, of which one is not always in control. Likewise with drawing and building. (I have to assume, having built very little, that one is always surprised when the transformation from two-dimensional to three-dimensional is complete). This is a complex analysis. After all, to think about the process of thinking (or drawing, building, speaking or writing) at the same time as one is attempting to "do" it, is difficult. Beatriz Colomina says it brilliantly: "If you think about how you ride a bicycle, you may fall off."[2]

Like Ingraham, I belabor the point because the idea of the gap between objects or different states is powerful and, particularly in this instance, appropriate. As Jonathan Hill writes, "sometimes, when a place is empty, it is actually full of what we did not see. A gap is an opening, for a period of time, between other, seemingly more substantial conditions. A gap implies incompletion, and invites completion, involving the viewer or user in the formulation of a work."[3] To start with, then, I offer these thoughts which, it would seem, have little to do with the topic of the conference, "Sites of Memory: Landscapes of Race and Ideology." Bear with me on this.

1 Catherine Ingraham, "Losing It in Architecture," *The Architect: Reconstructing Her Practice*, ed. F. Hughes (Cambridge: MIT Press, 1997), 151.

2 Beatriz Colomina, "Battle Lines: E.1027," op cit., Hughes, 4.

3 Jonathan Hill, extract from PhD thesis, by kind permission of the author.

"Body, Strap" by M Savini,
Bartlett School of
Architecture, London, 1994
Photo: J. Hill

III. FRIDAY, MARCH 26, 1999 *(Cambell Hall, Room 153, 3:24 pm)*

Someone claps rather loudly and the rest of the audience follows. Happily, I've timed my slides correctly and the last image—that of a white former student bound in a leather straightjacket, a project of his own making and beautifully crafted—floods the room. It's been a long day, I'm the sixteenth speaker and I sense the audience's attention is waning. In some ways this is fortunate, for me. "Body.Memory.Map" is not a paper in the traditional sense, nor is it an "event." However, it draws on the conventions of paper and event as well as those of the conference and the lecture for support. It has a complex structure, drawn from the analysis of "slippage" and "gaps" offered above. It attempts to provoke, rather than instruct, the viewer. It is not a text describing architecture, a drawing representing architecture, or a representation of building. Like its subject matter, "race," it remains inconsistent and misappropriates at will. It consists of twelve segments, brought together in the manner of a verbal, visual, and aural montage. The juxtaposition of image, text, and speech is important as is the placement of "gaps." It follows no given logic. The segments do not align themselves, chronologically or spatially. They are presented as a series of events, complete with their own language, tense, and references. Yes, I'm interested in landscapes, as the title of the conference has directed us, but primarily those in the mind's eye.

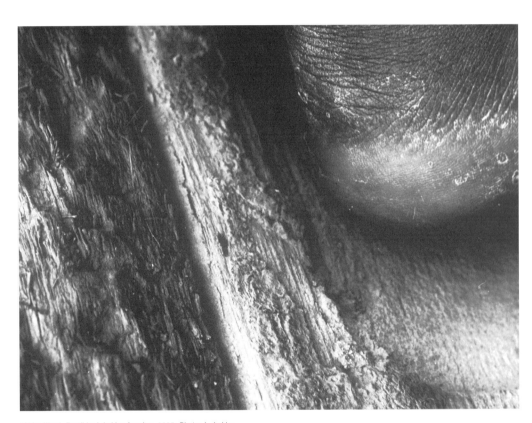

"Skin, Wood, Foot" by L Lokko, London, 1995. Photo: L. Lokko

IV. FRIDAY, JANUARY 29, 1999 *(at home in Chicago, 5:55 pm)*
A happy coincidence. My computer keeps track of important things like date and time, making at least the notion of montage fairly easy.

abstract

It is the thing that is most perceptible and least material. It is the archetype of the vital element. It is the first condition and the hallmark of art, as breath is of life: breath, which accelerates or slows, which becomes even or agitated according to the tension in the individual, the degree and nature of his emotion. This is rhythm ... it is composed of a theme—sculptural form—which is set in opposition to a sister theme, as inhalation is to exhalation, and that is repeated. It is not the kind of symmetry that gives rise to monotony. [4]

Imprisoned by four walls
(to the North, the crystal of non-knowledge
a landscape to be reinvented, to the South, reflective memory
to the East, the mirror, to the West, stone and the song of silence)
I wrote messages, but received no reply. [5]

Memory: the power or process of reproducing or recalling what has been learned and retained, especially through associative mechanisms; a capacity for showing effects as the result of past treatment or for returning to a former condition. The precise relationship between memory and architecture is difficult to define. The word itself suggests an intangibility, an immateriality, a certain presence in the mind's eye ... clearly a phenomenon that is more cerebral than physical. Architecture, although rooted in the cerebral, is traditionally made manifest in the material, physical world.

In "Body.Memory.Map," I propose to look at the question of "sites of memory" through the eyes of the one group in the United States for whom memory—both literally and conceptually—remains problematic: African-Americans. Within African-American culture, memory plays a crucial, fragmented and often contradictory role, not least because "[it] is also a struggle of memory against forgetting." [6] Severed from the mother culture(s) through slavery and colonialism, notions of "self," "home," and

4 Leopold, Senghor, "Ce que l'homme noir apporte," quoted in *Nordey*, source unknown.

5 Octavio Paz, "Envoi," quoted in Lefebvre, H., *The Production of Space*, Blackwell, (Oxford, 1991), 3.

6 Bell Hooks, "Choosing the Margin," *Yearning: Race, Gender and Cultural Politics*, (New York: Turnaround Press, 1991), 148.

"place" have become hotly contested terrain in which memory plays an increasingly complex role. Who remembers what? When? And how?

"Body.Memory.Map" is an exploration of the black body as repository of this history. Through a combination of photographs, texts, and photo-montages, the project offers a re-interpretation of both "site," "self," and "space" as these relate to the African-American experience. It uses the traditional and familiar tools of architectural investigation—scale, form, material, occupation, program, etc.—to suggest new and often unexpected relationships between race, space, and architecture.

V. THURSDAY, MARCH 18, 1999 *(driving south towards Tuskegee, Alabama)*
This is my first trip to the South. *The South*. I love the sound of the word, rolling it around in my mouth, repeating it again and again to myself as we drive. We are taking five African-American students on a visit to Tuskegee University in Alabama. We drive from Atlanta to Tuskegee via the Martin Luther King historic district, several identical sites of the 1996 Olympic Games and acres and acres of red clay soil along the side of the freeway that remind me of home. It is March and it is very, very hot. My partner is driving, and I am thinking about my paper, about coming to the South, about the term "landscape," and about African-Americans, and wondering what the students are thinking, if at all. They are all asleep.

"Look," I say to him, excited. "the soil. It's red, like in Ghana."

"Mmm." He says. I turn back to the landscape, pleased. I hadn't expected this link.

VI. FRIDAY, MARCH 19, 1999 *(Days Inn Motel, Montgomery, Alabama)*
Time to read the introduction again. There may be some changes.

Coming to the issue of the black American landscape as something of an outsider (firstly as an African, secondly—and perhaps more noticeably—as a European[7]), it occurs to me that my own interpretation of events, places, and this particular history is spatially marked in an interesting, albeit subconscious, way. In writing this paper, during the difficult process of thinking, drawing, editing, re-thinking, and re-drawing, I was acutely aware of the literal, metaphorical, and physical spaces I entered and exited as the project unfolded. Beginning at the beginning, with the body and exam-

---

7 Brought up in Ghana and later educated in the UK, I have retained a strong British accent.

"Wall, Thatch" by I Ward Kouao, Kusanaba, Ghana, 1997. Photo: I. Ward Kouao

ining its material presence at 10:1 and 1:1, passing through real and imagined land-scapes from Alabama to Accra and back again, moving back and forth in time and place, the idea of "position"—i.e., inside or outside, margin or center, here or there—and "direction"—coming or going, forward or backwards, circumnavigating the sub-ject or "going straight at it"—became much more than the organisational tool I initially imagined as an aide to reading the various pieces. It comes to me slowly that the condition of being "foreign" or "exterior" to the subject, or imagining oneself in the third dimension (as opposed to the third person) vis-à-vis the texts is important in a number of ways. From the opening quote, "History has its dimension of the unex-plorable, at the edge of which we wander, our eyes wide open," to the closing state-ment "A place on the map is also a place in history," it is clear to me that certain notions of space, scale, and movement were always already present. "Space" slips into the texts via a network of connected peoples and places, some real, some not. Similar, in other words, to the "map" that black Americans have constructed for themselves out of their fragmented history.

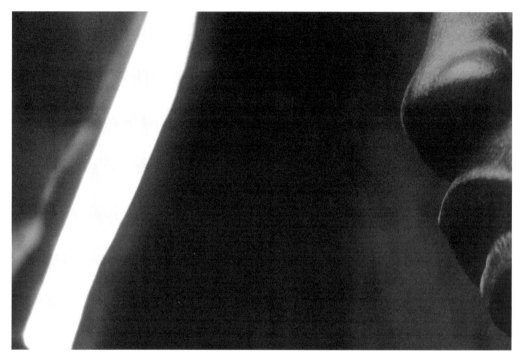

(above) **"Lips, Nose, Steel, Wall", by L Lokko, London, 1995.** Photo: L. Lokko; *(right)* **"Cloth, Memory, Face, Bleach" by Graduate Student, Ames, Iowa, 1997.** Photo: L. Lokko

VII. FRIDAY, MARCH 26, 1999 *(Campbell Hall, Room 153, 3:01 pm)*

ON BODIES

To be in the margin is to be part of the whole but outside the main body.[8]

In many traditional African cultures, there is one site into which many of the issues that are the focus of this conference—memory, history, language, home, self, and place—collapse: the body. Oral history, bodily art practices, tribal affiliations, architectures based on social—as opposed to formal—relations are all manifestations of a deep, spiritual, and aesthetic covenant with the body as the primary site of memory and expression. Appropriately too, within the history of African-Americans in the United States, it is the body that has been the primary site of experience and pain. Quite aside from the familiar descriptions of "bodies in space," the "active user" and discussions of architecture as the "envelope" of the body, I want to suggest that the fractured history of African-Americans, perhaps more so than other black Diasporic cultures, dramatically opens itself to the notion that memory, place (landscape), and space are awkwardly tied, like the three-legged runner, by the "black" body and all it has seen.

The very idea of the "body" in discourses of race—and here I refer to all discourses: African, African-American, Black British, Carribbean, etc.—is, of course, charged. From Sarah Baartjie—the Hottentot Venus—to Robert Mapplethorpe to Mike Tyson, images of the black body—whether naked, clothed, situated or siteless—have dominated the ways in which peoples of African descent are seen, are regulated (spatially and otherwise) and, crucially, are recognized. For blacks in the global Diaspora, a persistent sense of "out of place-ness" accompanies each and every move.

Out of Place. There is (has been) a project here. Whilst still in graduate school, my studio colleagues and I were set an unusual brief: "Occupied Territories." We were asked to "occupy the cultural condition of a fellow student, one from which you are routinely excluded." As the only black member of the studio, I asked for permission to occupy more than one territory. Permission granted. The project, entitled "These Are Your Cultural Weapons," looked at the surnames of twenty-one studio members. Out of the twenty-one students, seventeen were British, two German, one Italian, and one Indian. (Hill; Lumley; Webb; Humphreys; Nossitter; Harpur; Ram; etc.) Somewhere

8 | hooks, op.cit, 149.

in London, there exists a street (or two or three), named after each and every studio member, save one. I spent a day traversing London, photographing street signs. Twenty small black-and-white photographs bind each student irrevocably to London and to the English landscape. Only one is absent. But I don't suppose these facts are strange, or new. I would like to turn your attention away from the streetscape and back towards the body, yet bring them together in another way. I would like to "return," in a sense, to an older, more naïve sense of bodies and the ways they inhabit and create a landscape.

Crowd in Nairobi, Kenya. Photo: source unknown

VIII. 1968–1976 *(Ghana—Scotland)*

Growing up in Ghana, in West Africa, some of my earliest memories intertwine the body and landscape in ways that I have only recently begun to understand. We (my siblings and I) left Ghana each "summer", to spend the three months from June to September which constitute the rainy season in the tropics, with my mother's family in Dundee, Scotland. At first there was only the excitement of the trip, of crossing the dusty, cracked tarmac at night (always at night) to the waiting Douglas McDonnell DC-10 or later, more glamorously, a Boeing 747, and the strange, suspended sensation of leaving the muffled red heat of Accra in one breath and awakening to the damp green coolness of England in the next. But then, upon arrival in London, something else changed: the color of the human landscape around us: at home, in Africa, it was black. On "holiday," in Europe, it was white. This visual (and also tactile) difference, more than anything—more than the cold, the damp, the backdrop of Cockney English rather than any of the Ghanaian languages—signified our arrival. What I remember most vividly about leaving the airport in both directions, either arriving on holiday or going home, was the silent landscape of flesh everywhere—black skin at home, white skin abroad. And yet there were other differences, more spatial ones. The specifically African acceptance of flesh, the closeness with which people move in and around one another marked a number of spatial boundaries that were not to be found in Europe, anywhere. If one were to have asked me then, somewhere between the ages of seven and ten, what I remembered about either place, it would have been this: the fusion of corporeal differences into a kind of landscape. Density of color, texture, and form on the one hand and a corresponding sparseness, a visual "apartness," on the other.

Years later, armed with a more sophisticated understanding of such differences, I am standing on a street corner in downtown Johannesburg, South Africa. All around me Africans (black Africans) are walking: to and from work, to the taxi ranks via the street vendors, and to the train stations. They too have formed a kind of landscape: the same closeness, the packing of flesh into impossibly tight "combis" (minivans), the proximity of one to the other in bus queues and shopfronts. It comes to me slowly that whites here do not walk—they drive, as in America, in ones and sometimes twos. The odd figure of a businessman, a tourist, a backpacker ... these stand out in sharp contrast to the moving walls of black Africans around them. I wonder what a child might make of this.

IX. FRIDAY, MARCH 26, 1999 *(Campbell Hall, room 153, 3:44 pm)*

When memory goes a-gathering firewood, it brings back the sticks that strike its fancy.[9]
What is the relationship between memory and architecture? A precise definition does not come easily. The word "memory" itself suggests an intangibility, an immateriality, a certain presence in the mind's eye: clearly a phenomenon that is more cerebral than physical. Architecture, although rooted in the cerebral, is traditionally made manifest in the material, physical world. The question of memory in African-American culture is problematic because, as Hooks has stated so eloquently, "our struggle is also a struggle of memory against forgetting."[10] Severed from the "mother" culture(s) through the experiences of slavery, colonialism, and imperialism, notions of "self," "place" and "home" are fiercely contested terrains in which memory plays an increasingly fragmented role. Who remembers what? And how?

In Kirk Savage's excellent essay, "The Politics of Memory: Black Emancipation and the Civil War Monument," Savage tackles the thorny issues of the monument, perhaps the most expedient route to collective memory. There is probably no better starting point from which to interrogate the politics of memory, race, and the American landscape. Race precipitated the Civil War and race finally ended it—how telling that, as Savage recounts, the black scholar Freeman Murray could count only three monuments depicting black soldiers. "Public monuments do not arise as if by natural law to celebrate the deserving; they are built by people with sufficient power to marshal or impose public consent for their erection."[11] Put quite simply, blacks did not possess the financial or cultural clout necessary to validate their perspectives and thus legitimize not only their material struggle in the war (blood, guts, and glory), but the equally important and vicious ideological role that race played—and continues to play—in the collective national memory. To "read" America through its Civil War monuments is a troubling exercise in editorial control and underscores perfectly the complexities of race and power that have dogged this nation since birth. As always, the question of representation is paramount: how to represent the (awful) contradictory impulses of slavery and democracy. How to represent warfare—not "which heroes or which victories ought to be celebrated, but what ideas deserved representation. Ideas of warfare itself—organised violence and destruction—were unfit for representation."[12]

9 Birago Diop, quoted in Trinh T Minh-ha's, "Mother's Talk," Nnaemeka's in *The Politics of (M)Othering: Womanhood, Identity and Resistance in African Literature* (London & New York: Routledge, 1997), 26.

10 Hooks, op. cit,148.

11 For a truly insightful account of the role of monument in the shaping of collective memory, see Kirk Savage's "The Politics of Memory: Black Emancipation and the Civil War Monument," in *Commemorations: the Politics of National Identity*, J.R. Gillis, ed (Princeton: Princeton University Press, 1994), 127–149.

12 ibid., 127.

But—and here's the rub—race is neither invisible, nor nameless. On the contrary, in fact. One could persuasively argue that the opposite is true: that African-Americans have been so named, made visible (albeit in very particular ways) that the struggle, to paraphrase Hooks, is actually about "re-memory," the process of undoing the narratives and representations that are so easily, carelessly available and re-inscribing one's own. For the architect—black or white—this poses an interesting dilemma. Like the African-American subject, architecture is visible, named. Its formidable presence is all around us, everywhere, at all scales and in all places. How then to take this history that is characterized by silence and displacement, and place it, literally, in, on, around, above, below, between … somewhere, anywhere. How then to make out of material, form, space, and light a response to the condition, as Cornel West puts it, of "natal alienation?"[13]

X. JANUARY, 1993 *(Swakopmund, Namibia)*
Dem heroischen Deutschen Soldaten.
In memory of dead Germans (heroes). But this is a *British* soldier, *n'est ce pas?* Surveying the familiar bronze sculpture, the flash of recognition is instantaneous, surfacing from some unknown source. War films? School trips? White, noble, upright, and strong, sometimes armed, sometimes not … perched astride a neo-classical stone base … only the inscriptions change. From the edge of South West Africa (now Namibia, formerly a German colony) to Montgomery, Alabama, the statues are identical. This suggests a kind of visual fusion—all statues become one, all causes are one (won). "White and Anglo-Saxon … not a neutral individual body but a collective body, conceived with certain boundaries and allegiances."[14] As a means of establishing a collective (albeit selective) memory and settling it within literal and psychological landscapes, monuments are crucial. They may, however, as Martin Luther King, Jr. famously did, be appropriated.

13 C. West, "Cultural Politics of Difference," in *Keeping Faith: Philosophy and Race in America* (New York: Routledge, 1993), 16.   **14** op cit., Savage, K., 135.

"Hand, Fence" by L Lokko, London, 1995. Photo: L. Lokko

XI. WEDNESDAY, JULY 28, 1999 *(at home in Chicago)*

A place on the map is also a place in history.[15]

For the European navigators who sailed across the Atlantic, America was literally blank space. North America became a continent only very slowly: for the initial explorers, America was a group of islands, similar perhaps to the Azores or the Canaries. With Ferdinand Magellan's circumnavigation of the globe in 1522 what was, in the colonialist eye, essentially blank space became measured space. The determined lines of latitude and longitude, those abstract intellectual inscriptions of measurement across the globe, fixed the Americas well within the boundaries of a European view of the world. Latitude and longitude: pure, Platonic, all-encompassing expressions of perfect spherical geometry. The history of the relationship between geometry, property, and divinity needs no further elaboration here, except to note that the European "discoverers" of the "New World" were driven by an unshakeable belief in the power of geometry and mathematical measure. As Dennis Cosgrove has noted, "measuring and mapping, imagining the landscape in the mind or inscribing it onto paper are more rapid, less dangerous and more secure ways of coping with unknown space than

15 A. Rich, "Notes Towards a Politics of Location," in *Blood, Bread and Poetry: Selected Prose 1979–1985* (London: Virago Press, 1987), 210–231.

penetrating the Appalachian forests with axe or trekking the featureless grasslands … in the settlement of America, each community faced the need to balance the freedoms and physical dangers offered by immeasured space against the safety and social constraint offered by measure, rule and boundary."[16]

How can this history be measured, recorded, represented against the experience of black America? This is not a community balancing "freedom" and "physical dangers," trekking courageously into the wilderness. For Africans arriving in this country as dislocated, violently separated communities, theirs is an entirely different history. In place of the myths of establishing oneself at the edge of the unknown, as various cultures arriving in the "New World" have done, their task was to make sense out of senselessness, re-make history, re-make culture, and forge different relationships to the land. To recognize other histories, other peoples, other languages and sounds and, crucially, other ways of occupying the same space requires, in addition, the ability to recognize those places in the very construction of the majority history and culture. Speaking of literature but applicable to place- and space-making, Toni Morrison explains that [American] "knowledge holds that traditional, canonical American literature is free of, uninformed and unshaped by the four-hundred-year-old presence of, first, Africans and then African-Americans in the United States."[17] Her argument focuses on the ways in which American society relegated its contradictions and internal conflicts to a "blank darkness,"[18] effectively silencing the black experience and collective memory. If cultural identities are, as she argues, [partly] formed and informed by a nation's literature, then what are we to make of the problematic forced construction of America as a new, free, democratic and—essentially—white man?

Historical analysis, as Tschumi states, "has generally supported the view that the role of the architect is to project on the ground the images of social institutions, translating the economic or political structure of society into buildings or groups of buildings. Architecture, therefore, was first and foremost the adaptation of space to the existing socioeconomic structure."[19] What, then, are the available options that might make it possible to search, spatially, for the hidden agendas in architecture that consolidate and articulate one set of narratives over another?

16 Dennis Cosgrove, "The Measures of America', in J. Corner & A. McLean, eds. *Taking Measures Across the American Landscape* (New Haven: Yale University Press, 1996).

17 T. Morrison, "Romancing the Shadow" in *Playing in the Dark: Whiteness and the Literary Imagination* (Cambridge: Harvard University Press,1992), 4.

18 ibid., 38.

19 B. Tschumi, *Architecture and Disjunction* (Cambridge: MIT Press, 1994), 5.

XII. TUESDAY, JUNE 20, 2000 *(at home in Chicago)*

The museum and the memorial are not the only available architectural explorations of "race"—and never have been.

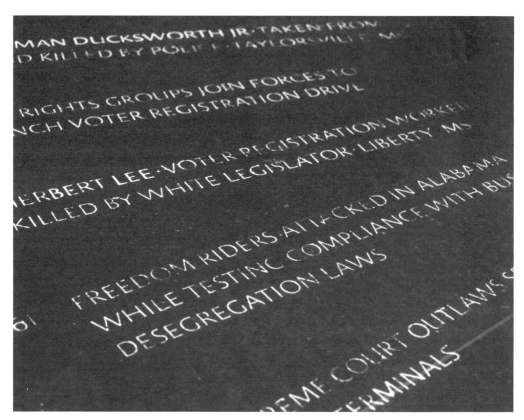

"Water, Memories, Civil Rights" by M Lin,
Montgomery, Alabama, 1998. Photo: L. Lokko

nine   sonorous urbanism

SPATIAL IMPLICATIONS OF THE AACM

There was a guy on Maxwell Street, that you could see from the expressway, that had all of these hubcaps in his junkyard: the sun was hitting them, and they were shining, it was just lighting up the whole expressway—it was blinding. So I came off the expressway to see what it was. And when I started looking at them, they were so incredible—looking at the coat of arms on these hubcaps, you know—when I was going through them, I would drop some trying to get to others, and I got involved in the sound when I was dropping them. I took some of them home and cleaned them up and began to beat on them and test them for sound; I designed a frame and everything and put it together. —Henry Threadgill

Chicago's zenith as an urban center of jazz occurred during the 1920s when musicians from New Orleans, such as Joe "King" Oliver and Louis Armstrong, steadily migrated north to further develop the collectively improvised music that is today known as the New Orleans and Chicago style. In a typical "arrangement," each band member would improvise a line in harmonic relation to the melody of a blues, rag, march, or stomp. However, Armstrong, after an extended visit to New York, returned to Chicago in 1926 and redefined this improvised music by creating distinctions between solo and ensemble play. In his Hot Five and Hot Seven recordings, he created a series of brilliantly inventive rhythmic and melodic solo flights that signaled the demise of both the collective improvisation of the New Orleans/Chicago style and Chicago's reign as the dominant site for new developments in jazz. Chicago would continue to support jazz, but the principal development of the styles that would later dominate, Swing and Bebop, would occur in New York.

In *Jazz City*, Leroy Ostransky proposes that some of the underlying urban structures of New Orleans, Chicago, Kansas City, and New York as transport cities provided the support for the development of jazz. Each city had an adequate density of resident and transient populations, with money to spend and a demand for entertainment, capable of sustaining a degree of musical activity that allowed for the diverse exchange of ideas that enabled jazz to flourish. However, on

Chicago's South Side, this configuration was challenged in the 1960s by the Association for the Advancement of Creative Musicians (AACM), which developed a free-form music practice in the midst of decreasing performance opportunities and the emergence of Black Nationalism.

The core membership of this nonprofit arts organization, founded in 1965 by Muhal Richard Abrams, Phil Cohran, and Steve McCall, was an experimental band that Abrams had started in 1961 with the intention of exploring new musical ideas through collective improvisations that deployed a vocabulary of written arrangements. Internalized, this vocabulary, which provided directive and connective themes while necessitating renewal, extension, and variation, enabled musicians to build "long multi-sectional compositions defined by elaborate instrumental variety; rapid and abrupt rhythmic, dynamic and textural successions; [and an] emphasis on multiple, disparate, instrumental voices that obscured any clear sense of tonality."[1] Sounds within silence, space as a medium of suspension, and autonomous improvisation were some of the musical explorations conducted within unscored performances. From this collective, numerous voices, such as the Art Ensemble of Chicago, emerged to become internationally recognized as principal contributors to the development of modern improvised music. This musical achievement makes the AACM and its base of operation, the Abraham Lincoln Center, a significant site in the cultural landscape of jazz history and Chicago's South Side. Moreover, the AACM is significant for its efforts to redefine these musicians and the spatial realm in which they operate.

The AACM offers a unique opportunity for considering the architectural and urban implications of processes that facilitate improvisation, such as composition as a point of departure or a moment by moment continuity, variable temporal flow, the body's relation to objects, and complex ensemble relations. For in its redefining efforts, the AACM applied those processes to its navigation of the city and developed a music offering a consideration of form and space that accommodates noise as defined by Jacques Attali in *Noise: the Political Economy of Music*:

1 Ronald M. Radano, *New Musical Figurations: Anthony Braxton's Cultural Critique* (Chicago: University of Chicago Press, 1993), 79.

A noise is a resonance that interferes with the audition of a message in the process of emission. A resonance is a set of simultaneous, pure sounds of determined frequency and differing intensity. Noise, then, does not exist in itself, but only in relation to the system within which it is inscribed: emitter, transmitter, receiver. Information theory uses the concept of noise (or rather, metonymy) in a more general way: noise is the term for a signal that interferes with the reception of a message by the receiver, even if the interfering signal itself has a meaning for that receiver.[2]

Situation and system dependent, noise, or that which is excluded or taken as interference, may in fact indicate a different ordering potential and meaning outside the range of an existing one. Significantly, Attali's consideration is not limited to music. Any system may be challenged through its noise, and a system or practice that looks to engage rather than suppress noise continually offers open and provisional rather than fixed and resolute definitions of form.[3] It is by privileging noise that the AACM's organizational and musical innovations challenged the prevailing perceptions regarding jazz musicians and their role, as well as the music's implications regarding the city.

NAVIGATIONAL TACTICS Ralph Ellison, in *Invisible Man*,[4] was the first to apply improvised music processes to develop a navigational understanding of urbanism. Recognizing the city's potential to provide renewal and invention even as forces within it strive to impose new forms of categorization, he proposed an improvisational relation to the city to optimize this fluid and tensioned dynamic. In *Jazz*,[5] Toni Morrison examines the role of jazz in relation to its makers in order to develop an alternative consideration of modernity, mobility, and the construction of the urban subject. Her resulting construction suggests that Ellison's navigational technique was operative as early as the Jazz Age. Morrison's narrator, omniscient yet flawed, embodies this tensioned dynamic as a voice that is unable to accurately account for all activities in the novel and is often contradicted by the narrative solos of the novel's main characters. The structure of the book reiterates both Ellison's and Morrison's essential point that no singular narrative is capable of fully rendering a subject's complexity, and in the

2 Jacques Attali, *Noise: the Political Economy of Music*, (Minneapolis: University of Minnesota Press, 1985) 26–27.

3 For a series of noise-based structural conceptions see Nathaniel Mackey, *Discrepant Engagement: Dissonance, Cross-Culturality, and Experimental Writing*, (New York: Cambridge University Press), 19–20.

4 Ralph Ellison, *Invisible Man* (New York: Vintage Press, 1972).

5 Toni Morrison, *Jazz* (New York: Plume, 1993).

engagement of that complexity the participant observer is also changed. In a succinct summarization, literary critic Gerald Early characterizes Ellison's novel as a contemplation of:

> *the fluidity of human life bumping up against human systems of categorization; ideologies as masks that humans adopt to manipulate or to delude; the individual finding freedom, not through politics, but through a kind of aesthetic and psychological 're-wiring.'* [6]

Although it is not directly political, this "re-wiring" is not without political implications. For both Ellison and Morrison, it permits the conduction of political and social undertones or noises present in the risk-laden dynamics of improvised music. Identified by Ellison as a finding and losing of the self through the solo's assertion of the individual within and against the group, this risk accompanies, indeed facilitates, improvisation and the emergence of developments that are unforeseeable by any single participant. Because the performance is responsive to both individuals and the group, yet controlled by neither, this improvisational risk, with potential consequences of stagnation (nonexistence), insanity (dysfunction), and completion (systemization, standardization, habit), is not limited to the soloist but is encountered by every participant. [7] Ellison's novel concludes with an appeal, "Who knows but that, on the lower frequencies, I speak for you?" Pitched to resonate physically as well as transmit sonorously, Ellison's invisible man strives to "re-wire" the reader's aesthetic understanding from fixed to vibrational conceptions to enable risk-laden navigational engagements of the city and society. [8] It is this interactive environment of developing individuals and forms emerging from the risk of improvisation that is sought in Ellison's and Morrison's proposals of improvisation as a means of negotiating the chaotic and alienating character of the city.

The AACM's efforts to extend these performance dynamics to an overall organizational structure, which treated each member as an individual who was free to participate in multiple collective groupings, constituted a manifestation of these political

---

6 Gerald Early, "Decoding Ralph Ellison," *Dissent* (Summer 1997), 114.

7 John Corbett summarizes this elaboration regarding the risk of improvisation made by Evan Parker in "Ephemera Underscored: Writing Around Free Improvisation," in Krin Gabbard, ed., *Jazz Among the Discourses* (Durham: Duke University Press, 1995), 223.

8 Ellison, op.cit., 568.

undertones into direct political action. Members could play in any band; however, a band led by an AACM member needed to maintain 60 percent AACM representation as a show of mutual support. The common language that the musicians were developing facilitated the meeting of this demand by enabling members to participate in a multitude of formulations both for performance opportunities and for the development of musical ideas. The AACM's signature group, the Art Ensemble of Chicago, best demonstrates this capacity, having survived as a group for thirty-four years, perhaps because of such fluid practices. Its members remain committed to the group, yet pursue outside projects in order to develop other musical ideas that, in turn, contribute to the Ensemble's musical vitality. This structuring also allowed groups to form and disperse in response to the parameters of their environment and the need to accommodate a greater variety of performance environments and opportunities.

The AACM sought to establish a more self-reliant community of musicians that offered an alternative to the recording and performance establishment, and demonstrated "how the disadvantaged and the disenfranchised can come together and determine their own strategies for political and economic freedom, thereby determining their own destinies."[9] With this emphasis, the AACM was not only responsive to the collapse of performance venues, but also responsive to the greater economic and social challenges confronting the South Side, historically black neighborhood. By the 1960s, numerous political and social organizations in Chicago and on the South Side began participating in civil rights efforts and seeking to improve the housing and educational conditions for black Chicagoans.[10] The Abraham Lincoln Center, the community services organization that provided the AACM with meeting space, was doubtlessly among those organizations. Founded in 1905 by Jenkins Lloyd Jones, it had operated with a mission to advance the intellectual, philosophical, and religious beliefs of people with whom they came in touch. Influenced by the efforts of such organizations, the AACM's included in its goals assisting other complementary charitable organizations. However, within what the master planners of the public housing projects, such as the Robert Taylor Homes, along the State Street corridor perceived as the chaos of the South Side, the AACM's biggest contributions were to the South Side's social vitality.

9 Muhal Richard Abrams and John Shenoy Jackson, "The Association for The Advancement of Creative Musicians," *Black World*, November 1973, 74.

10 See Radano, op. cit., 91–99 for a comprehensive discussion of the political, social and artistic environment that surrounded the AACM.

Museums and university campuses as well as South Side community centers, churches, art galleries, coffeehouses, and private homes were developed and promoted by the AACM as a new network of spaces for playing improvised music. In these spaces, which were free from the definitions that limited improvised music to an entertainment spectacle, the AACM positioned improvised music's fluid, transient, and creative play as a more integral part of daily life available to anyone, anywhere, and through a multitude of means. They also actively encouraged others to adopt this creative practice by repairing instruments and giving them to inner city youths and by developing a tuition-free music school to educate others in the music that the AACM was developing. Through such outreach, the AACM challenged the notion that jazz musicians were an unreliable and disorganized fringe group of society and revealed how the musician could contribute to the everyday character of the urban environment. In defiance of these stereotypes, the members of the AACM established an environment that sustained an ongoing effort "to use music to build a new culture ... through the production of a new music outside of the industry with implications beyond the musical."[11] It is within its music that the AACM developed a set of qualitative rather than quantitative formal practices that enable these navigational techniques and understandings to impact the understanding of the physical character of the city.

AACM AESTHETICS AND ATTALI'S NOISE Equally influential on the AACM's development as the South Side social and political organizations were Chicago area art organizations that promoted black nationalism, a movement that actively developed expressions of black heritage and culture and its African roots, and provided positive affirmations of blackness. In its most radical and revolutionary manifestations, this movement projected an essentialist black cultural identity by proposing an exclusive and integral relation between black art forms and expressions and black people. Presented as "great black music," the distorted, atonal characteristics of the AACM's music have been considered to be reverberant expressions of black militancy, anger, and alienation evident in cultural nationalism. (A similar consideration was made regarding the explorations of free improvisation by black musicians in New York at the time.) However, while all of these musicians pursued free improvisation by explor-

11 Attali, op. cit., 138.

ing the limits of their instruments, the intensely kinetic streams of sound and energy that characterized performances in New York were not the same as the sparser qualities of isolated sounds produced by members of the AACM. By limiting the range of their musical expression to manifest their verbal criticisms and frustrations, these character-izations fail to acknowledge the differences between these developing free music explo-rations or account for the range of expression found within the music. Additionally, these characterizations fail to acknowledge the development and presence of other atonal music or the presence of other free and collectively improvised music in the United States and Europe.[12] Contrary to both of these claims, the result of stripping away traditional principles and practices through the group's reexamination of black musical expressions and principles was a new form of musical practice with implica-tions not limited to black nationalist concerns. Producing sounds that are at times contemplative or humorous, as well as critical, in character, it is in the AACM's struc-ture for making creative music (the other term that the AACM used to describe its music) rather than its particular sound that makes the AACM's music revolutionary.

AACM stage shows involved a collage of disparate performative elements from the traditions of black music culture and included theatric stage actions, spoken word, and music. Explicit black nationalist sentiment and other political content could often be found in the stage actions and spoken words, but these same actions were also a part of the music and often used to trigger transitions in the direction of the musical perfor-mance.[13] All of these elements, presented as an interwoven series of spontaneous events, placed an emphasis on the inherent theatricality of making music while critiquing and emptying music of the entertainment content that had historically permitted the reduction of jazz to a marginalized backdrop. By dressing in different outfits, using face paint, and surrounding themselves with multiple instruments, the members visually reinforced this collage of activity. The surrounding instruments were not limited to the expected instruments of jazz of which a musician might have thorough knowledge or facility. A reed player, for example, might have an array of saxophones and other wind instruments as well as an assortment of little instruments, such as bells, whistles, gongs, toys, and other unconventional or homemade instruments that could be used as per-cussive augmentation.

12 For a discussion of contem-porary improvised music and black or "afrological" character-istics see George E. Lewis, "Improvised Music after 1950: Afrological and Eurological Perspectives," *Black Music Research Journal*, vol. 16, no. 1, (1996), 111–113. Lewis, a mem-ber of the AACM, identifies three predominant forms of contem-

porary improvised music: the "open" improvisation of the AACM, European "free" improvi-sation, and the "downtown" (New York) school. Musicians of each category have been known to play in groupings with one another. Lewis also notes the cross-cultural nature of contem-porary improvised music explo-rations.

13 See Ekkehard Jost, *Free Jazz* (New York: Da Capo, 1994), 171–173 for an extended discussion of the AACM's use of spoken word and stage action in their music.

As conceived by the AACM creative music places emphasis on a set of rules, or a vocabulary of open potential, which are tools for exploration and the stimulation of creative thinking. As well, emphasis is on the development of the individual voice and the ability to contribute to the collective improvisation. Rather than focusing on the proper technique and correctness of gesture necessary for insuring the accurate production of particular notes in written musics, an individual develops techniques and gestures that enable their ability to facilitate and meet the needs of the creative moment. These processes, in fact, underscore all improvised music, but this is not merely a stylistic shift, or a simple return to the collectively improvised forms of the New Orleans/Chicago style. In their rejection of the traditional rhythm section as support for limited solo flights, the AACM developed ensemble relationships in which each musician simultaneously improvised to a collectively developing piece. Access to multiple instruments was necessary given the AACM's desire to permit "the absolute ability to instantaneously organize sound, silence, and rhythm with the whole of his or her creative intelligence."[14] The free-form implication of these musical relationships, coupled with the absence of harmonic chord progressions, regular rhythmic intervals, or melodic line structures are noted by Leo Smith, who considers such work the second phase of improvised music as

> *the original intention of all great music: to create and express original ideas without being inhibited by certain prescribed forms. In free-music we have many forms: structured forms that supply a beginning leading into improvisation; link form, whereby several different predetermined elements are linked together to form improvisations; and, at its highest level, improvisation created entirely within the improviser at the moment of improvisation without any prior structuring.*[15]

Joseph Jarman describes the challenge of the AACM's improvised music:

> *This was about goal and purpose and mental attitude. It's about, what do I want to paint, what colors do I want to use, it's about, will I have the nerve to step out there on a limb? It's about, will I be creative?*[16]

14 Leo Smith, "Beyond Categories," in Robert Walser, ed., *Keeping Time: Readings in Jazz History* (New York: Oxford University Press, 1999), 317.

15 ibid., 322.

16 John Litweiler, *The Freedom Principle: Jazz after 1958* (New York: Da Capo, 1984), 179.

The AACM brought the structures that facilitate improvisation into sharp focus through their reduction of music to a collective exploration of creating sound.

The effect of their reductive performative approach was the transformation of these creative processes into a new form of musical practice; an alternative mode of production accessible to anyone. This practice is a form of abstraction that is intimately tied to its makers, and because it is developed collectively, one that eludes any singular control. Jacques Attali elaborates on the impact of this music, produced through collective labor, as a mode of production that "heralds the negation of the tool-oriented usage of things," and is "a reconciliation between work and play":

> *Thus in a reversal of the current process, which starts with the conception and ends with the object, the outcome of labor no longer "pre-exists ideally in the imagination of the worker." To modify the meaning of form in the course of its production, to empty exchange/use-value of its alienating content, is to attempt to designate the unsayable and the unpredictable.* [17]

He also notes the impact of this mode of production on the object:

> *Each production-consumption (composition) entity can call its program into question at any moment; production is not foreseeable before its conclusion. It becomes a starting point, rather than being an end product; and time is lived time, not only in exchange and usage, but also in production itself.* [18]

The AACM's simultaneous acts of inhabitation and musical development describe a potential environment, "a truly different system of organization" waiting to be actualized. [19]

17 Attali, 142.

18 ibid., 144–5.

19 ibid., 137.

LOCAL AND GLOBAL DISPERSION The group's sense of organization does not concentrate on forms but on their emergence and dissolution in the continuous play of an unbridled set of forces. The urbanism that corresponds to this production is not one that places a primacy on fixed order or form. Its most opportune moments are in the spaces that architecture and urbanism do not traditionally account for—the spaces called noise. These are spaces of development, not through their erasure or formalization, but through the nurturing and maintenance of their free and shifting play. Commenting on the influence of the AACM on other musicians, Muhal Richard Abrams emphasizes the idea rather than the music:

> From what they've told us, we've commanded the respect of musicians all over the world, especially in the states. And it's not so much because of the music, itself, but the idea. Because if the AACM is anything, it's a very excellent idea. It's not so much what is or isn't done, it's the idea and what it could mean to different groups, depending on their energy. The idea: to pool our energies to a common cause. [20]

Given that the contemporary city is increasingly less described by its physical form than its processes, it would seem that for architecture and urbanism the application of the AACM's principals of collaboration and engaging the potential of noise are, likewise, a provocative set of ideas.

Noting that noise is an interference that prevents the complete repetition of an earlier set of conditions, art historian George Kubler proposes that noise is irregular and unexpected change. [21] Historically, he notes that since, "Human perception is best suited to slow modifications of routine behavior," we have sought to regulate rather than embrace the sources of noise. [22] Perception limits the rate of change and invention; however, in their acknowledgment and encouragement of noise, the AACM's structures permit an opportunity to challenge and increase the range of our perception and thus our ability to comprehend and incorporate invention and change. Or as Roscoe Mitchell challenges, "If something sounds good to you, then it has a structure. It's just a matter of going and figuring out what that structure is." [23] Architecture might

20 Litweiler, 196.

21 George Kubler, *The Shape of Time* (New Haven: Yale University Press, 1962), 60–61.

22 ibid., 124.

23 Quoted in Lewis Porter, Michael Ullman, *Jazz: From Its Origins to the Present* (Englewood Cliffs, NJ: Prentice Hall, 1993), 394.

encourage a similar increase in perception and the emergence of the new by amplifying the locations of noise in the cultural and social as well as physical routines of contemporary urban life. Residing in such releases of routines into transient, fluid, and creative play is architecture, which, rather than seeking to define places, might seek to develop opportunities and means for creatively engaging the cultural, social as well as physical spaces of noise. The continued potential of these principals and processes is for an open means for the development of both the city and its individuals.

Attali admits the difficulty in fully conceptualizing the implications of a political economy based on this system of organization. Similarly, the outcome of an architecture permitting and encouraging the engagement of noises within routines does not reveal itself in the fixed moments of architecture's tools of representation. Architecture, in structuring such relations, must wait for the impact of this engagement to reveal itself over time. The AACM was transformed in 1969 when it splintered into distinct, yet tethered, bodies that still permitted a local community presence by establishing the AACM School. The development of its internationally known music continued even when many members departed for Europe to further explore improvisational forms. The school continues to operate as the group's headquarters and has, in continuation of its advocacy that inner-city youths be creative, nurtured the development of new generations of musicians operating in Chicago. The thirty-five-year lifespan of the AACM has revealed the departures of its members to be a dispersal rather than a break because of the resiliency of their structural ties, which continue to enable their pursuit of this music. The collective formulation has permitted a continued development and a sense of connection and support across distances despite turbulent financial, recording, and performing opportunities as groups quickly form and disperse. Lester Bowie commented at a festival celebrating the AACM's twenty-fifth anniversary, "As far as achieving our goals we haven't. There have been results, though, and we're not finished yet. . . . We always understood this was going to be a long distance run."[24]

24 Lester Bowie, quoted in Howard Mandel, *Future Jazz* (Oxford: Oxford University Press, 1999), 46.

To the Colored Citizens of the United States.

NICODEMUS, GRAHAM CO., KAN., July 2d. 1877.

We, the Nicodemus Town Company of Graham County, Kan., are now in possession of our lands and the Town Site of Nicodemus, which is beautifully located on the N. W. quarter of Section 1, Town 8, Range 21, in Graham Co., Kansas, in the great Solomon Valley, 240 miles west of Topeka, and we are proud to say it is the finest country we ever saw. The soil is of a rich, black, sandy loam. The country is rather rolling, and looks most pleasing to the human eye. The south fork of the Solomon river flows through Graham County, nearly directly east and west and has an abundance of excellent water, while there are numerous springs of living water abounding throughout the Valley. There is an abundance of fine Magnesian stone for building purposes, which is much easier handled than the rough sand or hard stone. There is also some timber; plenty for fire use, while we have no fear but what we will find plenty of coal.

Now is your time to secure your home on Government Land in the Great Solomon Valley of Western Kansas.

Remember, we have secured the service of W. R. Hill, a man of energy and ability, to locate our Colony.

Not quite 90 days ago we secured our charter for locating the town site of Nicodemus. We then became an organized body, with only three dollars in the treasury and twelve members, but under the careful management of our officers, we have now nearly 300 good and reliable members, with several members permanently located on their claims—with plenty of provisions for the colony—while we are daily receiving letters from all parts of the country from parties desiring to locate in the great Solomon Valley of Western Kansas.

For Maps, Circulars, and Passenger rates, address our General Manager, W. R. HILL, North Topeka, Kansas, until August 1st, 1877,,then at Hill City, Graham Co., via Trego.

The name of our post-office will be Nicodemus, and Mr. Z. T. Fletcher will be our "Nasby."

REV. S. P. ROUNDTREE, Sec'y.

NICODEMUS.

Nicodemus was a slave of African birth,
And was bought for a bag full of gold;
He was reckoned a part of the salt of the earth.
But he died years ago, very old.

Nicodemus was a prophet, at least he was as wise,
For he told of the battles to come :
How we trembled with fear, when he rolled up his eyes,
And we heeded the shake of his thumb.

CHORUS :   Good time coming, good time coming,
Long, long time on the way ;
Run and tell Elija to hurry up Pomp.
To meet us under the cottonwood tree,
In the Great Solomon Valley
At the first break of day.

Leaflet promoting Nicodemus from Minorities Collection,
Kansas State University

ten   waiting on the dawn at demus

REFLECTIONS ON HISTORIC LANDSCAPE DOCUMENTATION

All colored people that want to go to Kansas, on September 5, 1877 can do so for $5.00. —Nicodemus, the "Promised Land" [1]

To persuade African-Americans to leave their homes, Kansas townsite promoters circulated handbills, throughout southern black neighborhoods in 1877. Although most of the advertisements exaggerated the environmental conditions and agricultural potential in Nicodemus, African-Americans were still persuaded to relocate to a desolate Kansas plain for a number of different reasons: the promotion of new towns, to escape southern atrocities, and to prove their equality. [2]

From emancipation in 1865 until 1920, African-Americans experienced the freedom to determine their economic, political, social, cultural, and physical lives and during this period the most prolific development of contraband camps, rural villages, and sustained urban enclaves evolved. Migration had begun even prior to the dark slavery era with Africans settling peaceably in the Bay of Fundy as early as 1792. Other Africans had migrated across the Atlantic to the West Indies. Migration to urban and rural communities of the northeast and midwest by southern African-Americans was common by the late 1880s.

In April 1877 seven Kansans formed the Nicodemus Town Company, the first trust association that attempted to develop an all-black town on the Middle Border, or Great Plains.

Settlers who migrated to Nicodemus did so as a means of survival. African-Americans in the South still faced discrimination, segregation, violence, and poverty; moving west meant another kind of freedom.

The Nicodemus Town company consisted of six African-Americans from the South and one white preacher who had heard of the availability of homestead land in Kansas through the preemption laws. The company founders envisioned a way to profit personally by homesteading property through the government and began recruitment efforts. [3] To accelerate recruitment among the largely illiterate former-slave population, the

---

1 Kenneth Marvin Hamilton, "The Settlement of Nicodemus: Its Origin and Early Promotion," in *Promised Land on the Solomon: Black Settlement of Nicodemus, Kansas,* (National Park Service, 1986), 4–5.

2 Kansas State University Minorities Collection, Manhattan, Kansas.

3 Hamilton, op. cit., 2–3.

African-American townsite boosters went to selected organizations in the upper South, accompanied by wealthy members of these communities who described the advantages of moving west. Without enough funds to employ additional boosters, the company distributed circulars in other towns to advertise their lots in Nicodemus. Eventually these men persuaded at least four colonization groups, approximately 750 people from Kentucky, Tennessee, and eastern Kansas, to form emigration associations and move to the Nicodemus area. For African-Americans in the South whose lives were often at risk, moving west meant freedom.

The first settlers arrived from the woodlands of Kentucky and Tennessee. They faced new challenges and many reacted negatively to their new home.[4] Some arriving by train were so disappointed and angry that they tried to hang the organizer, the Reverend W. H. Smith, and return eastward the same day. Many had sacrificed large amounts of money and sold possessions to pay for their rail transport, although they assumed their way had been paid for by the promoters. The Reverend Smith did not pay in full the rail transportation cost, thereby misrepresenting the financial obligation of the travelers. Families arriving between September and December had little time to plant crops for spring or prepare for the harsh winters. Many were ill prepared for the isolation; Nicodemus was twenty miles in any direction from mail, food, or building supplies. Since building materials were not available as advertised, the new residents used indigenous materials—sod and grass—for underground dugouts and above ground sod houses, known as "soddies."

Despite the hardships, over 600 people lived in Nicodemus Township (the agricultural land surrounding the town) by the late 1870s, most of them on the townsite (the unincorporated sixteen-acre center). Houses, businesses, public buildings, two churches, hotels, and livery stables dotted the landscape. These buildings were arranged by de facto zoning with the residences and churches at the west end side of town and the livery stables, hotels, and cafes to the east. Newspapers in the region promoted the town and contributed to a short period of growth that in turn enhanced the attractiveness of Nicodemus to at least four railroad companies. Nicodemus residents had become politically savvy and hoped to secure a rail stop along their dedicated easement.

4 ibid, 7–8.

Aerial photograph of Nicodemus, Kansas, in 1953. Seventy-six years after its founding, the townsite still looked desolate and barren. Only a few trees, at the lower left, appeared to mark the town park. Photo by Bernice Bates

These positive developments did not last long, and a number of misfortunes befell the town. In 1889, Nicodemus lost its bid for the county seat to Hill City and saw the first of many poor harvests. When it became evident that neither the Central Branch of the Union Pacific Railroad nor the Missouri Pacific Railroad would lay tracks adjacent to the townsite, people started to move their businesses to places with more opportunity. Some left the county entirely and many moved their stock of goods, and in some cases their buildings, to the new town of Bogue, a railhead established by the last railroad company offering service in that area, six miles south of Nicodemus. Some of the more determined African-American farmers who anticipated prosperity for the townsite returned to their original Nicodemus Township homesteads and townpeople who were not business owners or farmers maintained residences on the townsite longer than the African-American entrepreneurs. White businesses left and discontnued their support. The entrepreneurs remained but discontinued all active promotion of the townsite.

Like most new towns in the Great Plains that failed to attract the railroad, Nicodemus could no longer efficiently perform its primary function of collecting and distributing goods. There was no way that the people of Nicodemus could compete with towns such as Stockton, Hill City, or Bogue that had secured a rail connection, and the townsite never experienced its long-sought revival. By 1950, the town had even lost its post office due to out-migration and the national mandate for consolidating rural service. Yet Nicodemus, which had always been based on a subsistence economy, continued to avert economic insolvency.[5]

Nicodemus' commercial core had long since disappeared by 1976 when the State of Kansas designated Nicodemus an Historic District. Only a handful of deteriorating houses peppered the landscape and families who once lived on homesteaded land in the satellite communities saw their children leave the area for opportunities in the cities. Aside from income earned from dry land farming, there were no funds appropriated for infrastructure repair in Nicodemus, and the townsite suffered from unimproved streets, inadequate utilities, and deteriorating housing stock. In the 1980s, federal money brought some relief through the creation of a new community core, anchored by a senior center and amenities like paved roads, a water tower, weatherized housing, and a volunteer fire service. In response to this effort, residents moved their families and farmhouses in from the township to the townsite. This moving and recycling of building materials had been practiced in Nicodemus for over a hundred years, beginning with the wholesale transport of commercial buildings to Bogue, a town created by the railroad company to avoid servicing Nicodemus.

Nicodemus has maintained a small population despite the difficulties of the past, and it is through the perseverance of the settlers and their descendants that the townsite has survived. Only 40 residents live in Nicodemus today, and the townsite is a quiet place to retire to. The community retains its historic rural charm and character with small frame houses painted an assortment of colors, vast skies, expansive views, and agricultural land. There is a tradition of African-Americans in the area visiting the townsite on special occasions like the annual Emancipation Day Celebration, also known as "Homecoming," and Founders' Day. Today, the three-day "Homecoming" still attracts several hundred people from western Kansas, including former residents

5 Clayton Fraser and La Barbara
W. Fly, "Nicodemus: The
Architectural Development and
Decline of an American Town,"
Promised Land on the Solomon:
Black Settlement at Nicodemus,
Kansas (National Park Service,
1986), 57.

of the area, many of whom are descendents of the county's early African-American settlers. A sense of community permeates the townsite as family and friends participate in talent and fashion shows, potluck dinners, outdoor games, horseback riding, and storytelling reminiscent of the early days.

The history of Nicodemus parallels that of most new towns in the Great Plains. Although unique as an all-black town, the saga of Nicodemus could have been the story of any settlement west of the Mississippi. The unique heritage of the African-American settlers limited their town's economy, and without the railroad, Nicodemus simply stopped growing. Relatively few nineteenth-century towns gained the rail service essential to the prosperity of an aspiring city, and the great majority were unlucky and eventually faded into insignificance. Historians of the day reported that the townsite died; thus giving birth to the myth. However, a more apposite theory might be that the townsite experienced a redistribution of population. The African-American farmers moved from town back to their farmsteads in the township, while the white and affluent African-American businessmen (who never resided on the townsite to begin with) moved on to the next opportunity. By the 1920s, Nicodemus, like other Great Plains settlements, had enjoyed its last days of prosperity.

When the National Park Service initiated the first cultural landscape documentation through the Historic American Building Survey (HABS) program in 1983, residents of Nicodemus were still hoping for recognition and rescue. Streets were paved and electricity and phone service were extended to the townsite. Community development programs had improved the quality of life for 58 people still living on the townsite. Nicodemus remained an unincorporated rural agricultural village, and now enjoyed a National Historic Landmark designation, albeit without federal support.

A four-member HABS team of landscape architects and an archaeologist, who was pursuing a graduate degree in architecture, moved to the townsite for three months in 1983 to document the history of Nicodemus. Their goal was to dispel the myth surrounding the death of the town. The wealth of information made available by historians and researchers about the early period of Nicodemus' development suggests that Nicodemus no longer exists. It was necessary, therefore, to the townsite's continued evolution to understand and interpret its status as a living place. The National Park

Service had placed Nicodemus at the top of the its endangered properties list II years earlier, but had not assessed the site conditions for strategic redevelopment planning, so the documentation this new group of researchers embarked on was paramount.

Cultural landscape documentation and interpretation was a new research method but a nonprofit organization specializing in community research and education, Entourage, Inc., had been conducting precursory research on African-American settlement patterns and seemed equipped to conduct a thorough investigation of the townsite. At over 800 settlements throughout the United States the group had used a multidisciplinary approach to understand the complex web of associations between people and the land. Students with experience in archaeology, architectural history, landscape architecture, and planning were included in the summer team.

Library research and deed searches enabled this exploration into the "genealogy of the land." The land was used as a primary source of evidence of occupation; it alone could offer an accumulative history of community occupation, since a great deal of the physical fabric had not been documented. There were unexposed layers of definition of the place, hidden by the passage of time. The researchers' task was to uncover these hints of the past to help foster a greater sense of history in the present. Seven developmental phases were hypothesized to explain the town's history. The first phase was the pre-1877 development on the slopes south of the townsite. The second phase occurred between 1885 and 1888, when the site experienced an unexpected commercial

above and right: **HABS team members spent most of their time identifying significant sites for further investigation. Ruth Parr, archaeologist (not shown), and Richard McNamara interviewed numerous landowners to reconstruct the townsite's evolution.** Photo by Everett L. Fly, HABS team.

boom. Running from 1889 to 1920, the third phase was an actual development cycle, when the township was redistributed and consequently experienced steady growth. From 1921 to 1939, the town experienced the fourth phase, the Dustbowl, when the main issue was survival. During the fifth phase, from 1940 to 1959 the town went through a period of resurgence that was then overcome by the sixth phase, which marked a period of decline between 1960 and 1974. During the seventh phase, from 1975 to the present, the town has experienced both resettlement and renewal.

The fieldwork and interviews jogged the memories of residents and subsequently uncovered long-hidden stories about the environment and the social life at Nicodemus. Several farmers assisted archaeologist Ruth Parr, in identifying likely "dugout" sites on their land. Dugouts were among the first shelters built by settlers who created homes by digging space out of the grass. The plotting of these early homes suggests a great number of townspeople must have settled close to the river south of the present townsite. This hypothesis was further strengthened by the probable location of the railroad easement through town, in the southernmost section of the town plant. The dugouts scattered along the river bluffs produced a vernacular pattern very different from the formal grid of the townsite as it later developed on the ridge. Although the land on the ridge seemed relatively flat, the grid looked imposing on the rolling landscape. The clustered dugouts were widely distributed or scattered across the bluffs of the South Solomon River. These dugouts and outbuildings, along with

the older residents' recollections of family stories, led the team to believe there that there were once three satellite farm settlements associated with Nicodemus—Samuel's Addition (the earliest to disappear in the late nineteenth century); Mt. Olive (a community west of the township that had stone houses, a church, and a community school which dissolved during the 1920s); and Fairview (the largest of the three, containing frame residences and a school which disappeared after 1950).

In addition to the scheduled interviews, the research team opened its on-site office to the residents. This "Open House", as they called it, at first, occurred on every Thursday, but later evolved into an everyday event, promoting an on-going dialog between the residents and the HABS team. Residents would wander into Township Hall, inquisitive about the drawings or the progress of the research. Over subsequent visits, they learned how to read the drawings and left notes for team members on their desks, citing corrections and making suggestions. One of the town's oldest residents, a shut-in who rarely left his home, came in one day eager to tell his story; with a little encouragement he offered his rationale for the nicknames he had given all the residents over time. Though not significant to the landscape documentation, most of the residents found the circumstances of their nicknaming enlightening, and their storytelling produced new ways of thinking and learning for both the team and the community.

Planners and designers often approach a project thinking only of professional responsibility. As the documentation of the townsite evolved over the summer, the researchers realized that their presence on the site had affected the community. The HABS team developed personal relationships with the residents—often riding bikes with town children, dining with older residents during the day, and hosting street parties at night when the farmers returned from their fields. Ernestine's Cafe stayed open during the week and Ernestine and her sisters played piano and sang during the evening meals. State officials periodically drove three hours to Nicodemus from the capital for Ernestine's cooking.[6] This "less sterile" social interaction encouraged rich storytelling and community building in contrast to the structure the HABS researchers worked within during the day. Experiences with the residents were essential to collecting personal histories and interpretations and understanding obscure socio-cultural patterns of the past and present.

6 Ernestine VanDuvall had
been Walt Disney's cook.

The majority of Nicodemus residents, like Ora Switzer, have lived in the area all their lives; they provided valuable information about the townsite's history. More important, there is still a concerted effort made by older residents to instill pride and knowledge of the town's heritage in its younger generation. Photo by Everett L. Fly

Since publication in 1986 (underwritten by the National Park Service), the result of this research, entitled "Promised Land on the Solomon, Black Settlement at Nicodemus," has helped the town garner restoration funding. The Historic Preservation Committee established by Nicodemus residents as advisors for the HABS project remained intact to oversee special projects long after the research was completed. Over the years, the National Park Service has secured several engineering companies who have completed assessments of structural changes necessary to stabilize vulnerable buildings.

Other groups, like Nicodemus West, Inc., founded in 1977 by former residents interested in maintaining ties to their hometown, have become increasingly active. They have invested in Nicodemus' future by granting personal loans and scholarships to residents in need. The Nicodemus Historical Society, founded in 1989 by the grandchildren of original residents, began efforts to upgrade the townsite's Historic District designation to that of a National Historic Landmark. Through presentations, newsletters, public school dramatizations, exhibits, and theatrical productions throughout the country, the Society guaranteed the national rediscovery of Nicodemus.

Today, Nicodemus has national landmark status and is now a National Park, dedicated in July 1998. The residents can finally see a better day dawning on their townsite. Historic Landmark status gives Nicodemus an opportunity to tell its story to America. It gives national voice to its history, and its struggle, even if the future is uncertain. Residents are experiencing a renewed ownership of their history, which has become a vehicle for change at the townsite; thus the design for the future comes from the process in which it was conceived. This national significance empowers Nicodemians to look beyond their years of distress towards a day when the nation will celebrate their endurance in the Promised Land, called Nicodemus:

> *Nicodemus. There was something genuinely African in the very name. White folks would have called their place by one of the romantic names which stud the map of the United States, Smithville, Centreville, Jonesborough, but these colored people wanted something high sounding, and biblical, and so hit on Nicodemus. A village like Nicodemus, with a population of colored folks, is not a novelty. To live in villages is a specialty of the race.*[7]

Nicodemus enjoyed a heyday in 1886 and historians labeled it dead by 1930. However, it persevered and today residents celebrate a new and different prosperity. Families left Nicodemus for better opportunities elsewhere, but they never relinquished altogether the idea of community they had built in Nicodemus. Former residents from all around the country return to Kansas annually for the Emancipation Celebration, a Nicodemus event since 1877 and renamed "Homecoming" in 1950. The collective efforts of these residents and their will to keep the town and its history alive make Nicodemus unique among early African-American settlements. Most settlements established between 1865 and 1920 either disappeared or were consolidated into expanding urban areas. Nicodemus, on the other hand, has maintained its historic identity, in part by reaching beyond Kansas to former residents for assistance.

Whether two families or two hundred families reside there in the years to come is not important, and is inconsequential to Nicodemus' survival. For Nicodemians,

7 Noble Prentis reported to
Atchison Weekly Champion,
1881, quoted in Fraser
and Fly, 60.

community is not just the physical place but people who share a common ideology of the place—a common goal or hope for tomorrow. Nicodemus survives because it is in the minds and hearts of those who have lived there. There will always be a dream for Nicodemus, just as its first residents had envisioned. This collective dedication to the vision will allow Nicodemus to transcend the realities of tomorrow because it will endure with the residents' commitment to the concept of "community,"[8] that begins in Nicodemus but reaches farther afield in the collective memory of others.

Founder's Day, like "Homecoming," provides another opportunity for celebration and storytelling in Nicodemus. Family members and nearby friends return to the Baptist Church site each September to enjoy a day of worship and fellowship. The 1909 church building shown in this photograph is scheduled for restoration under the National Park Service management plan. photo: La Barbara James Wigfall

8 Fraser and fly, op. Cit., 80.

top: **The Drawing Room, Jessie Lott, artist;** *below:* **Project Row Houses, Houston, Texas.**

eleven

african-american art and architecture

A THEOLOGY OF LIFE, DEATH, AND TRANSFORMATION

Scholars of African-American culture have emphasized that the underpinning of African-American creativity is marked by constant improvisation: *"While improvisation is a universal characteristic of imaginative humans, the extensive sense of improvisation commonplace in the Afro-American experience is rather special. For this case spontaneous change represents a cultural norm rather than single independent inventions. It is an integral part of the process of African art to constantly reshape the old and reinforce the image of the community."*[1] —John Michael Vlach

For many African-American artists, art objects are often dressed in the accouterments of the ordinary, the discarded, and the abandoned. Self-taught Houston artist Jessie Lott refers to his sculptures welded from salvaged found objects as an "art of circumstances"[2]—an art that emerged from the convergence of financial lack and the ability, with divine insight, to *"see* what God has put in front of you." Art is the vehicle of revelation. Out of this tradition of improvisation and transformation has emerged an important proto-typical public art project in Houston, Texas—Project Row Houses. This project has transformed an abandoned lot of twenty-two identical "shotgun" houses of the Third Ward community into revolving art installation sites for artists whose work deals with issues pertinent to the African-American community. Melding art and architec-

ture, vernacular and academic, Project Row Houses acts not only as a historical retrieval of African-American material culture but also as a mirror of a distinctive African-American way of being in the world.

Project Row Houses is a spatial unfolding of artist John Biggers' paintings in which the shotgun house is a powerful symbol of the African-American cultural landscape. The narrow, gabled elevation of the shotgun house, with domestic elements placed prominently on the front porch, represents a mythological archetype that gives form to the collective African-American ancestral experience. The modest house form is abstracted as a temple-like symbol and domestic chores are treated as sacred rituals. Seemingly charged with the accumulations of long-gathering ancestral energy, Biggers' portraits of shotgun houses sug-

1 John Michael Vlach, *Afro-American Tradition in Decorative Arts* (Cleveland: Cleveland Museum of Art, 1978), 3.

2 Jessie Lott's sculptures which he describes as "an art of circumstances" has been featured in several outside art exhibits across the United States.

gest a transcendent metaphysical relationship between people, house, and place. The shotgun house is one room wide, one story tall, several rooms deep, has its primary entrance in the gable end, and has no hallways. The term "shotgun" was coined because one could shoot a bullet straight through the house without penetrating any walls, and its linear plan also made the narrow houses well-suited for cross ventilation in the tropical climates where they proliferated.

According to American folk culture historian John Michael Vlach, the shotgun house was introduced to the U.S. by free Haitians who settled in New Orleans after the Haitian slave rebellion against the French in the early nineteenth century. Essentially, the Haitians reconnected African-Americans with the socially intimate housing that many historians believe evolved from the narrow, one-room units of the Yoruba compound in West Africa—where most Americanized slaves originated. The form of the shotgun house reflects the value placed on extended family in traditional African society and a reverence for one's ancestors. In contrast to the western model of aggressive individuality, African culture promotes the interwoven lives of family and clan members to the point that boundaries between self, family, and community are ambiguous. A person is viewed as being born into a society that is at the very source of his being. Like Buddhism, traditional African beliefs assume the continuity of generations—believing that ancestors are reborn in the young. Although a person is an individual, he or she is not an autonomous individual. African-American aesthetic values grew out of this complex belief system that interweaves the bonds of family, the continuing influence of the ancestor on the descendant, and the connection of the human spirit to one's earthly dwelling place. The architecture of the Yoruba compound demonstrated the lack of importance the Africans placed on the individual within the

*right: **Shotguns Fourth Ward**, 1987, **John Biggers, artist, acrylic and oil on board,** Hampton University Museum, Hamptopn, VA

dwelling unit. The emphasis was instead on the celebration of family life and the development of interpersonal relationships. Mostly used for sleeping, the one room units of the Yoruba compound surrounded a large communal space where day-to-day activities took place.[3] Even as it was transformed by Caribbean and European building techniques, the shotgun house continued to express the enduring social values and cultural traditions of generations of African-Americans. For newly freed African-Americans emulating the shotgun house type of the free Haitian community, it was not only a symbol of their emancipation, but also a means of defining themselves as a united community outside of the confines of slavery.

A SPIRITUALLY PROTECTED LANDSCAPE

I have seen things that neither Beckett, nor Ionesco nor any of the others could have thought possible; and to see these things I did not need to do more than look out of my studio window above the Apollo Theater on 125th Street. So you see, this experience allows me to represent in the means of today, another view of the world.[4] —Romare Bearden

American cultural historian, Grey Gundaker, writes that for the early African-Americans the establishment of a dwelling place meant building a secure place not only for one's children, but also for one's ancestral memory. Burial rituals symbolized the preservation of this memory for present and future generations.[5] West Africans brought to the U.S. as slaves believed that death was merely a transition to a more powerful spiritual realm. The Kongo cosmogram—a cross, inscribed inside a circle or diamond—symbolizes the continuous cycle of life and death in traditional West African culture. Within this continuous cycle of life, it is believed that the dead exist in the more powerful realm and are able to manipulate good or evil in the world of the living. Remnants of this belief system, overlapping with Christian beliefs forged under slavery, persisted in African-American burial practices well into the twentieth century. Believed to contain fragments of the deceased's spiritual self, the last-used possessions of the dead were inverted on the grave site to direct the spirit to the world of the dead

3 John Michael Vlach, "Sources of the Shotgun House: African and Caribbean Antecedents for Afro-American Architecture," Vols. 1 and 2, (Ph.D diss., Indiana University, 1975).

4 Bearden, Romare, Campbell and Patton, *Memory and Metaphor: The Art of Romare Bearden* (New York: The Studio Museum in Harlem, 1991), 44.

5 Gundaker Grey, "What Goes Around Comes Around: Temporal Cycles and Recycling in African-American Yard Work," *Recycled Re-Seen: Folk Art from the Global Scrap Heap,* (New York: Harry N. Abrams, Inc. 1996), 79.

that mirrored our own. Through their root systems, which could travel deep through the earth surface, trees were thought to be a source of connection to the dead. Spirits were not only to be feared, but could also be called upon for healing and guidance in earthly matters. The nsiki, a portable charm or shrine made of roots, stones, and grave dirt[6] could be activated by the spirit of one's ancestors for the healing and protection of its owner.

The landscape depicted by Biggers emerged from a collective memory of this protected environment: the "dressed yard" in which ordinary domestic elements are transformed through contact with natural elements into protective charms to ward off evil spirits that might threaten the household. Hung from trees, brightly colored bottles are believed to bring rain, make trees bloom, bring luck, and entrap evil. Articles like broom straws and rice grains act as sieves filtering evil spirits. Paths through the yard are made to meander, and in many instances the doors in the linear shotgun were shifted because "evil travels in straight lines." Art historian Robert Farris Thompson refers to Biggers' *Shotguns* as a "nsiki painting" created for spiritual healing and compares it to Grant Wood's *American Gothic*:

On the front porch of each of the five closest shotgun houses appears a key feature of traditional African-American yard art: vessels by the door. They stand for African-American culture in practical, domestic acts: preparing soap, cooking pork, bathing infants. But they also signify covert spiritual protection, Grant Wood's pitchfork taken underground. The pot before the door cooks or contains more than meets the eye. It metaphysically caparisons the traditional African American yard and houses, as do African-American bottle trees and bottle shelves and bottle-lined walks and garden beds."[7]

The work of contemporary African-American yard-artists recalls this mystical connection between man, his dwelling place, and daily life. In the hands of African-American folk artists, guided by divine insight, discarded household goods take on new meanings beyond mere make-do decoration. Gundaker writes: *In African-American yard work [recycled materials] permit profound meanings to recycle through virtually whatever comes to*

6 Robert Farris Thompson, *Flash of the Spirit, Afro and Afro-American Art and Philosophy,* (New York: First Vintage Books Edition, 1984), 117–119.

7 Thompson, 108.

hand. By creating new configurations out of formerly divergent components, the makers of yards establish networks of associations between objects and ideas, cueing and channeling interpretations without closing down alternative readings. One such network of associations is, logically, the grave, the burial mound. A commonplace [association] of recycling as a mode of expression is that objects that have died through being discarded are 'reborn' when put to new uses."[8]

Houston Third Ward artist Robert Harper (who lived only blocks away from the Project Row House site until his house burned) continuously tinkered with the three-dimensional collage of wheels and hubcaps in his front yard. A consistent theme of Harper's art and the African-American dressed yard is circular movement and motion, which are concepts intertwined with cultural ideas of beauty and a belief in the ever continuing cycle of life as articulated by the Kongo cosmogram. Objects that move in the wind, like Harper's wheels, are decorated and treated as special objects that communicate the power of unseen spiritual forces. The role of the artist in African society and in African-American culture is that of intercessory between the divine spirit and man and the dressed yard acts as a kind of visual prayer. The aesthetic experience lies with the ability of the viewer to perceive an otherworldly presence. Created from salvaged, discarded objects, these gardens reveal the connection of our everyday lives to our existential essence. Art, life, land, philosophy, religion, and politics are interconnected with the divine spark that Thompson calls "the flash of the spirit": an improvisational individuality informed by a transcendent spiritual presence that energizes all of African-American culture and creates a powerful resistance to total Western encapsulation.

PROJECT ROW HOUSES

I see them as I walk the Third Ward of Houston, the rhythm of their shadow, the square of the porch, three over four like the beat of a visual gospel.[9] —John Biggers

As with Biggers's *Shotguns*, the striking presence of the Project Row House site comes from the repetition of the houses' spare, identical elements: factory made double-hung windows, standard-sized wooden attic grills, prefabricated concrete steps, and a single

8 Gundaker, 79.

9 Thompson, 23–30.

right: **Project Row Houses, detail;** *opposite:* **Exterior Courtyard, Project Row Houses.**

square post on the front porch that link the houses to the directness and minimalism of modern architectural expression. Devoid of ornamentation, the houses reveal rhythm, interval, scale, and proportion that, without affectation, restore the connection between the experience of art and architecture. While the stark, rough appearance of the shotgun house is usually associated with "financial lack," the minimalist expression of the shotgun house, as depicted by Biggers, is not one of real need, but rather a renunciation of luxury and display and has taken on an aura of spiritual discipline not unlike that of the Japanese tea house. In Biggers's *Shotguns* "the female figures clasp tiny versions of the houses held like lanterns to guard the purity of the people." The flying birds in the upper left corner and the vertical washboards on the porches symbolize ascension to the heavens.[10]

The modest 600-square foot, one-story houses are elevated on stone footings and are separated by side yards only three feet wide. The shotgun unit in and of itself lacks significance and gathers meaning from its relationship to the whole: the identical elevations of each in a row of shotgun houses create a sense of collective identity. Front porches transform the street edge into a public gathering space. One row of houses faces a major thoroughfare, the other faces a narrow alley. The two rows of houses frame an outdoor courtyard. Much of life on the Project Row House site, not unlike the Yoruba compound, took place outside the tiny houses in the collective outdoor

10 Thompson, 108.

"room" framed by the two rows of houses. Punctuated by large trees, rusted clothes-line posts, and the porches that Biggers called "talking places" where men can discuss the meaning of the Bible, this common green space gives the site a distinctive rural character although it is located in what has become an inner city neighborhood. While the houses are in fact more of a hybrid form of the shotgun house and the com-pressed bungalow, with gabled tin roof tops, long narrow plans and shallow rear porches, the project's clapboard houses are typical of the shotgun house in their gen-eral appearance. The Third Ward houses represent one of the many variations on the shotgun house found in African-American communities across the country. By the time the project's houses were built in the late 1930s, the shotgun house had been nationally adopted as an affordable housing type. The Third Ward was a flourishing business district, and the neighborhood's population was evenly split between African Americans and immigrant whites. Frank and Katie Trombatore, an immigrant Italian couple, developed the site as rental properties adjacent to the corner two-story store-front where they lived and operated a grocery store.

When Rick Lowe stumbled upon the site of identical shotgun houses in the Third Ward, he felt its resonance with Biggers' paintings and the housing of the com-munity; "the physical houses have relevance to the people in the area, those who grew up in the houses or lived near them." Since Lowe conceived of the housing site as a potential public art project, each of the houses have been opened to the public with revolving art installations. Artists spend six-month residences at the site and in the surrounding community developing concepts to transform a single house. The vitality of domestic life still exists on the Project Row Houses site: seven of the abandoned houses have been adapted as living spaces for single mothers who are in the process of completing their high school or college degrees. The remaining houses have been converted into spaces for community service programs.

ART FOR THE SOUL

A world through art in which the validity of my Negro experience would live and make its own logic.[11]

For Project Row Houses the shotgun house acts as a transparent, accessible material link to the African-American past that connects not only art and life, but also the particulars of the African-American experience to universal truths. The site and houses provide an infrastructure of content to which the artist must respond. With the space of the houses as a backdrop the artist has an opportunity to transcend the personal by providing a window onto a set of collective cultural values expressed by the shotgun house type.

Before the restoration of the houses was completed, artist Jessie Lott transformed the boarded-over windows of the houses into a collective canvas for the work of individual artists, the first art show on the site, "A Drive-By Exhibit." This inaugural exhibition set the stage for the project's challenge to individual artists: to interweave personal visions with those of the community vis-à-vis the unique form and space of the shotgun house—echoing the traditional African artisan's creative process of melding collective values and personal visions. Biggers' *Shotguns* capture this philosophy in the imagery of the collective identity of the shotgun house that contrasts sharply with the individuality of the women on the porches and improvisational quality of the dressed yards in the foreground.

Drawing upon the direct experience of the house in her installation *Recollections,* Annette Lawrence created one of the project's most holistic yet personal expressions of art, place, and culture. Preferring the purity of a single vaulted space, Lawrence removed the house's interior partitions and ceiling, exposing its wooden rafters. She

11 Romare Bearden in Campbell
and Patton, 44.

finished the roof and walls with sheetrock, creating a light, pristine space interrupted only by the remains of a brick chimney. The space was layered with vertical planes of strings strung from the rafters to the floor. Woven between the harp-like strings are tiny paper bag notebooks made by neighborhood children, who tell their own story of the community. Lawrence, whose work often has musical overtones, compares her stringed installation to the "inside of a piano" and "bars of music." "I wanted my piece to be as light as possible and quiet. The strings in my piece refer to the lines of clapboard siding on the houses." Lawrence's delicate installation seems like a melody played against the heavier cadence established by the rhythm of the identical houses along the street.

Many of the artists' installations transform the houses with narratives and metaphysical metaphors, echoing reoccurring themes of spiritual healing in the African-American yard-art. Artist Tierney Malone transformed the shotgun house into a mythical drugstore, *Hope Apothecary*, a rich installation of rooms filled with bottles and cans containing various potions for curing the ills of the community. Stacked on shelves, Malone's containers are collaged with images of African-American heroes like Langston Hughes and Jackie Robinson and juxtaposed with scenes of poverty and violence. The installation was created as a reflection upon the "societal, spiritual, and

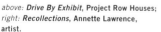

*above: **Drive By Exhibit**, Project Row Houses;
right: **Recollections**, Annette Lawrence,
artist.*

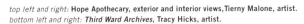
top left and right: **Hope Apothecary, exterior and interior views,**Tierny Malone, artist.
*bottom left and right: **Third Ward Archives**,* Tracy Hicks, artist.

psychological problems we face as a country and as individuals." Malone left the walls as they were: rough and textured with bent nails, staples and remnants of wall and newspaper recalling the African-American tradition of "dressing" the house to ward off evil spirits. The rooms, filled with beautifully detailed and well crafted collaged containers, transcend the sentiment and nostalgia of the artist's message.

In another house the "spirits" of the community members are captured on film with disposable cameras disbursed throughout the neighborhood. The photographs framed inside mason jars echoed themes of the nsiki, the spirit-evoking containers for the healing and protection of its owner. According to artist Tracy Hicks, the "spiritual guidance the community members seek is found within themselves." The mason jars are stacked on free-standing shelves. Filtering the heat and light from the windows the house takes on an other-worldly presence.

George Smith, an artist-in-residence at Rice University, has often alluded to African and African-American burial rites and traditions in his sculpture. Like Biggers, Smith has interpreted the narrow form of the house as an ancestral shrine:

> *this shrine represents an African-American interpretation of the Mbari shrines that are built by the Ibo people of Nigeria. These public shrines were used for celebration whenever it was felt that a community needed spiritual renewal or strengthening after a crisis caused by drought, war, famine or similar adversity.*[12]

Smith, in an early study for his house-shrine, explored the domestic link between African-American house and grave. In keeping with the African-American tradition of placing broken, inverted cups, saucers, dishes, and other possessions of the deceased over the grave site to keep the spirit content, Smith created a sacred ring of broken white dishes in the middle of the house. "Gathering together to eat is life-affirming and china was always the family's most revered possession," he notes. Smith's idea of creating a shrine to African-American ancestors evolved into the construction of a wood-frame altar around a brick chimney that was once connected to a wood stove, providing warmth in the winter and a means for cooking.

12 George Smith, *Project Row Houses*, (Artists Notes, April, 1995).

Its [recycled materials] just cast off stuff people throw away. Like people who've been cast off, and everybody thinks that they're worth nothing—I've been there. Beat up, broken down at the bottom. But I had this dream in my head, and that made me more than a piece of junk.[13]

Ultimately however, the project is less concerned with the individual work of art than it is with its ability to transform an economically and socially depressed community. Project Row Houses founder Rick Lowe, like artist John Biggers, has always believed that art was capable of the healing and transformation of the human spirit. Now considered one of Houston's pockets of poverty, the Third Ward's economic and social depression is evidenced by the large numbers of boarded up and abandoned houses and empty lots scattered throughout the neighborhood. Despite thriving African-American churches and public institutions, the neighborhood's lack of a viable private enterprise has fostered a high unemployment rate and its associated ills—poverty crime, deteriorating housing, and poor health care for the community's citizens. Lowe says: "One cannot be a victim [of situations and circumstances] while participating in the creative act." Jessie Lott explains: "when one transforms a discarded article into a work of art, one transforms and gives new life to himself." Art and imagination are the means of revealing the beauty in an object once its function is gone. Inherent in this act of restoration is the African-American theology of birth, death, and redemption.

The soulfulness of the African-American-landscape comes from the common-place convergence of matter and spirit in everyday life, providing a subtle but potent resistance to a western technocratic way of life. The art and architecture of Project Row Houses is a powerful visual and spatial expression of the spirit-filled way of being that informs the whole of African-American life and reveals to us the interconnectedness of things: of culture and circumstance, of past and future, of the individual and the collective, of the everyday and the existential.

13 Charlie Lucas, an Alabama sculptor, quoted in "What Goes Around Comes Around: Temporal Cycles and Recycling in African-American Yard Work," *Recycled Re-Seen: Folk Art from the Global Scrap Heap* (New York: Harry N. Abrams, Inc. 1996), 81.

twelve   storing memories in the yard

REMAKING POPLAR STREET, THE SHIFTING BLACK CULTURAL LANDSCAPE

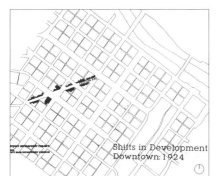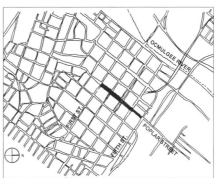

(top left and right) **African-American urban settlement patterns, downtown Macon, 1924; downtown Macon, 1997.**
(bottom left and right) **Existing view of Poplar Street, 1997.**

NARRATIVE I	Time	Characters/ Locations	Rep. Jeffrey Long,
	1926	The Walton family,	*(first black elected*
		(notable black	*to U.S. House of*
	Setting	*Victorian family)*	*Representatives.)*
	Downtown:	The Hutchings family,	Iola Bailey,
	Cotton Avenue	*(funeral home owner)*	*(beauty parlor owner)*
		The Duvall family,	Mile's Café
		(upholsterers)	Kyle's Drug Store
			Mose Miles,
			(pharmacist)

African-American businesses along Cotton Avenue, 1930s. Reprinted from *Macon's Black Heritage*, Tubman African American Museum (Macon, GA, 1997).

Macon, Georgia is a city of boulevards. Wide canyons made of brick. They form a pattern that resembles an 'H.' If we assume lore and tale are true, then the ancient city of Babylon emerges before our eyes. The boulevards only fill up when people come out with their objects and transport. They empty when people go away, taking their things with them. The most magnificent sight is when bales of cotton come to town. Bound in burlap, they instantaneously metamorphose, occupying the middle of the boulevard.

The only street that follows its own path is Cotton Avenue They say it was a native Indian trail that led to the Ocmulgee River. It cuts the terrain, slashing deliberately through the orthogonal city grid. As you stand at the highest point along Cotton Avenue looking downhill toward the river, you see that a bustling black aristocracy has built churches, law offices, and commercial businesses. Standing in opposition to City Hall's neoclassical girth, the site seems to be consciously overlooking the industrious freedmen and women.

MACON YARDS Macon is situated in the once mighty agricultural black belt of middle Georgia. The city's architecture is a mix of old and new buildings featuring the highest percentage of antebellum buildings in the American south and the recently constructed State of Georgia's Music Hall of Fame and Sports Hall of Fame. Macon's black history is chronicled in literature and local museums highlighting its indigenous musicians; namely, Little Richard, Lena Horne, and Otis Redding. But between the lines of historic texts, museum exhibitions, and rhythm and blues lyrics and licks, and in the stones of new and old buildings, reside deeper memories of a city where cotton was king. De Certeau characterizes this juxtaposition of old historic relics and the common rituals of daily life as a haunted landscape—one that can tell a story through its memory.[1] As it turned out, the kings were white and the paupers were black. Racial and social injustice prevailed; strong black businesses thrived and failed as the landscape of urban blacks became characterized by instability and mobility. A shifting black landscape emerged from institutional displacement of the black working class and gentry. This landscape of work and play can be documented over time, revealing causal effects of racial injustice, planning, and class perpetuated fears. Contemporarily, the shifting landscape has come to rest on Poplar Street in downtown Macon. I characterize this as the backyard of downtown Macon. Whether cotton bales, markets, fire stations, clubs and bars, or parking occupied the street, Poplar Street's functions have remained a place for storing the city's everyday rituals and memories. These histories and events create a different lens to observe the contemporary black street life of Poplar Street that is organized around public parking and a meager transit system.

(*left*) **View of Poplar Street with parks, 1910.**
(*above*) **Cotton bales down middle of Second Street, Macon, Georgia, 1905. Both photos reprinted from Vickie Leach Prater,** *Macon in Vintage Postcards* **(Charleston: 1999).**

1 Michel De Certeau, Luce Giard and Pierre Mayol, *The Practice of Everyday Life*, (Minneapolis: University of Minnesota Press,1998).

The analogy of Poplar Street as the city's backyard provides a framework to better understand cultural transformations that have a direct influence on the design and use of Macon's urban landscape. The yard, as a landscape type can be examined within this context, focusing specifically on its cultural attributes and utility, while serving as the link between the past and present. The southern yard typology is employed as a cultural vessel and receptacle in the current re-making of the street's public landscape. This appropriated landscape type is the vehicle for an improvisational design process that is at once gesture and archive. Utilizing this gestalt in the design process it is possible to uncover the city's cultural past while rehabilitating present and future memories within a familiar context—stabilizing the once shifting landscape in which blacks and others occupy Macon's downtown.

YARD AS ARCHIVE The yard is particularly endemic to the understanding of everyday southern life and domestic landscape. The yard in southern culture hosts common and everyday rituals in connection with the home. The southern yard can at once be a garden, a place to while away the day, a landscape of cultivation and utility, and a landscape where personal objects are collected, displayed, and sometimes forgotten. The yard is seen as an archive. De Certeau writes, "Gestures are the true archives of the city, if one understands by 'archives' the past that is selected and reused according to present custom. They remake the urban landscape every day. They sculpt a thousand pasts that are perhaps no longer namable and that structure no less their experience of the city." [2] Although the yard is an abstract concept when we think of the urban street, its many meanings and functions can be reused as a framework for making new histories.

Reviewing the etymology of yard we ascertain that it is derived from the Old English word "geard," which meant "to enclose," and in Old High German its derivation was "gart"—meaning "garden". Cultural geographer Paul Groth writes, "by the 1500s, urban writers in England commonly used the phrase "house and yard," and noted that one could keep dogs or a cow in the yard." [3] He further states that there are historic English examples of yards adjacent to aristocratic houses in the 1500–1600s and that by the early 1700s the term yard also described great sweeping spaces around

2 Ibid, 141–142.

3 Paul Groth, "Lot, Yard & Garden," *Landscape* 30, no. 3, (1990): 29.

4 Ibid, 30.

country houses. His description reinforces the yard's etymological transformation. Most importantly, Groth suggests that yard is situated in the triad of American urban landscape types: the lot, yard, and garden. "When we call something a yard, it generally implies more value than something called a lot. In turn, we often treasure something called a garden."[4] In the southern landscape this triad is not always clear as seen in Richard Westmacott's seminal study *African-American Yards and Gardens in the Rural South* (1992) and Richard Wilhelm's *Dooryard Gardens and Gardening in the Black Community of Brushy, Texas* (1975). Both studies describe a hybrid meaning and use for the yard, inferring that it is a landscape valued for functional purposes and also a treasured garden landscape.

The yard's importance as an everyday cultural landscape coupled with the ephemeral nature of Macon's black cultural landscape is further diffused by particular memories of a segregated Macon. However, particular episodic narratives from the past can force a bond with new memories by articulating the yard's spatial and social construct within a new setting. Moving from archive to gesture, it is possible to activate the site's history, altering the cultural backdrop from which to engage a collective and not segregated past. Aldo Rossi quotes Halbwachs's *La Mémoire Collective,* stating, "When a group is introduced into a part of a space, it transforms it to its image, but at the same time, it yields and adapts itself to certain material things which resist it. It encloses itself in the framework that it has constructed. The image of the exterior environment and the stable relationships that it maintains with it pass into the realm of the idea that it has of itself."[5] Thus, the yard as archive is a tangible landscape that holds specific cultural memories. The yard as archive weaves new black cultural narratives with the old, rendering a new gesture to remake the Poplar Street landscape.

5 Aldo Rossi, *The architecture of the City.* trans. Diane Ghirardo and Joan Ockman, (Cambridge,: MIT Press, 1982) 130.

Hog gutting in a southern yard. Reprinted from Richard Westmacott, *African-American Gardens and Yards in the Rural South* (Knoxville: University of Tennessee Press, 1992).

Blind blues guitarist in downtown Macon. Reprinted from
Macon's Black Heritage.

STREET AS ARCHIVE "Can you imagine people no longer making music, painting, making pictures, dancing ... ? Everybody would answer no to this." [6] Rob Krier ponders this question, addressing the street as an urban typology. Surely, this is a question more relevant to the European community than for American communities. This is not to say that American cities do not contain streets where people act out artistically and socially. Most American cities feature special or counter-cultural streets where true democracy can be found: South Street in Philadelphia, Telegraph Avenue in Berkeley, Bourbon Street in New Orleans, and almost any street in Manhattan. But these are far from the norm in most city neighborhoods. Contemporary American streets have been de-democratized, redesigned by modern engineering practices in order to facilitate our penchant for the automobile. The car has become more important than people. We can imagine people no longer making music, painting, making pictures.

Aside from the streets mentioned above, there are others that can be examined for their rich cultural life and everyday expressions. These are the streets that pass through ethnic enclaves. They portray social patterns usually deemed unsightly, disorderly, and counter to the norm. They are street landscapes where democracy is practiced in the everyday. Whether Latino, Asian, or in black working-class enclaves, the streets are cacophonous landscapes where cultural patterns and practices win out. In contrast,

6 Rob Krier, *Urban space*
(New York: Rizzoli, 1979) 20–21.

they are not Elm Street, the tree-lined bucolic ideal with picket fences and neat lawns, or the commercial street with ubiquitous site elements. Our tendency in the last century has been to clean up this democracy by legislating their design, in order to reform human use. Under the pretext of streetscape design, use is standardized and subordinated to the automobile's circulation and storage.

Idiosyncratic use and appropriation of the street by common folk is the true archive. For many Americans similar practices were abandoned at childhood. In association with the yard, street use in ethnic enclaves represents an archive that is slowly disappearing. In Macon, Georgia, Broadway Street existed in the mid-twentieth century before becoming Martin Luther King Boulevard. Looking at specific time periods the street in this ethnic enclave is a lens to understanding the tragic life and death of a black cultural landscape, but most of all, Broadway as archive uncovers what was, and what most Maconites still remember.

NARRATIVE II	Time	Characters	Butterbeans
	1950	Little Richard	and Susie
		James Brown	Cab Calloway
	Setting	Otis Redding	Duke Ellington
	Downtown:	Bessie Smith	
	Broadway Street	Ma Rainey	

Broadway is a black nexus. A cacophony of movement and sound fill the muggy August night. It is a landscape of filling stations, motels, hotels, theaters, dance halls, clubs, bars, flop houses, and used car lots. White Maconites go out of their way to avoid the density of blackness.

This is the black side of downtown. People strut their stuff, unconstrained by the predicament of segregation. As soon as people arrive from the train and bus, they are entertained by the melodious rhythms of everyday activities. By day everyone seems to be preparing for the night, getting haircuts and straightenings, shopping, or working. They anticipate when the work will be done.

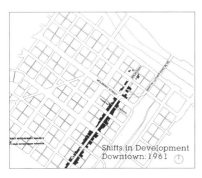

(left) African-American urban settlement patterns, downtown Macon, 1961. *(right)* 1959 view of Douglass Theatre on Broadway. Reprinted from *Macon's Black Heritage.*

On Broadway you find the Douglass Theatre. They say that Bessie Smith sang here. On any night names synonymous with blues or R & B grace the stage. It is a southern version of New York's 42nd Street—hot blues to go with hot nights.

Broadway Street's transformation reveals urban redevelopment under the guise of progress as the tool for dismantling black cultural life. Regional transportation routes between Savannah and Atlanta emphasized Macon's geographical location along the I-75 corridor, a corridor that eventually replaced train and bus service. Here, suggestions of the processes responsible for urban restructuring are illuminated. Suburbanization, the emergence of the rent gap, and demographic changes in consumption patterns eventually led to the erosion of Macon's urban core. Housing and business divestments in the city center increased as money shifted to new edge developments. Racial strife was exacerbated by new visions of the city modernizing at the expense of the black community. In addition, the rural to urban migration patterns concentrated on urban areas speeding their erosion by overcrowding and intensified use. Tensions increased further as fewer jobs existed for unskilled workers—jobs moved to the urban edge where cheap land facilitated the building of factories for efficiency. Retail followed the move to suburbia and, coupled with the systematic dismembering of mass-transit, made travel impossible without an automobile. During this time period development in Macon stretched across the Ocmulgee River east of the city center and along Interstate 16 connecting to Interstate 75. Public spaces and dwellings overrunning with black citizens and thriving businesses were prime targets for redevelopment utilizing blight as a rationale. To blacks, Broadway was their entertainment district, but to city fathers it was a slum that needed cleaning up.

The landscape of Broadway was reconfigured, beginning with the redesign of the street. The street was increased in size and buildings deemed blighted were removed. A two-lane paired roadway was inserted, breaking away from the city's historical grid. A large suburban style intersection was created at the intersection with Mulberry Street, connecting Broadway to 5th Street and onto Interstate 16. Most of the businesses along Broadway were impacted by this development, leaving only one major building that city leaders saw as the most important memory worth saving, the Douglas Theater. The theater eventually closed and later would be refurbished and renovated as a historical and civic building.

Black businesses along Broadway never regained their physical and spatial form and pattern. The mix of entertainment, commercial, and residential uses that sustained and created a distinct cultural episode in the black history of Macon would be lost forever—giving way to an automobile landscape. Broadway's name would eventually change to Martin Luther King Boulevard. As in other cities the street that bears King's name is central to redevelopment and modernization projects that were prevalent after the time of his assassination. They became places that were structurally improved at the expense of cultural life.

Etched in black Americans' memory are streets and places such as Birdland on 42nd Street, Slim Jenkins on 7th Street, the Fillmore district, Harlem, and Beale Street to name a few. They were streets and places where black culture acted out in a time of segregated rule. They were black landscapes. When the landscape shifted, the music stopped. The ghosts of Bessie Smith, Duke Ellington, Ma Rainey, and Little Richard haunt Martin Luther King Boulevard in Macon, Georgia. It is no longer a street. The engineers call it a connector. Driving through this landscape it is visually and physically impossible to imagine the heyday of black cultural life. Gone are the continuous building walls along the street and, in their place, large parking lots and post-modern buildings occupy large lots. But the memory of Broadway lives on in the minds of most black residents. The contemporary black nexus has moved to Poplar Street. But unlike its predecessor the street has failed to bring back the music. Each chance has been thwarted by aggressive politics and deep-seated prejudice that remembers Broadway Street. But, more important, it is a different street...it is a boulevard, 180 feet wide. Times have changed; Poplar Street is a parking lot and the buildings are empty. Utilizing the street archive as a link to the past, Poplar Street can be remade to reflect an understanding that streets are for people. Streets are the last democratic public space. Merging the yard and street archive into one landscape brings the past forward into the present day, thus exorcising the ghosts that haunt the city landscape.

Narratives emerge from the cultural context that haunts Macon's urban fabric. The yard and street as archive hold past memories that reside deep in the subconscious; as gesture, it binds previous episodes, current use, and future dreams. It is possible to interpret Macon's physical landscape through the research of Sanborn Fire Insurance maps. Once the physical remains of Macon's black cultural heritage are uncovered, they can be pieced together to tell a story that begins with the city's origins and its transformation to the current-day landscape. In contrast, written and oral histories and archival photographs present story and tale, illuminating the other cultural landscape that exists in the subconscious of black Maconites. Selected narratives can reveal liminal episodes that actively contribute to the city's story through remembering.

LANDSCAPE AS MEMORY The prospect of uncovering a particular episode from the past relies on the ability to trigger the mind to remember what was. "In our everyday lives, memory is a natural, perhaps automatic, by-product of the manner in which we think about an unfolding episode."[7] Unfolding implies that episodes are not static but dynamic recollections. They are encoded and retrieved, evoking the exploration of stored memories.

Henri Bergson suggests that "whenever we are trying to recover a recollection, to call up some period of our history, we become conscious of an act sui generis by which we detach ourselves from the present in order to replace ourselves, first, in the past in general, then in a certain region of the past—a work of adjustment, something like the focusing of a camera."[8] Memory, like a camera, zooms in and out of focus and

7 Daniel L. Schacter, *Searching for Memory: The Brain, The mind and The Past* (New York: Basic Books, 1996), 45.

8 Henri Bergson, *Matter and Memory*, trans. Nancy Margaret Paul and W. Scott Palmer, (London: G. Allen & Co. Ltd., 1929), 133.

frame of reference; images and place unfold from the subconscious only when present day events, places, and things trigger past episodes.

Landscapes inhabited by blacks in downtown Macon, Georgia, during the last hundred years represent meager holdings in the present-day city surroundings. Their sum does not constitute a landscape to trigger particular environmental episodes from the cultural past. Dismantled and erased, the black landscape is shadowed by Macon's more formal and more grand Victorian and neo-classical landscapes. As well-preserved memories, the formal landscapes are set aside like cherished family portraits. Collectively, they are framed and in focus, reconstructed for us to remember a particular past. The other landscapes, inhabited and created by blacks, are nothing more than a scattered set of memorials and disparate historic buildings. They are not included in the family portraits. A collage of discrete artifacts, these remnants stand in odd juxtaposition to their evolving built surroundings and preserved antebellum memories, a telling tale of fragmented cultural and social change. Though meager landscapes and artifacts remain, we can encode their specific past from the social and built memory of Macon's black inhabitants. These dynamic episodes live on through story, tale, and historic artifacts and archives. Blacks have labored in Macon as artisans, builders, and professionals; their contributions are literally in the stones and mortar of the built landscape. Old cotton warehouses, asphalt streets that suppress beneath them hand-made bricks from the local kilns, restored vaudeville era theaters, and single-bay office buildings bear testimony to Macon's black heritage. The shadow of their past life haunts the contemporary built environment.

Kenneth Foote explains in *Shadowed Ground* that the "concept of memory provides an important bond between culture and landscape, because human modifications of the environment are often related to the way societies wish to sustain or efface memories."[9] The dominant society in Macon throughout the twentieth century effaced the landscapes created and maintained by blacks. This speaks directly to cultural fragmentation and racial segregation. Its implicit impact and manifestation in the landscape is separate landscapes, one black and the other white. Modification and change to Macon's downtown in the twentieth century are manifested within the context of segregated societal views and memories.

Tourist brochure
cover page

9 Kenneth E. Foote, *Shadowed Ground. America's Landscapes of Violence and Tragedy*, (Austin: University of Texas Press, 1997), 33.

Most notable from a review of these landscapes is that the dismantling of black institutions and businesses follows the story of many black southern communities during the same time period. The causal agents, primarily economics, class, and racism, precipitated the movement of blacks to grounds unoccupied and unwanted by whites. This created the beginning of a shifting cultural landscape. Emblematic of the fragmentation caused by steady migration and uprooting, the black cultural landscape today is represented by selective memories and histories drawn from artifacts left behind. However, they present a skewed nostalgia. Macon's black heritage is preserved in the landscape exogenously. Only particular physical landscapes and artifacts were deemed important for preservation by the city's administration. Everyday landscapes that hold the memories of blacks were not preserved.

This story is not an isolated one; it is true for many urban landscapes inhabited by blacks throughout the twentieth century in America. Borchert describes the northern migration of blacks to the back alleys of Washington, D.C. and their successive demise and change;[10] Crouchett describes the demise of the 7th Street entertainment and commercial centerpiece in West Oakland, California, due to infrastructure development.[11] In both cases urban blacks shifted their place of residence. The shifting urban landscape, by its very nature, makes difficult the accretion of collective memories. Sites are scattered and lost, leaving the concentration of shared memories diluted.

Macon's black cultural landscape is dynamic and episodic despite a history of obstacles. The region has a long history of slavery and racial discrimination. Institutional planning and urban restructuring processes physically fractured the black downtown community. These conditions were further exacerbated by the decline of the southern agriculture economy, the boil weevil infestation, and the great migration[12] as people moved north for better means of income. Modern urban renewal, aggravated by race and class based planning, led to the further dismantling of the city's everyday black landscapes along Cotton Avenue, Broadway Street, and Poplar Street. In the end, simply because specific memories were not shared by all, the black landscape was modernized and improved, erasing a century of black occupation and progress.

A patchwork of pawn shops, boarded-up buildings, and check cashing stores supplement a bakery, barber, and beautician. Only one club is left on the street—Grants

10 James Borchert, *Alley Life in Washington: Family, Community, Religion, and Folklife in the City, 1850–1970* (Urbana: University of Illinois Press, 1988).

11 Lawrence P. Crouchett, *Visions Toward Tomorrow: The History of the East Bay Afro-American community 1852–1977* (Oakland: Northern California Center for Afro-American History and Life, 1989).

12 Donald L. Grant, *The Way It Was in the South: The Black Experience in Georgia* (New York: Birch Lane Press, 1993).

NARRATIVE III	Time	Characters	Doctors
	2000	Barbershop	Bus riders
		Club owner and	
	Setting	son Bakery	
	Downtown:	Marco Denese	
	Poplar Street		

Lounge. Inside, polaroids and snap shots define the Wall of Fame. The musicians and clubs are long gone—the polaroids are the only documentation.

The street is a parking lot from sidewalk to sidewalk, all 180 feet; 210 cars in all can be parked over three blocks. They say that pecan trees were planted here once; that a market and fire station graced the street; that parks flowed up the street's center; that a creek sprouted in the lower block; and that the mayor once brought a tank down the street to quiet the club rousers. It is hard to imagine these things when the sun is beaming down on you in July with no tree in sight. It is hard to imagine these things today.

Most of the people on the street are black. Most of the people on the street are waiting for the bus, under the wooden shelter, for good times. When I first visited downtown, my hosts never drove down Poplar Street. Instead we toured the mansions on the hill. I think they were ashamed to show me the street with the Daughters of the Confederacy obelisk and the black folks.

African-American urban settlement patterns, downtown
Macon, 1998. *(right)* Poplar Street bus shelters, 1996.

View of Biddy Mason Wall,
downtown Los Angeles,
1994.

GESTURES IN THE LANDSCAPE The small number of landscape projects recalling
and interpreting episodes from the American black cultural landscape have been futile
in their attempts to prompt memory of past events or episodes. Those created are static monuments and memorials that bear didactic displays in lieu of real landscape
experience. The Biddy Mason Park and Art Wall in downtown Los Angeles, for example, document the homestead and life of California's first midwife. The story is an
important one to California's black heritage and Mason's family. An eighty-one-foot
wall of narrative and images provides visitors with a historic account and placement of
the homestead. An image cast in stone of Mason's home and picket fence graces the
wall. Her portrait, which is also placed on the wall, is still clear in my memory. But
within the existing context, adjacent to a parking lot, the juxtaposition and setting
contribute very little to induce any episodic memory of a particular place and time.
Hayden writes, "set against a Masonic skyline, this small place devoted to history
encouraged a viewer to contemplate change on Spring Street in both space and
time."[13] The juxtaposition does force you to come to terms with the transformed landscape. However, the simple fact that Mason's homestead has been effaced, reduced to a
wall, leaves us to ponder why this ground, important enough to be singled out, does
not contribute to the contemporary landscape in a more integrated and interactive
way. Could the stones be assembled not as a static monument in time but as a part of
that new mid-block landscape?

13 Dolores Hayden, *The Power
of Place: Urban Landscapes as
Public History*, (Cambridge: MIT
Press, 1995), 187.

Nothing can replace real landscape experience. When we attempt to remake these landscapes, we must fully understand what we are trying to bring back. Michel de Certeau suggests that "renovation does not, ultimately, know what it is bringing back—or what it is destroying—when it restores the references and fragments of elusive memories. For these ghosts that haunt urban works, renovation can only provide a laying out of already marked stones, like words for it."[14] Once removed, the stones cannot be put back together in the same way. Their re-assembly gives way to the construction of new histories. The story evolves and changes. In Macon, the stones have been re-assembled to tell a story that is different than that remembered by black inhabitants.

Yearly, Americans flock to great European cities in multitudes to bathe in glorious histories and past memories that are literally written in the cities' stone and mortar. Returning home our environments seem sterile, void of the same richness. We yearn for the same qualitative experiences and connection to the past. What we cannot articulate or see in the environment is the simple fact that past histories have been subtracted out of our everyday landscape. Le Corbusier's mantra of "when the cathedrals were white" continues to haunt American renovation. The American modern landscape is characterized by the disregard for the old, whereas in mature cities and cultures of the world the past is valued even in the face of modernization. The stones are carefully subtracted and put back in place literally one by one. In time they change and give way to new memories as each stone is understood for its past and present contributions. In Rome, the twentieth century exists within the stones of emperors and popes. And within the walls of Raphael Moneo's Roman Artifact Museum in Merida, Spain, the visitor is immersed in a visual cacophony of Roman centurions marching along the roadway discovered beneath the city. As you view art works under the roof of a modern structure, past episodes come alive through juxtaposition and program. The past haunts the built environment and remains familiar to all visitors and inhabitants.

These thoughts suggest that maybe a more thoughtful and fruitful endeavor is to wed old, diverse, and disparate artifacts with newly constructed landscapes and built constructions. American society today more than ever requires a bond between cultures and a willingness to share memories. The most important and telling landscapes, those which are used everyday, are the landscapes least discussed or studied, yet they

14 de Certeau, 143.

are the sites that generate the strongest memories, the strongest associations with place and time. If these stones, the rebuilding blocks of collective memory, are removed, how do we reclaim them and reassemble them?

A bricolage approach, as illuminated in American vernacular building traditions and improvisational characteristics exhibited in African-American cultural arts,[15] can be a useful design strategy to extend the lineage of memory and time into the present landscape. Other black American cultural art forms reveal the process of improvisation as seen in the work of Bearden, Parker, and Ailey. They suggest ways to reverse normative trends and validate the existence of the other in our public landscapes.[16] This process does not seek to diminish or eradicate the existence of European cultural influences on the public landscape, but instead attempts to validate acculturation by utilizing the norm as a point of reference to begin an extemporaneous design exchange, introducing familiar spaces and objects based on other cultural experiences, social patterns, and practices. These strategies necessitate inclusion of the past through an additive design process, counter to normative site demolition and subtraction strategies.

Landscapes can incite episodic memories in the physical. Even though it is a subjective endeavor, this can present a proscenium for understanding setting, time, and place of spatially articulated social relations and landscapes, forcing us to recollect our past within the setting of the present. To fuse objects and space with the past a cultural backdrop must be in place to serve as a structure for juxtaposition. This does not mean that we simply mix together the old and new, but carefully commingle past and present through formal gestures and narrative. De Certeau writes of these two as a condition for a new urban aesthetic. They are chains of operations, like a spoken language. Improvisation facilitates personal expression and freedom within the structure of specific site and building design. De Certeau sees "two distinct modes, one tactical and the other linguistic."[17] He further explains that "gestures and narratives manipulate objects, displace them, and modify both their distributions and their uses."[18] Story can be distinguished from form, incorporating the physical landscape from the past and present through real landscape and built constructions, allowing narratives to reach back, extending the past to the present and future. In this way, we can clearly see where to place the fallen and misplaced stones.

15 John Michael Vlach, *The Afro-American Tradition in Decorative Arts* (Cleveland: Cleveland Museum of Art, 1978).

Robert Ferris Thompson, *Flash of the Spirit: African and Afro-American art and Philosophy* (New York: Random House, 1983).

16 David Sibley, *Geographies of Exclusion: Society and Difference in the West* (London: Routledge, 1995).

17 de Certeau 1998, 141.

18 Ibid, 141.

The project for the re-making of Poplar Street in Macon, Georgia, utilizes the yard and the street as historical archives to bridge the gap between the past and present. The yard is a simple gesture that refocuses the street into small identifiable spaces where people come together to socialize or for other leisure activities. Current uses such as parking and transit continue. They are juxtaposed with new building structures that sit atop previous building sites, water features that emanate from previous sources, spaces, and places where music can be played, and landscape elements and plantings can create space. The new objects and spaces take on new meanings through human use and change in context.

NARRATIVE IV	**Time**	**Characters**
	2002	Citizens of Macon
		Hood Design
	Setting	City of Macon
	Downtown:	Bibb County Road
	Poplar Street	Improvement Program

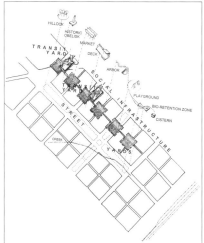

Hybrid street diagram

View of Yard #1 and Yard #2

YARD AND STREET AS GESTURE Located in the heart of the city of Macon, Poplar Street is a wide boulevard featuring public yards where automobiles, people, water, light, trees, and flowers create a cacophony of activity and sound. Storefronts of buildings are full of merchandise as tourists flock to buy souvenirs and southern edible delights. The building uses are mixed, featuring housing, retail, restaurants, and civic functions. The new transit system has buses and trolleys for locals and tourists.

The yards are synonymous with the street. As you walk up and down the sidewalk you notice spatially that activities and movement are taking place in the street itself.

On this day the yard has a market with a group of pickup trucks backed in selling apples. Another has a trellis structure with beautiful vines draping its center and big oak trees along the edges. Kids are running through the space chasing the butterflies that from a distance seem like blossoms in air. A local band is set up in another yard playing the blues on the porch structure. The latter is full of people reclining in yard chairs. The hot sun is reflecting off of the fountains that shoot water horizontally across the ground.

At the top of the hill, the obelisk dominates the yard where the water overflows into a big trough. The shadow and reflection make the yard seem full. At the bottom of the hill children are playing on the swing and racing sticks in the fountains that channel along for a block before disappearing into the ground.

There are a few strange and unfamiliar objects in the yards that hold your attention. The lights are big and animated like the windmills in George Ervin's yard; they are giant tripods. In several yards the ground appears to have been cut; big chunks of yellow rock are visible in wire cages on the ground. Along the cut's broadside the ground seems like a layer cake. You can see dirt, stone, brick, and asphalt as if someone sliced it in half with a knife. The fountains seem to be seeping the water out of the ground. They are like shallow wells that you do not need to pump. In certain places there seems to be some sort of old foundation walls. One is really big but the bus stop shelter sits on top of it in some places. The others fade out under the porch where the musicians are and along the sandbox where the kids are playing. They cannot be old foundations … they shine too much and are made of stone.

Looking up and down the street you see black and white alike, eating, playing, parking, walking, talking, and just hanging out in the yards.

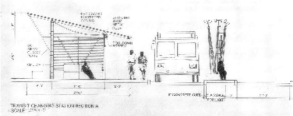

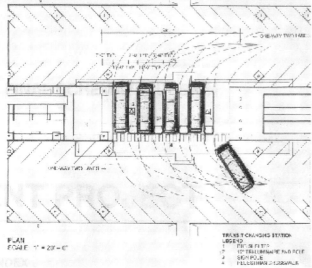

(clockwise from top) **Poplar Street looking towards City Hall; the transit changing station—elevation and plan.**

contributors' bios

CRAIG BARTON

Craig Barton is an associate professor of architecture and the Director of the Urban Studies program at the University of Virginia School of Architecture. Through his practice, scholarship, and teaching Mr. Barton investigates issues of race, African-American cultural practices and their implications in architectural and urban design. In collaboration with Marthe Rowen and others, he has completed various projects and competitions including the design of a museum and memorial for the National Voting Rights Museum. His work exploring constructions of race and identity has been widely presented and published.

NATHANIEL Q. BELCHER

Nathaniel Belcher is currently an assistant professor in the Department of Architecture at Florida International University. He has worked to establish the Jazz Architectural Works Shop, an independent research based program dedicated to the development of critical theoretical ideas and the production and documentation of objects/environments which recognize marginalized influences on architecture and its related disciplines. He has lectured on architecture as it relates to African-American culture, and on modern architecture in Brazil.

DAVID P. BROWN

David P. Brown is an assistant professor of architecture at Rice University. He is currently working on a book, *Noise Orders: Jazz, Modernization and Modernity*. By examining the work of the AACM, Louis Armstrong, John Cage, Le Corbusier, Ralph Ellison, Rashaan Roland Kirk, Meade "Lux" Lewis, Piet Mondrian, Toni Morrison, and Mies van der Rohe, this work identifies some of the structures and thought that facilitate improvisation and speculates on their potential application to architecture and urbanism.

MELISSA ERIKSON

Melissa Erikson is a graduate student in landscape architecture at UC-Berkeley.

FELECIA DAVIS

Felecia Davis, is an assistant professor at Cornell University School of Architecture. A principal in the design firm of Felecia Davis DesignCollaborative, Ms. Davis began her professional career with several architectural and engineering firms in California, New York, and London, including Pei, Cobb, Freed and Partners and Margaret Helfand Architects. Her Memorial and Museum for the African Burial Ground in lower Manhattan and, Goree Monument to Ship Navigation and Slavery in Senegal engaged the boundaries constructed between history and memory in the formation of narratives for these sites. She has constructed an extended context of African-American historic sites in Manhattan on the web, which is titled, "Places of Memory: Walking Tours of Manhattan," to more clearly understand the significance and meaning of these spaces and the urban fabric.

KENRICK IAN GRANDISON

Kenrick Ian Grandison is Assistant Professor of landscape architecture in the University of Michigan's School of Natural Resources and Environment in Ann Arbor. He studies and university campuses in the Deep South, an interest that was stimulated in part by his involvement in campus planning as a landscape architect with Johnson, Johnson and Roy, Inc. between 1990 and 1993. Exploring historically black college campuses as spatial records of the contentious history of race relations in the Deep South in the postbellum moment, he raises theoretical and methodological questions regarding incorporation of multiculturalism in discourses on the built environment.

BRADFORD GRANT

Bradford C. Grant is the chairperson of the Department of Architecture at Hampton University in Hampton, Virginia. He most recently served as professor of architecture at California Polytechnic State University, San Luis Obispo, California. His research on the status and role of the registered African-American architect can be found in The Survey and Directory of the African-American Architect (University of Cincinnati, CPSA, 1996), co-authored with Dennis A. Mann.

WALTER HOOD

Walter Hood, Associate Professor and Chair of the Department of Landscape Architecture and Environmental Planning at UC-Berkeley, is trained as both a landscape architect and architect. He was the recipient of the 1996–97 Rome Prize in Landscape Architecture. Mr. Hood participated in the Cooper-Hewitt Museum 2000 Triennial and in the San Francisco Museum of Modern Art Revelatory Landscapes Exhibition 2000-2001. Recent professional projects include Poplar Street Urban Design in Macon, Georgia, the new de Young Museum with architects Herzog and de Meuron, and Yerba Buena Lane in San Francisco. Published works include *Urban Diaries* (Spacemaker Press) and a pamphlet entitled "Jazz and Blues Landscape."

LESLEY NAA NORLE LOKKO

Lesley Naa Norle Lokko, was born in Scotland, UK, of Ghanaian-Scots parentage. She is the editor of the forthcoming anthology, *White Papers, Black Marks* which explores the relationship between race and architecture. She is currently on the faculty of the University of Illinois at Chicago where she runs a graduate design studio focusing on issues of race and cultural identity in architecture.

DELL UPTON

Dell Upton is a professor of Architectural History in the College of Environmental Design, University of California at Berkeley. Professor Upton's publications include *Architecture in the United States*, *Holy· Things and Profane: Anglican Parish Churches in Colonial Virginia*, *Madaline: Love and Survival in Antebellum New Orleans*, *America's Architectural Roots: Ethnic Groups That Built America*, and (with John Michael Vlach) *Common Places: Readings in American Vernacular Architecture*. He teaches courses on the history of architecture and urbanism, vernacular architecture, material culture, cultural landscapes and research methods.

AMY WEISSER

Amy S. Weisser serves as Director of External Affairs/Assistant Director for Beacon at Dia Center for the Arts in New York City.† In addition, she writes on the social and architectural history of institutional buildings. Weisser received†her Ph.D. from Yale University's†Department of History of Art in the spring of 1995, with a dissertation on the architecture of modern American public schools. In 1997, she moderated the session "The Space of Race in American Architecture" at the Society of Architectural Historians annual conference. Weisser has taught at Yale University and has held administrative appointments at the American Museum of Natural History.

LA BARBARA JAMES WIGFALL

La Barbara James Wigfall is an associate professor in the Department of Landscape Architecture/Regional and Community Planning at Kansas State University. Her research on African American communities and community empowerment emphasizes the cultivation of cultural elements as a vehicle for community survival, preservation, and/or redevelopment.

MABEL O. WILSON

Mabel O. Wilson is a partner in the design collaborative KW:A, whose most recent undertaking— an installation and book project called an *Away Station*—investigates the architectural spaces of urban migration. Along with various competitions and projects, Ms. Wilson has written extensively in journals and books on the implications of race and urban life. She is currently an assistant professor at CCAC in San Francisco.

SHERYL TUCKER DE VAZQUEZ

is an assistant professor of architecture at Tulane University where she teaches design and theory. She received a grant from the National Endowment for the Arts Design Arts Program to produce design and construction documents adapting a two-story corner building into a gallery/gathering space for Project Row Houses. Her proposal received a design award from the American Collegiate Schools of Architecture.